The Phenomenology of Questioning

Bloomsbury Studies in Phenomenology and Existentialism

Bloomsbury Studies in Phenomenology and Existentialism showcases first-rate scholarship in the fields of existentialism and phenomenology, with a key aim of pushing boundaries. Looking beyond the traditional canon, it encourages the discussion of existentialism and phenomenology across a broad range of traditions, viewpoints, genders and religions, whilst also welcoming scholars examining how existentialism and phenomenology relate to and influence other areas of philosophy and contemporary culture.

Areas of interest include, but are by no means limited to:
- Phenomenology and art
- Phenomenology of depression, addiction and psychiatric disorders
- Existential psychoanalysis
- Existentialist ethics
- Cross-cultural existentialism
- Indigenous existentialism
- Race and existentialism
- Phenomenology of technology
- Phenomenology and film
- Existentialism and political philosophy
- Existentialism and feminism
- Feminist phenomenology and gender theory
- Existentialism and literature
- Existentialism and religious belief
- Phenomenology and the theological turn

Editorial Board

Alia Al-Saji (Associate Professor, McGill University, Canada)
Kate Kirkpatrick (Professor, University of Oxford, UK)
Steven Crowell (Professor, Rice University, USA)
Kwok-ying Lau (Emeritus Professor, The Chinese University of Hong Kong, Hong Kong)

Nathalie Nya (Lecturer, John Carroll University, USA)
Alastair Hannay (Emeritus Professor, University of Oslo, Europe)
Helen Ngo (Research Fellow, Deakin University, Australia)
Rafael Winkler (Professor, University of Johannesburg, South Africa)
Jon Webber (Professor, University of Cardiff, UK)
Skye Cleary (Lecturer, Columbia University, USA)

Also Available from Bloomsbury
The Bloomsbury Handbook of Existentialism, 2nd edition, ed. Felicity Joseph, Jack Reynolds, Ashley Woodward
The Phenomenology of Virtual Technology, Daniel O'Shiel
Chance, Phenomenology and Aesthetics, Ian Andrews
An Existential Phenomenology of Addiction, Anna Westin

The Phenomenology of Questioning

Husserl, Heidegger and Patočka

Joel Hubick

BLOOMSBURY ACADEMIC
LONDON • NEW YORK • OXFORD • NEW DELHI • SYDNEY

BLOOMSBURY ACADEMIC
Bloomsbury Publishing Plc, 50 Bedford Square, London, WC1B 3DP, UK
Bloomsbury Publishing Inc, 1385 Broadway, New York, NY 10018, USA
Bloomsbury Publishing Ireland, 29 Earlsfort Terrace, Dublin 2, D02 AY28, Ireland

BLOOMSBURY, BLOOMSBURY ACADEMIC and the Diana logo
are trademarks of Bloomsbury Publishing Plc

First published in Great Britain 2024
This paperback edition published 2025

Copyright © Joel Hubick, 2024

Joel Hubick has asserted his right under the Copyright, Designs and Patents Act, 1988, to be identified as Author of this work.

Series design: Ben Anslow
Cover image: Aerial view of beautiful natural shapes and textures in lake. Taken via drone. (© temizyurek / Getty Images)

All rights reserved. No part of this publication may be: i) reproduced or transmitted in any form, electronic or mechanical, including photocopying, recording or by means of any information storage or retrieval system without prior permission in writing from the publishers; or ii) used or reproduced in any way for the training, development or operation of artificial intelligence (AI) technologies, including generative AI technologies. The rights holders expressly reserve this publication from the text and data mining exception as per Article 4(3) of the Digital Single Market Directive (EU) 2019/790.

Bloomsbury Publishing Inc does not have any control over, or responsibility for, any third-party websites referred to or in this book. All internet addresses given in this book were correct at the time of going to press. The author and publisher regret any inconvenience caused if addresses have changed or sites have ceased to exist, but can accept no responsibility for any such changes.

A catalogue record for this book is available from the British Library.

A catalog record for this book is available from the Library of Congress.

ISBN: HB: 978-1-3503-5815-7
PB: 978-1-3503-5819-5
ePDF: 978-1-3503-5816-4
eBook: 978-1-3503-5817-1

Series: Bloomsbury Studies in Phenomenology and Existentialism

Typeset by Integra Software Services Pvt. Ltd.

For product safety related questions contact productsafety@bloomsbury.com.

To find out more about our authors and books visit www.bloomsbury.com and sign up for our newsletters.

For Rachael and Felix.

Contents

Abbreviations	xi
Introduction	1
§1. The elusive phenomenon of the activity of questioning	1

1 The phenomenon of questioning 21
   §2. The role of questioning in phenomenology 21
   §3. Husserl's path from phenomenological questions to
       phenomenological answers 26
   §4. Heidegger's return to and preservation of Husserl's
       phenomenological questioning 33
   §5. Patočka's undaunted phenomenology of the question
       'what is history?' 44
   §6. The unique type of questioning employed by phenomenology 50

2 Husserl's 'To the questions themselves' 57
   §7. Chapter introduction 57
   §8. Husserl's motto precedes his methods 59
   §9. The experiential, philosophical and historical flux
       of phenomenology 65
   §10. What is the phenomenon for Husserl? 70
   §11. Phenomena understood as pregnant objects and logical predicates 74
   §12. The multiplicity of singular unities: A phenomenon and
        its manifold 78
   §13. Phenomenology as systematic but not merely a system 86
   §14. Chapter conclusion: Phenomenological questions precede
        their answers 95

3 Heidegger's 'possibility' of phenomenology 97
   §15. Chapter introduction 97
   §16. Heidegger moves away from Husserl 98
   §17. Heidegger on the structures of an explicitly formulated question 107

§18. Heidegger's *BT* as an introduction to phenomenology as possibility   113
§19. What does phenomenology mean for Heidegger?   117
§20. The four terms of *phenomenon, semblance, appearance* and *mere appearance*   119
§21. The concepts of logos and aletheia within the activity of phenomenology   126
§22. Chapter conclusion: The uncovered power of question preservation   135

4   Patočka's questioning phenomenology   137
§23. Chapter introduction   137
§24. The centrality of questioning in Husserl & Heidegger's phenomenology   139
§25. Provisional, religious and philosophical definitions of heresy   141
§26. Patočka's heretical approach to phenomenology   143
§27. Patočka's encounter with Husserl's questioning of the lifeworld   147
§28. What is phenomenology for Patočka?   151
§29. Patočka's heretical phenomenology as using Heidegger to further Husserl   160
§30. Patočka's philosophy of history as an example of his phenomenology   163
§31. Patočka's phenomenology as shaken but undaunted philosophy   166
§32. Chapter conclusion: the method of Patočka's heretical phenomenology   170

5   The logos of questioning   175
§33. Chapter introduction   175
§34. Philosophy as a call to genuine questioning   176
§35. Regular questioning correlates with an experience of curiosity   184
§36. Philosophical questioning correlates with an experience of wonder (*thaumasein*)   186
§37. The stability and instability of questioning   189
§38. The flux of wonder and curiosity   192
§39. Chapter conclusion: Thinking in a mode of possibility   196

Conclusion   199

Notes   214
Works Cited   242
Index   249

Abbreviations

Each work is referenced in detail on first mention; some works are then abbreviated thereafter to avoid repetitive referencing. A complete list of works is cited in the bibliography.

Edmund Husserl

Crisis	= *Crisis of European Sciences and Transcendental Phenomenology*
FTL	= *Formal and Transcendental Logic*
Ideas	= *Ideas for a Pure Phenomenology and Phenomenological Philosophy*
Inaugural Lecture	= *Pure Phenomenology, Its Method and Its Field of Investigation*
LI	= *Logical Investigations*
PRS	= *Philosophy as a Rigorous Science*

Martin Heidegger

BQP	= *Basic Questions of Philosophy*
BT/SZ	= *Being and Time/Sein und Zeit*
HCT	= *History of the Concept of Time*
IPR	= *Introduction to Phenomenological Research*
"My Way"	= *My Way to Phenomenology*
Ontology	= *Ontology – The Hermeneutics of Facticity*

Jan Patočka

BCLW	= *Body, Community, Language, World*
HE	= *Heretical Essays in the Philosophy of History*

IHP	= *An Introduction to Husserl's Phenomenology*
PE	= *Plato and Europe*

Others

CPR	= Immanuel Kant's *Critique of Pure Reason*
Enquiry	= David Hume's *An Enquiry Concerning Human Understanding*

Introduction

§1. The elusive phenomenon of the activity of questioning

Growing up on the flat plains of Saskatchewan, one quickly becomes fascinated with the horizon line. Add to this an automobile culture wherein driving a return trip of five hours in a single day is a common occurrence, contemplating the nature of something that is as equally present as it is permanently out of reach, comes naturally to us. The same may be said of the activity of questioning – a curious experience that is as simple and straightforward as it is mysterious and perplexing. What exactly is this ability that everyone already seems to understand and use so well and yet, like the horizon line, remains in view albeit at a distance, becoming all the more elusive the more one attempts to reach it?

I can recall that on the first day of my postsecondary education I encountered the issue of which is more valuable: a question or an answer. At my college during lunch, I just happened to sit down beside my philosophy professor. He asked me what I hoped to get out of this year of education and I proudly told him that I intended to acquire all the true answers to all of my questions. He kindly responded that after a year of study I might have more questions than I had started with. I frowned in response because I was unsure of what to make of such a reply. Surely a university was a place to learn, and learning involves the acquisition of answers. The idea that I would leave university with more questions than I had arrived with completely inverted what I took, at that time, to be the most important aspect of education: answer acquisition and answer mastery.

What is the allure and power of an answer? Why do we celebrate the discovery of truth? Why do we put aside questions and consider them 'finished' after a powerful and true answer has been found for them? When it comes to research grants, publications and obtaining teaching positions, it is safe to say that academia values answers more than questions. At present, it seems that it is very hard not to view every philosophical topic, concept or issue from the perspective of *answers* (or its more austere synonym: *results*). However, when thinking is only pursued from the perspective of answers, questions are likewise reduced in value to the answers they either provide or fail to provide. Furthermore, questions are de-valued in this perspective when they appear to give no answer at all. Philosophers are usually suspicious of questions that are openly considered to be un-answerable by definition, but, what about questions that remain worthy of asking a second or third time, even after excellent answers have been uncovered? Of those most wondrous experiences that seem to disappear entirely through what they make possible, I suggest we reconsider the activity of questioning.

At what age do we learn how to question? Although many students will recall the various moments at which they were taught how to question in a particular way or within a particular discipline (e.g. how to solve a simple arithmetic problem or how to apply basic logic to a truth claim), who remembers learning how to question in the first place? Children, who require extensive instructions on how to be polite, share and to get along with one another, do not seem to require any instruction in the art of asking questions. In fact, as most anecdotes indicate, parents usually have to stifle their children's incessant questioning rather than foster it. In our daily lives, there seem to be very few projects or areas of thinking that do not require the activity of questioning. And yet *what* this activity is, *how* it gets underway and what it fully *means* remain somewhat invisible to the thinking that so effortlessly employs it. Indeed, for it is the effortless use of questioning that in part keeps it so invisible to inquiry.

What does the activity of questioning accomplish and is it always productive? Do we question because we find ourselves ignorant or do we find ourselves ignorant because we question? Questions confound thinking in both, an edifying way that leads to and from wonder and in a pejorative way that leads to and from frustration. Some questions resist being answered, even after thousands of years of wonder, whereas others are answered so quick and easily that the very means of arriving at an answer are overlooked entirely for the prize they deliver. There are many ideas, thoughts and concerns that seem initially clear to us that become perplexing the more they are questioned.

What makes a question worthwhile? Obviously, many different factors affect the worth of a question, but one common assumption is to value it based on whether or not it leads to a meaningful *answer*. Although valuing a question for its potential answer(s) is reasonable, prior to engaging with it directly, no one can really know beforehand whether or not it will lead to a worthwhile answer. That a question needs to be engaged with or experienced directly before this can be known is usually overlooked. Thus, there is a strange impasse located right at the source of every question in that no one can truly know in advance of genuinely raising a question, whether or not it is worth asking. Furthermore, even after asking and answering a question, it remains an open possibility to raise it in a new way and, in so doing, to uncover a new answer. As will be discussed at great length, much of the great philosophical discoveries throughout history were made using a question that had hitherto been 'fully' answered; and yet, these 'closed' or 'resolved' questions nonetheless yielded novel insights, new avenues for further thought and a plethora of overlooked problems. Despite the goal of answering a question 'fully' or 'once and for all', it seems that among all things, questions reveal themselves as unquenchable possibilities. As sources of unstable flux, questions need to be respected and always given the benefit of the doubt. The fluctuation of thought caused by the activity of questioning need not undermine the search for answers, the value for truth or the rigorous attempts to epistemologically secure knowledge for science, but then again neither should one disrespect the very means by which all these valuable and worthwhile objects are uncovered through and clarified by.

The activity of questioning is an elusive phenomenon because it comes so effortlessly to thinking. Like a fish trying to understand water, questioning thoroughly permeates nearly all of conscious thought. As this activity is the very means by which a thinker inquires into problems, analyses objects and pursues various possibilities, it is difficult to make it itself into a problem. Furthermore, there is no way to inquire into the activity of questioning without using the very 'thing' under investigation. This self-reflexive quality of an analysis of questioning tends to produce messy results at best.

Provisionally speaking, the activity of questioning is a powerful way to relate to the experience of ourselves and to the world around us. When we wonder about something, we make efforts to be receptive to it and when we inquire after it, we make efforts to grasp and to understand it. Since a large portion of conscious life is composed of wondering about, and seeking to understand our experience of the world, it might be beneficial to first consider a few of the different ways the activity of questioning initially appears to us before attempting a detailed description of what questioning fully entails; for as it turns out, we can question in many ways.

Beginning with the most general experience of this activity, it is important to let the experience of questioning self-reveal its own multiplicity as this will safeguard against overlooking the full scope and range of its power. We can identify at least four senses in which questioning initially and generally appears to us: colloquial, contemplative, rhetorical and genuine. This is not an exhaustive list, but merely a starting point of departure for the following analysis.

Colloquial questioning is when we question in a way that concerns day-to-day issues that simply require being 'figured out' or merely resolved. This kind of questioning takes for granted that an answer already exists for it and simply needs to be found out. In this sense, among the four kinds, colloquial questions show the most stability for thought. This kind of inquiry takes the form of a means, as something that entirely disappears through what it aims to facilitate: we can inquire for information (who are you?, what is that?, where is it located?, when will it take place?, etc.); we can seek an explanation (why did that happen?, how does it work?, etc.); we can exercise our ability to doubt (is it really true or does it just seem that way?, how can you be sure?, etc.); we can seek to problem-solve (how do x and y relate?, what is the result of a particular mathematical operation?, etc.) and so on. If one will permit the personification, this kind of questioning does not seek to call attention to itself so much as it works to make communication, thought or the conveying of ideas as fluid as possible. In such cases, a thinker rarely considers a question as a question, but rather more as a way through which to arrive at some point, end or destination. Acting primarily as a means, colloquial questioning enables a fluidity of thinking to reach its particularly designed end or goal (whatever that may be depends on the context or situation in which it is employed). In this sense, colloquial questioning represents the most stable way to utilize the activity of questioning as its question-to-answer relation is more or less a one to one system. However, not all questions work in the same way, as others instead of facilitating an ease of thought confound, perplex and problematize thinking, even halting it altogether.

Contemplative questioning is when we question in a way that concerns reflective issues that require deeper thinking. This form of inquiry also seeks a specific answer like colloquial questioning, but it does not take for granted that an answer already exists. Rather, this kind of questioning is performed with the recognition that its target answer might need to be 'coined' or be developed from scratch. Contemplative questions include those questions we raise for further consideration and reflection (what is the good life?, what is justice?, etc.); questions that seem to always resist being fully resolved even after we have found answers for them (who am I?, how shall I live?, what may I hope for?, etc.); questions for which we already have excellent, powerful or traditional answers (what is knowledge?, how do we know what we claim to know?, what is being?, etc.) and so on. In this sense, contemplative questions elicit instability for the sake of their inquiry, but this instability is brought about ultimately for the sake of finding a novel answer and, hence, more stability.

A contemplative question is simply an issue that refuses to fully stabilize into a colloquial question in that its question-to-answer relation resists being reduced to a one-to-one system. Although these questions have yielded excellent and true answers, the original question nonetheless remains worth raising again and again. What makes it contemplative is that the issue under investigation takes the form of an object that draws attention to itself, holding the questioner within its particular orbit of thought despite the answers it yields. For example, the question 'what does it mean for a human to be alive?' can be easily answered with the definition of 'an entity that breaths, eats, perceives, moves, and communicates'. However, this answer only really speaks to a biological definition of life. When asked again, this time in light of a concern for spiritual, moral and or ethical life, the very same question can yield an additional answer of human flourishing (the human need for something beyond mere biological persistence). Both of these responses to the same question qualify as excellent, and yet even in light of them both, the original question still remains worth asking and answering nonetheless. Contemplation comes about when we recognize that our hitherto uncovered answers do not fully eclipse the originary object in question; when an answer does fully eclipse the originary object in question, then a contemplation question changes into a colloquial one. Once the work of contemplation is completed and a stable answer has been developed, it is common for a contemplative question to resemble a colloquial question as the relation of question-to-answer has been fully stabilized. When a thinker needs to push a colloquial question back into a contemplative form, they may appeal to a rhetorical device.

Rhetorical questioning is when we question in a premeditated way that aims to confirm or to elicit a preconceived idea. Rhetorical questions can be used to modify colloquial questions in at least two powerful ways: (1) to further stabilize the question-to-answer relation or (2) to destabilize it and in so doing change it into a contemplative question. In the first rhetorical sense, questioning does not really raise something for consideration as much as it aims to lead a thinker to a specific claim about something (e.g. the question 'who would not want to live freely?' is a rhetorical way of claiming that 'everyone wants to live freely'). Pedagogically speaking, rhetorical questions are used to prompt a particular answer or to enable a student to see and understand something for themselves. Returning to the example of 'what does it mean for a human to be alive?', we can imagine that in the context of a elementary science class, this question might be raised by a teacher in the first rhetorical way in order to help their students see the value of the answer 'an entity that breaths, eats, perceives, moves, and communicates'. To accomplish this, the science teacher might repeatedly ask and answer this question in a rhetorical way in order to highlight the stable connection between the question and its answer. This would impress upon the students that the rhetorical question be understood as a colloquial one befitting the aims of an elementary science class. However, we can also imagine how a few years later, when that same class is now being introduced to the basics of philosophy, the teacher might raise the same rhetorical question 'what does it mean for a human to be alive?' in order to get their students to give the ready-made biological answer, only to problematize it (e.g. show that merely existing biologically is not enough to count as human flourishing). Doing this would effectively destabilize the one-to-one question-to-answer relation originally presented for the students in their science class, but not simply to show how the biological answer is wrong. Rather, this would show how the original question, despite the excellence of the biological answer, is still worth further contemplation and that this additional thought yields additional answers (e.g. human flourishing). This is how a rhetorical device can be used to destabilize a colloquial question and push it back into a contemplative form.

Perhaps the most famous philosophical example of using a rhetorical question to teach takes place between Socrates and the slave boy in Plato's *Meno*, wherein, through merely asking questions, Socrates enables the slave boy to recollect an understanding of geometry he has never been taught. Socrates famously states that 'if [the slave boy] were repeatedly asked these same questions in various ways, […] he will know [things] without having been taught but only questioned, and find the knowledge within oneself' (*Meno* 85c-d). In addition to the pedagogical use of rhetorical questions to teach, another famous example of using a rhetorical question to destabilize, that is, to break a thinker out of a one-to-one question and answer system, is observable within Augustine's famous inquiry into the nature of time. In *Confessions*, he asks '[w]hat is time then? If no one asks me, I know: but if I were desirous to explain it to one that should ask me, plainly I know not' (*Confessions*, 11.14). In a simple sense, time is the way we measure the flow of our experience. We break it into units and use various means to count and divide it. Thus the question 'what is time?' can be easily answered as 'the measured division of our passing experience'. So long as no one really asks me to interrogate my answer and it is for the most part left unsaid, I will experience no anxiety. However, as Augustine convincingly points out, the more we directly engage with the question itself and forgo the easy answer, the more confounding the question can become. These two ways of using rhetorical questions to either stabilize or destabilize thought is perhaps what makes them so useful in an educational setting as they both provide a stimulating starting point for discussion and a means for further exploration of any given topic. The experience of being confounded by the destabilization of a question makes room for further contemplation, but what happens when this instability is pursued absolutely?

Genuine questioning is when we question in an honest way that follows the 'train of thought' wherever it may or may not lead, to allow a question to open a path for further thinking. This kind of questioning is exploratory thought *par excellence*, and as such, may open up new avenues of thought, uncover phenomena, crystalize in clarity or, in fact, do none of these things at all. What makes this kind of thinking *genuine* is that it provides the least amount of 'preconception' and/or 'perceived used'. Genuine questioning brings about instability in thinking for the sake of instability; this may prove useful but it also may prove useless. Unlike the other forms of questioning, there is no specified end or goal other than free thinking. This is also why genuine questioning can be the most fruitful and/or most fruitless: the exploratory thinking of genuine questioning will frequently solidify into the other three forms of inquiry (colloquial, contemplative and rhetorical) and, in so doing, provide meaningful results; whereas in other instances, genuine questioning will only facilitate exploration and destabilization without yielding any use whatsoever.

Usually, but not always, genuine inquiry requires that one not know a question's possible answer(s) in advance although even when we do know in advance, we can still be surprised by what a question yields. This kind of questioning is usually elicited in response to an experience of wonder. When we encounter something wondrous, we generally respond to it with a genuine desire to further explore and understand that experience. Where a rhetorical question might break our understanding out of our one-to-one question-to-answer relation, when we seek to further explore what we have found wondrous, this is genuine questioning. What makes genuine questioning so multidirectional, dynamic and ripe with possibility is that we have the least amount of control over it. Whereas colloquial, contemplative and rhetorical questioning remains thoroughly within our grasp and control, genuine questioning is primarily characterized by *letting go* of that control and letting the question take a thinker wherever it may or may not lead. It is an easy task to question in a colloquial way, perhaps a bit more difficult to do so in a contemplative and rhetorical way, but when it comes to genuine questioning, it is not something we properly enact by intention so much as *let something happen to us*.

As the analysis of this text aims to put first the experience of the activity of questioning, it is clear that nothing less than a phenomenology is required. As Martin Heidegger elegantly puts it in *Being and Time* (henceforth *BT*): 'The expression "phenomenology" signifies primarily a *methodological conception*. This expression does not characterize the *what* of the objects of philosophical research as subject-matter, but rather the *how* of that research. [...] Thus the term "phenomenology" expresses a maxim which can be formulated as "To the things themselves!"' (*BT* 50/28). This means that the phenomenon of questioning will always be held before and above any concept, definition or description made of it in order to maintain a value for *how* this activity emerges through experience over and above *what* comprises it. In other words, this is to maintain and preserve the phenomenological maxim for 'going back to the activity of questioning itself' over and above any descriptions made of it. This maxim does not originate in Heidegger but in his great teacher and founder of phenomenology Edmund Husserl.

Given the provisional descriptions of how questioning generally appears to us in these four forms, the activity of questioning has been somewhat introduced. Although the activities of colloquial, contemplative and rhetorical questioning lend themselves to stable thinking, the instability of genuine questioning rules out any analysis that is merely conceptual or systematic. Furthermore, it is clear that we cannot investigate questioning without using the very activity we are trying to clarify. This does not preclude an investigation of questioning from taking place, but it does situate it as requiring more than just an analytic analysis. Thus, instead of merely trying to conceptualize, systematize and or define in advance *what* questioning entails, the following analysis lets the activity of questioning self-reveal in *how* it emerges as an experience, on its own, in action and in use. This comprises doing a phenomenology of the experience of questioning: although this text puts forth descriptions, highlights many of the various facets and emergent layers of questioning, and attempts to conceptualize and argue for various structures of this activity, its primary goal is to provide a phenomenological path for the reader to follow and return to this activity for themselves. To go and see it for themselves, to find and test the evidence discussed in this text for themselves, and to experience this activity so they may verify any claims made of it for themselves. It is my hope and intention that this text be viewed like a map, that does not simply provide claims and arguments, so much as really show how the reader can return to the phenomenon of questioning in a new and edifying way.

Phenomenology, as originally envisioned by Husserl, provides an embryonic instantiation of the activity of questioning. In addition to providing a set of ideas, distinctions and methods, phenomenology also provides a unique practice of returning to phenomena *again and again* in order to test and verify any and all descriptions, concepts and structures.[1] Thus, in addition to reading and thinking about the content of phenomenology (its many concepts, definitions, descriptions and methods), the beginner phenomenologist must also make efforts to see and experience for herself what this content *correlates* with. This practice of perpetually returning to experience is encapsulated by Husserl's motto 'to the things themselves' (*zu den Sachen selbst*).[2] This will not only allow the activity of questioning to appear as an abundance, in various multifaceted and dynamic ways, it will *also* ensure that we are not limiting, pre-defining or forcing it to appear in any way other than in how it genuinely shows itself. Furthermore, no claim will be permitted that does not immediately call for the reader to re-elicit for themselves the very same evidence under consideration used in support of any assertion in this text.[3] However auspicious this may sound, it also has the unfortunate effect of demanding much more on the part of the reader than, perhaps, a usual text might require. Keenly aware of this higher demand, I have striven to make each and every claim as transparent as possible. That being said, only the reader may judge, *via* reflection on their own experience, whether or not these efforts are ultimately edifying or not.

This activity of perpetually returning to the matters themselves is one of the often-overlooked discoveries of phenomenology, usually eclipsed by its equally valuable conceptual systematicity, many layered distinctions and sophisticated complexity. However, in order to be considered at all, all ideas, ways of thinking, concepts and or definitions are initially encountered as a phenomenon with correlating appearances; as such, *every given phenomenon will always be more than the sum of its appearances and descriptions*. In phenomenology, this requires one to distinguish between the hitherto collected descriptions of any given phenomenon and its originary potential to re-reveal itself anew. At first, this may sound like a descriptive account of experience will be impossible due to its inherent Heraclitean flux; however, for Husserl, the consistency, efficacy, power and truth of phenomenology lie not in its capability to stabilize an idea beyond reproach (once and for all) but to base every claim upon a perpetually repeatable experience of verification (the stabilization of truth remains 'present', but it is further revealed to be based upon an underlying fluctuating dynamism out of which it perpetually re-emerges *as stable*). Therefore, whatever is true phenomenologically speaking is only such when it is founded upon the experience that verifies it. Sharing in the knowledge of truth, therefore, amounts to being able to elicit for oneself the experience that verifies the knowledge claim in question. For these reasons the call to return to the matters *themselves*, to see how they are initially and continually experienced alongside their descriptions, turns out to be more than just a motto or slogan; for without it, phenomenology merely amounts to just another collection of empty claims.

In addition to Husserl, I also consider how his students Martin Heidegger and Jan Patočka take up, reinterpret and modify Husserl's practice of questioning within their own particular development of phenomenology. These three thinkers collectively demonstrate that the activity of phenomenological inquiry transcends its tradition in that it offers something more than just a perspective, a novel system or a set of ideas: it also offers a *questioning practice*. The emergence of questioning within the historical development of phenomenology (Husserl-Heidegger-Patočka) is therefore revealed as a uniquely appropriate starting point for an investigation of the activity of questioning.

Given that questioning appears in many ways, how then should one begin a phenomenology of it? The first step requires that we allow the phenomenon of questioning itself to become questionable. This is no philosophical word play nor is it a simple task. The most challenging aspect of any phenomenological investigation is the assumption that one already understands the object of inquiry, given that this threatens to eclipse the original phenomenon under investigation. In other words, the most obfuscating obstacle that threatens a genuine engagement with a question is an already-held answer. Attempting to bring the very activity of questioning *itself* into consideration, to let it appear without pre-figuring it in any way, requires one to suspend this activity's *familiarity* and *ease of use*. In so doing, this activity will become all the more peculiar in a phenomenologically edifying way.

There are instances in the history of philosophy when a question is considered unanswerable for long periods of time only to be suddenly answered rather well; there are also other instances when a question has been answered *so well* that it becomes unthinkable to raise it anew, that is, until someone genuinely and edifyingly does so.[4] Within the gravity of an excellent answer there also lurks a hubris that can undermine a genuine engagement with the original question it aims to resolve. In light of this, answers should be valued separately to questions and, furthermore, a question should not be judged merely in terms of its potential to provide an answer. How exactly can one value a question on its own, without referring to a potential answer or a lack thereof?

The second step in a phenomenology of questioning is to suspend our natural tendency to judge questions by their potential answers. The worth of a question is found in being able to ask it properly, not just being able to answer it well. In his seminal work *Truth and Method* Hans-Georg Gadamer states that '[a]mong the greatest insights that Plato's account of Socrates affords us is that, contrary to the general opinion, it is more difficult to ask questions than to answer them' (Gadamer 356). It is initially reasonable to believe that the difficulty of a question lies primarily in mastering its answer(s) as coming to a clear grasp of an answer can be incredibly difficult. It is one thing to have an answer memorized, but it is quite another to try and to understand what an answer really means. For example, although many students can recite the definition of Kant's transcendental philosophy, many will likely find it difficult to explain in their own words what it really means or fully entails. Merely memorizing an answer is not the same as fully understanding its meaning and, likewise, merely memorizing an answer in relation to a question is not the same as being able to ask it properly. Being able to ask a question properly, independent of the concern for answers, is to fully engage with it, to let its possibilities 'run wild' as it were and to follow these tangents without prejudice wherever they may or may not lead. As we usually know in advance what we want and or do not want from a question *via* answers, letting go of this answer-oriented view of questioning turns out to be the initial difficulty in suspending the natural tendency to judge questions by their potential answers.

With a provisional description of questioning and answering now distinguished, one can address whether a particular approach to questioning is superior to others. Regarding the process of questioning well, Gadamer states that '[t]here is no such thing as a method of learning to ask questions, of learning to see what is questionable. On the contrary, the example of Socrates teaches that the important thing is the knowledge that one does not know' (Gadamer 359). Thus, one way to begin genuinely questioning is to simply acknowledge one's own ignorance. Although this acknowledgement is reasonable for straightforward questioning, we can develop Gadamer's suggestion to include a form of genuine exploration when considering more complicated questions: a willingness to follow the question like Socrates follows the argument 'wherever, like a wind it may lead us' (*Republic* 394d). In this sense, honesty in genuine questioning need not simply coincide with the admittance of ignorance, but also with a willingness to pursue a question to its full end. Gadamer states that

> [i]n order to be able to ask [a question], one must want to know, and that means knowing that one does not know. In the comic confusion between question and

answer [...] there is a profound recognition of the *priority of the question* in all knowledge and discourse that really reveals something of an object.

(Gadamer 357)

Gadamer here connects questioning with appearance: when we genuinely question something, we make efforts to let it appear to us. Gadamer states quite beautifully that '[d]iscourse that is intended to reveal something requires that that thing be broken open by the question' (Gadamer 357). Something being 'broken open by the question' or being brought back into a state of questionability connotes a kind of receptivity on the side of the questioner to let the phenomenon appear in a way that does not interfere or pre-modify it. As a kind of reflection that occurs within a mode of questioning, now distinct from the mode of answering, it is possible to contemplate a question while keeping its potential answer(s) in suspension. This not only reveals how the activity of questioning can be pursued independently of answering, it also shows how this can be valuable: as a *means of exploration* that allows for phenomena to maintain their potentiality to further self-reveal. Husserl's motto proves to be an exemplar for how to practise questioning, but merely making or agreeing with this claim does not clarify why this is the case; for that we must see the practice of his motto in action for ourselves.

To view the practice of phenomenological questioning in operation, we may turn to an essay written by Adolf Reinach, one of Husserl's assistants and an excellent conveyor and teacher of phenomenology. Husserl said that Reinach 'was among the first who could understand, creatively and perfectly, the peculiar meaning of the phenomenological method and could view [it] in its entire philosophical range' (Reinach 2002 196). Reinach valued the *practice* of phenomenology, what it could bring into view for a thinker as significant among the many important aspects of Husserl's method. According to Herbert Spiegelberg, author of *The Phenomenological Movement: A Historical Introduction*, 'what Reinach appreciated in Husserl was chiefly the "cautious and thorough mode of working," not his results' (Spiegelberg 1960 196). This is not to say that Reinach did not also value the results of Husserl's phenomenology, but like many of Husserl's students he was perhaps inspired more by Husserl's practices than by the results of those practices.

One practice in particular that Reinach noticed in Husserl is the re-questioning of the things themselves. In his essay 'Concerning Phenomenology', Reinach states that 'if we bring ourselves to the point where, as philosophers, we must bring ourselves – through all signs, definitions and rules – to the [matters][5] themselves (*zu den Sachen selbst*), things will present themselves to us quite differently than is [initially] believed' (Reinach 186). In order to illustrate the activity of returning to the matters themselves, Reinach uses the problem of number, specifically the phenomenological question '*of what are numbers predicated?*' (Reinach 186). Using this question, Reinach makes the distinction between the original experience of numbers themselves (what we genuinely experience when count or perform mathematical operations) and the various concepts we develop to predicate these experiences. When we think about numbers, it is easy to skip the original phenomena and jump right to the concepts we already have for them. However, if we enact Husserl's motto, and try to return to the numbers themselves, that is, the original experiences that our concepts *conceptualize*, Reinach shows us that we can distinguish between our original experiences of numbers (as phenomena) and the traditional concepts that attempt to organize and *conceptualize* these experiences (the descriptions *of* those phenomena). Thus, behind the ready-made concepts of number, we find what those concepts predicate: the originary phenomena of numbers.

Reinach's investigation distinguishes between the experiences of original phenomena from the already-available conceptualizations of them provided by tradition or history. Specifically, one may turn to their own experience of number in order to see the difference between it and the two (non-exhaustive) traditional concepts of *ordinal* and *cardinal* numbers. Reinach states that '[t]he division of numbers into ordinal and cardinal is generally accepted today. But people do not agree on which type of number, the ordinal or the cardinal, is primitive, and on whether we may or may not designate one as more primitive than the other' (Reinach 2002 186). Ordinal numbers are defined under the organizational concept of order (first, second, third, etc.), whereas cardinal numbers are defined under the organizational concept of size (small, medium, large, etc.). Both concepts are ways to predicate the original experience of number itself (that is of our own experience of counting). In other words, we can ask 'what is a number?' and can consider at least two answers in response to this question: the ordinal conceptualization or the cardinal conceptualization. Were we to take up the question 'which is more primitive?', we would have to bring into view both concepts (ordinal and cardinal) and compare them with the original experience of number itself. In this sense, we can see that the *very experience of number is itself not a third concept*, but the original target-experience that both concepts aim to predicate, explain or account for (namely, the originary phenomenon). Genuinely taking up Reinach's question 'of what are numbers predicated?' provides a way to bring oneself back to this original experience of number as a phenomenon and to re-consider it as an experience that is *unaccounted for* (that is, to restore its questionability). Once the originary phenomenon of number has been made questionable, we are then in a position to contemplate which concept (ordinal or cardinal) best *accounts* for the experience of the phenomenon itself.

Were one to begin with an already-developed answer-concept, the original experience of the phenomenon of number in its many-sidedness could be entirely covered up or missed altogether. However, when one begins with the question 'of what are numbers predicated?', one observes that this question elicits the original experience of number itself, in its entire scope and breadth; in this way, enacting Husserl's motto revitalizes the originary phenomenon. In other words, when we begin with an *answer*, the dynamism of any given phenomenon may be unnecessarily collapsed or missed, due to the stability of the answer (description, definition, concept, etc.), but when we begin with a *question*, the dynamism of phenomena is kept in view as a source for further thinking (even after it is fully stabilized into a clear and concise concept). This reveals why it is important to begin any investigation with questions rather than with answers, given that the stability of answers tends to threaten or eclipse the originary dynamism of experience. Balancing the dynamic power of questions with the gravity of answers proves tricky, given that most philosophical investigations are ultimately judged for the concepts they establish or clarify.

In phenomenology, concepts remain important and valuable; however, they are also recognized as *conceptual responses* to original experiences and, therefore, are understood as stable appearances of the dynamic phenomena they aim to predicate. In this sense, all concepts are *conceptualizations of experience* and, as such, all concepts are 'built' upon an originary phenomenon as the original 'thing' or matter that is predicated by them.[6] Husserl's phenomenology instructs us that one ought not to merely perform concept construction and concept analysis, but should also make efforts to see and consider how well such concepts correlate to the original experiences they are designed to predicate: the thing, matter or phenomenon that aims to be *conceptualized by* and therefore correlates *with* its definition, notion or concept. Spiegelberg puts it another way when he writes that 'what philosophy must begin with are the phenomena and problems themselves; all study of theories, however significant, must take second place' (Spiegelberg 1960 122). Thus, concepts and theories remain important but must be kept from eclipsing the original experiences of phenomena that they are intended to account for and clarify. Following on Reinach's example of number, it is clear how a question can enable one to return to and reveal the underlining phenomenon that is conceptualized by an answer.

The very activity of *returning to the matters themselves* is accomplished by returning to the original source-phenomena within experience and this is, in turn, accomplished by recollecting, re-asking and preserving the questions that elicit such phenomena. In this way, the phenomenological practice of Husserl's motto is not restricted to *just* conceptual analysis, *but furthermore and in addition to this* throws a thinker back into what must always come prior to concepts: their correlates within the flux of experience.⁷ That phenomena always emerge in tandem with a plethora of appearances reveals reciprocity between the many hitherto collected and accounted for *appearances* and the *phenomenon's* potential to further reveal additional appearances: each moment of appearance throws a thinker back onto the generating potential of the phenomenon that subsequently purports additional appearances, and so on. As will become clearer throughout this text, the flux of experience is incompatible with the stability of concepts and, as such, the only way to keep the experience of the matters themselves in view and in thought without restricting or modifying them in any way is to keep them in question. In this way, one can interpret Husserl's motto as a charge to 'return to [re-question] the things themselves'.

The guiding theme of this text, then, is the question: 'what is questioning?' However, in keeping with Husserl's motto, this investigation will go beyond merely describing the formal structure or functional power of a question, given that I will also seek to explore the very experience of possibility elicited by questioning. The possibility of questioning is unique in that we can genuinely experience its dynamism for ourselves when we question. However, as I have already provisionally shown, this strange kind of dynamism and self-reflexivity elicited by questioning makes it a rather elusive target to investigate. There are questions we bring to experience and, in so doing, wonder about them, and there are phenomena that bring questions to us and in so doing bring us into wonder. In the foreword to his work *Ontology-The Hermeneutics of Facticity* (henceforth *Ontology*), Heidegger describes philosophy as '[p]utting forth *questions* – questions are not happenstance thoughts, nor are questions the common "problems" of today which "one" picks up from hearsay and book learning and decks out with a gesture of profundity. Questions grow out of a confrontation with [the matters themselves]' (*Ontology* 4). How exactly, then, does one 'put forth' the question 'what is questioning?' How does one return to the activity of questioning itself and allow it to self-reveal?

My strategy is to begin with the emergence of questioning through the historical development of phenomenology in the work and thought of Husserl,

Heidegger and Patočka. I argue that there is an opaque appearance of questioning that emerges within and alongside the phenomenological practice of returning to the matters themselves (specifically in Husserl's motto and how it is taken up and developed by Heidegger and Patočka's own reinterpretation of phenomenology). This leads to the question of how exactly one questions the things themselves. To answer this, I argue that one of the central discoveries of phenomenology is *that* phenomena emerge prior to their correlating appearances.[8] This leads to the next question of what enables a phenomenologist to see and to investigate original appearances of phenomena prior to their conceptualization. To answer this, I argue that phenomenology rediscovers a special power of questioning that enables one to stabilize or destabilize the flux of phenomena in thought, perception and reflection. The flux of experience and phenomena cannot be fully accounted for with an answer, but it can be 'pointed to', 'picked out' or 'identified' with a question. Phenomenology concerns the ability of consciousness to destabilize or to stabilize the flux of experience through the activity of questioning and answering respectively. Precisely explaining how the activity of questioning can in fact accomplish these feats of de-stabilization and what this fully means is the more sophisticated way of answering the question 'what is the role of questioning in phenomenological inquiry?' Thus, a close examination of how phenomenology takes up and interprets the activity of questioning in Husserl, Heidegger and Patočka will provide a way to inquire into the meaning of questioning itself.

The old adage that 'failed research is still research' seems to be in keeping with phenomenological pursuits and coincides with Husserl's 1907 reference to his own work as 'just preliminary work, mere struggle on the way to the goal and not the full goal itself [...] Thus I am, after many years, still the beginner and the student. But I want to become the master! *Carpe diem*' (*The Idea of Phenomenology* 1). This is likewise confirmed by Heidegger's claim that 'thinkers learn from their shortcomings to be more persevering' (*Kant and the Problem of Metaphysics* xx). Patočka similarly states that

> to uncover what is hidden in manifestation entails questioning, it means discovering the problematic character not of this or that but of the whole as such, as well as of the life that is rigorously integrated into it. Once, however, that question has been posed, humans set out on a long journey they had not traveled hitherto, a journey from which they might gain something but also decidedly lose a great deal. It is the journey of history.
>
> (*Heretical Essays* 25)

Whatever efforts that are required to allow the activity of questioning to reveal itself, they will essentially and inherently require one to struggle with the matters themselves. This struggling with the things themselves, then, is revealed to involve more than the provisioning of a set of answers but, furthermore, a *way of questioning*. It is for this reason that this text attempts to establish a path towards a clear grasp of what the activity of questioning entails, in order to let it show itself and self-reveal. Navigating this path involves taking the followings steps.

Chapter 1, entitled 'The Phenomenon of Questioning', is preparatory in that it attempts to bring the original phenomenon of questioning itself into view for investigation. In order to do this, I first trace some of the broad strokes of phenomenology's historical developments through Husserl, Heidegger and Patočka and then argue that this development can be interpreted as a re-discovery of the power of questioning. In particular, special attention is paid to how each individual thinker raises and answers the questions 'what is phenomenology?' and 'what is the phenomenon?' Although Husserl, Heidegger and Patočka each provide very different (and in many cases completely incompatible) definitions, concepts and philosophical systems, they may nevertheless all be unified under phenomenology's central concern to return to and re-experience the things themselves *via* questioning. The preservation of questions is, therefore, revealed to be the way in which phenomenology preserves original experiences from becoming eclipsed by powerful descriptions.[9] With the phenomenon of questioning itself located within the historical development of phenomenology, a closer textual analysis of each individual thinker (Husserl-Heidegger-Patočka) is then performed in the subsequent three chapters.

Chapter 2, entitled 'Husserl's To the Questions Themselves', establishes Husserlian phenomenology as a point of departure for an investigation of the activity of questioning. This is accomplished by performing an in-depth textual analysis of Husserl's thought on how to define phenomenology and the phenomenon from *Logical Investigations* (henceforth *LI*)[10] to *Ideas for a Pure Phenomenological and Phenomenological Philosophy Books I-III* (henceforth *Ideas*),[11] specifically using his inaugural lecture at Freiburg entitled: 'Pure Phenomenology, its Method and its Field of Investigation' (henceforth *Inaugural Lecture*) as a key to viewing his development throughout that time from around 1913 to 1917. I argue that Husserl's motto 'to the things themselves' can be reinterpreted as 'keeping the things themselves' in *question*. Husserl's efforts to keep his phenomenological questions preserved, in order to let them continually reveal and re-reveal new phenomena (or reveal new layers or appearances of the same phenomenon), are not something he develops explicitly in his particular methods; instead, it emerges implicitly through the continual *practice* of his motto.

Chapter 3, entitled 'Heidegger's Possibility of Phenomenology', continues with a close textual examination of Heidegger's departure from Husserl as he claims in 'My Way to Phenomenology' (henceforth 'My Way') and his reinterpretation of phenomenology and the phenomenon in *BT* §7. In particular, Heidegger insists that his philosophical perspective seizes upon and understands phenomenology *as a possibility*. Exactly what Heidegger means by this phrase, and how he reinterprets Husserl's phenomenology to revolve around the central activity of questioning, is examined in detail. I argue that Heidegger further develops how the activity of questioning can be used to investigate phenomena that remain in flux (e.g. phenomena that resist total stabilization and phenomena that disappear through the very stabilization of their appearance). Heidegger further develops Husserl's questioning practice by raising, establishing and *preserving* the meaning of the question of being in *BT*.[12]

Chapter 4, entitled 'Patočka's Questioning Phenomenology',[13] examines how Patočka takes up and further develops Husserl and Heidegger's practice of phenomenological questioning. For Patočka, this takes shape as *philosophical heresy* understood as maintaining a thinker's questions while at the same time proposing contrary answers (a method clearly indebted to both Husserl's penchant for revision and to Heidegger's self-description of taking up Husserl's questions over and against Husserl's answers). By the end of this chapter, the activity of questioning is thoroughly in view as a vague and un-thematic appearance understood *via* Heidegger's notion of '*Erscheinung*', a hitherto not yet fully revealed phenomenon that has only been announced (*BT* §7). With the activity of questioning now clarified and situated within phenomenology, a direct analysis of how a thinker genuinely perceives and experiences the notion of 'raising a question' will become possible.

Chapter 5, entitled 'The Logos of Questioning', seeks to further develop that the activity of questioning has only been partially and opaquely revealed as an appearance within the historical period of phenomenology highlighted in Chapters 1–4. In response to this, I then make further attempts to clarify and make transparent just what the activity of questioning fully entails on its own in order to show how it may be used in any area of thinking.[14]

As a work that is also phenomenological, in addition to providing arguments and textual interpretations in support of my thesis, efforts are made to bring the activity of questioning itself in view for the reader, so they may see and verify for themselves any claims and descriptions I make.

Elucidating the activity of questioning cannot be conceptually fixed in advance, given that the activity of questioning is a dynamic phenomenon that emerges from the fluctuating flow of experience. Instead, one must consider its varying stable appearances (e.g. colloquial, contemplative, rhetorical and genuine questioning) in light of its source located in an unstable phenomenon that perpetually re-reveals itself. It is, however, in the face of such experiential and conceptual dynamism, in which no pre-guarantees are possible, that phenomenology genuinely begins.

1

The phenomenon of questioning

§2. The role of questioning in phenomenology

This chapter introduces how we can view the historical development of phenomenology, through Husserl-Heidegger-Patočka, as a trajectory that rediscovers the power of questioning. Phenomenology teaches us not only to raise new questions within this historical and philosophical development, but also to preserve old questions. These are questions that have been raised repeatedly by the history of European philosophy, such as what a number is, what logic is, what being is, etc. Contrary to our tendency to seek out and to collect answers, phenomenology teaches us to retrieve and revive the original questions that form the basis of any uncovering or understanding. In his *Vienna Lecture*, Husserl states that the philosopher must maintain 'his resolve not to accept unquestioningly any pregiven opinion or tradition so that he can inquire, in respect to the whole traditionally pregiven universe, after what is true in itself, an ideality' (*Vienna Lecture* 286). Such investigations, characterized by re-questioning tradition, need not compete with traditional answers; in fact, renewed questioning tends to open up hitherto un-thought ideas or novel ways of thinking that are beneficial when they are explored alongside traditional models. In this way, phenomenology promotes the preservation and repetition of asking questions alongside their already-valued answers.

The following sections, §§3–5, elaborate on the specific role the activity of questioning plays in the phenomenology of Husserl, Heidegger and Patočka. After the activity has been introduced, how each individual thinker takes up and modifies the activity of questioning through their own particular philosophical development of phenomenology is then considered from Husserl in §3, to Heidegger in §4 and Patočka in §5. Once the activity of questioning has been worked out and introduced for each thinker, §6 draws provisional conclusions that setup the more in-depth analysis and investigation that subsequent chapters undertake.

Phenomenology is primarily concerned with describing all of the many multiform, dynamic and static ways we experience phenomena. In phenomenology, the idea of experience does not limit itself to a pre-figured definition but maintains openness for any and all real, ideal, possible and/or even impossible experiences. However, all experience must be *experienced by a consciousness* and, as such, phenomenology also includes a concern for the recipient of experience: consciousness and/or conscious life. Importantly, although description is the primary 'means' of phenomenology, prior to becoming objects capable of being described, all phenomena must *appear to consciousness* in the first place. Thus, in addition to concerning objects of appearance, phenomenology also concerns the many *ways* in which the phenomena themselves come into appearance for a consciousness.

Phenomenology also concerns itself with questions of methodology as well as those oft-repeated, open questions, and against the idea that phenomenology only provides a fixed method: how does one study the things themselves? (Husserl), what does it mean to exist in an everyday way? (Heidegger), what is history and why is it important? (Patočka). Within phenomenology, the very questions taken up and contemplated are revealed to be as important as any of the answers developed for them. Thus, the special concern for keeping questions in mind that occur within phenomenology makes it a viable point of departure for an analysis of the activity of questioning itself.

Husserl's phenomenology, in particular, aims to describe the essential structures of perception, consciousness, the constitution of meaning, the structure of objects and horizons of temporality. However, to understand or value Husserl only in terms of how *successful* his descriptions of essences are is, ironically, to miss something essential about his work. Alongside these powerful phenomenological *answers* one also finds an incredible *tour de force* of phenomenological *questioning*. Thus, alongside the collection of robust descriptions of phenomena, Husserl's phenomenology also concerns the perpetual *appearing of phenomena*, the different ways they appear, fail to appear or even disappear through their very appearance. In a clear summary of just how difficult it can be to return to the matters themselves, scholar R. Philip Buckley states that

> [t]he guiding dictum of phenomenology is 'to the things themselves.' This saying conveys a sense that the 'things,' the 'phenomena' with which we are confronted and into which we seek some insight are not as immediately accessible as may be imagined. Phenomena, however, are often hidden not by their distance from us, but by their very proximity, by the fact that they are taken for granted as being self-evident and understood by all. Even the most common, everyday

phenomena and the words used to describe them often reveal, upon closer inspection, a degree of complexity which has previously been unsuspected. Upon interrogation, that which had been taken to be self-evident and widely understood shows itself otherwise.

(Buckley xv)

The obstacle to overcome in phenomenology is the very self-evidence and proximity of the things themselves, and the challenge is to make efforts to keep such 'obviousness' at bay somehow, to work against the ease of 'what we already think we know' in order to let the things themselves self-emerge and self-reveal. The phenomenologist appeals to the activity of questioning in order to fully appreciate the many different ways phenomena in fact appear to consciousness. By perpetually questioning and re-questioning the things themselves, one maintains a special kind of receptivity to the possibility of phenomena to further generate additional appearances.

Husserl remains concerned with the dynamism of experience. Sustaining a question for further consideration is to maintain its *problematicity*, which may be defined as maintaining a question so as to allow phenomena to further reveal additional appearances. Preserving questions despite already having excellent answers for them forms the basis of phenomenology. Recalling, recollecting and preserving questions are the fundamental ways through which phenomenology is pursued and, in this sense, Husserl's motto may also be understood in the form of 'back to the [questions] themselves'. For example, after finishing his PhD in mathematics, Husserl began his career in philosophy with the question 'what is a number?' His blunder into and analysis of psychologism led him to investigate logic itself. These investigations eventually led Husserl to consider ideas pertaining to phenomena and to phenomenology. This exploration reveals that the very idea of phenomenology is never something fixed, even for Husserl, but instead comprises an ongoing pursuit to understand 'the things themselves'. It is the instability and inexhaustibility of the things themselves, taken as a whole and as a problem, that Husserl's phenomenology aims to investigate, account for and to describe.

In order to pursue an understanding of the things themselves, they need to be kept in question. Husserl's philosophical development reveals that his approach to phenomenology was continually being modified and developed throughout his entire career. Spiegelberg states that

> [w]hile is it is true that Husserl is the founder and remains the central figure of the Movement, he is also its most radical representative, and that not only

in the sense that he tried to go to the roots, but that he kept digging deeper and deeper, *often undermining his own earlier results*; he was always the most extreme member of his Movement and hence became increasingly the loneliest of them all.

(Spiegelberg 1960 xxviii, my emphasis)

Husserl's extreme radicalism in his own philosophical efforts notwithstanding, his actions can be taken as something isolating or even pathological; however, his willingness to re-question his entire project may also be interpreted as something incredibly positive, fruitful and valuable. A teacher of mine once said that he 'admired Husserl for his philosophical passion, intellectual honesty, hesitations, and mistakes as much as he did for his philosophical successes'. There certainly is something fascinating as well as edifying in Husserl's own dedication to re-questioning everything again and again. His penchant for revision is also visible in as much as nearly all of Husserl's published works were designated to be *introductions* to phenomenology, or introduction to the 'new' (recently developed) method on how to do phenomenology. From his writings as well as his *practices*, one can thus observe that studying phenomenology requires more than merely taking on a particular paradigm; it requires one to continuously engage and wrestle with its central questions.[1]

Husserl's willingness to re-question everything is very influential on Heidegger's conception of phenomenology. In his attempt to clarify the meaning of phenomenology for himself in BT, Heidegger suggests that '"phenomenology" [...] does not characterize the *what* of the objects of philosophical research as subject-matter, but rather the *how* of that research' (*BT* 50/27). To clarify this difference, one can consider the *answers* derived through phenomenological research to be its 'what' (understood as a collection of descriptions, concepts, definitions, structures, etc.), whereas phenomenological *questions* comprise 'how' this research is undertaken. Provisionally, to say that 'phenomenology is concerned with questioning the appearances of objects, ideas, meanings, and their corresponding modes of thinking and experiencing' is to highlight that it takes special efforts to consider *how* phenomena reveal themselves, in addition to studying *that* they reveal themselves.

In holding a central concern for 'how' phenomena reveal and re-reveal themselves, both Husserl and Heidegger's phenomenologies maintain a concern for the stability and instability of phenomena in addition to their various modes of givenness in intellectual and intuitive modes of experience. Thus, every definition, concept or description is correlated with an original and dynamic source experience; whereas definitions, concepts and descriptions are stable and can be grasped as *answers*; their correlating experiences are experienced in a mode of fluctuation that may reveal or re-reveal themselves in perpetual new ways. The many ways in which phenomena appear provide a difficult problem for phenomenology, as something that resists ever being fully stabilized or fixated. Although this fluctuation resists stabilization, it may nonetheless be kept in question. Understanding 'how a fluctuation can be kept in question', therefore, turns out to be a key aspect of clarifying the power of phenomenological questions. How then does one describe, account for or even talk about something that always remains in flux?

The issues of stability and instability play crucial roles in phenomenological questioning. In the face of stability, phenomenologists accept and anticipate that every appearance, mode of experience or concept may re-reveal itself in new ways, or, to put it in Husserlian terms, that new evidence may require that we review and correct earlier accounts of experience. In the face of instability, phenomenology investigates the way phenomena, unities and manifolds originate in a flux prior to their stabilization. Phenomenological research also concerns the very way such appearances either come into or fail to stabilize themselves. In addition to the stability of concepts, definitions and descriptions, research also maintains a concern for the fluctuation and dynamism of phenomena. Although the very *fluctuation* and *dynamism* of phenomena resist the stabilization of description, we still experience them nonetheless. This is where the activity of questioning becomes a helpful tool in that it allows us to demarcate the dynamism of phenomena with *questions* (to pick them out of the experiential flow of consciousness) alongside our ability to stabilize experience with *answers* (already collected stable appearances in the form of concepts, descriptions, structures, etc.).

The activity of questioning plays a central role in securing a way to phenomenologically view or to think about that which remains in a dynamic flux. The very notion of instability remains invisible to a perception that operates only with pre-established definitions, concepts or fixed systems. In order to investigate and phenomenologically recognize instability – understood in various ways as the unconcealment of entities, to form a definition, to conceptualize something, or to develop and establish a system or mode of thought at all – one has to be able to first wrestle with the dynamism of experience itself. When one questions with a ready answer in mind, one thinks in a mode that is aiming for stability, whereas when one genuinely questions in an open way for an answer one does not already possess, then one thinks in a mode that embraces instability. When we question in general, we open ourselves up to a kind of possibility that is multidirectional and dynamic. When we actively question an idea, its structures, capacities and limits are placed in flux. This flux makes the idea malleable and opens its various aspects to change. It is this fluctuation of possibility that we turn our gaze towards and observe when we investigate phenomena in a questioning manner. This dynamic possibility is made accessible through questioning in general, but phenomenological investigation utilizes a more precise form of reflection that also differs in how it is interpreted by each individual phenomenologist.

§3. Husserl's path from phenomenological questions to phenomenological answers

For Husserl, phenomenology concerns the fidelity of our knowledge to correlate to the evidence provided by the genuine experiences of the matters themselves. Whatever is suggested as 'knowledge' may be tested for its experiential correlate as evidence, and, in turn, whatever is experienced may be tested in the search for what may be developed as evidence to further support knowledge claims. Phenomenological investigation is, therefore, taken up when one raises the question 'to what extent do our knowledge claims correlate to our genuine experience?' An immensely powerful and open enterprise, the vast breadth of phenomenology may even cause one to pale in the recognition that *any kind* of knowledge and *any kind* of experience may become a proper object of phenomenological investigation.[2]

Husserlian phenomenology seeks to make phenomena transparent by using the general activity of questioning to modify ideas, and to fully clarify their eidetic structure. The process of suspending various attitudes, ideas or ways of thinking (the *epoché*) in order to fully explore the diverse manifestations of a phenomenon (through eidetic variation) and examining their essence requires questioning what something is and how it appears to consciousness. However, Husserl is not just seeking to develop his own personal descriptions of these experiences; rather, he seeks to collect *essential descriptions*, what is true for every instance of consciousness. In this sense, Husserl's approach can be identified as a radical kind of questioning that seeks to return to source experiences in order to clarify how consciousness, thinking and object constitution function. Due to the radical nature of Husserl's questioning, it proves to be rather difficult to follow; furthermore, the evidence of Husserl's radical re-questioning is found more in his practices than in his specific claims.

Starting with another of Husserl's assistants might prove beneficial in beginning to clarify the role of questioning in Husserl's work. Eugen Fink was Husserl's last assistant and in his essay 'The Problem of the Phenomenology of Edmund Husserl'; he clarifies the difficulty involved in reviving a philosopher's or a text's central question. In it Fink states that although texts 'must provide the basis for [their own] interpretation, and thus the fundamental question must be elicited from them [...] just how this question is included in the texts cannot always be univocally ascertained' (Fink 1981 21). This testifies to the difficulty of tracing back in order to find the original question a text or philosopher aims to address or answer. Regarding phenomenology, Fink states that 'given that access to the fundamental question of phenomenology is uncertain, the indication of the problem of Edmund Husserl's phenomenology can only be an interpretation that concedes this risk from the start' (Fink 1981 21). I take Fink here to suggest that the best way to approach Husserl's phenomenology is to first try to understand the questions that Husserl takes seriously, prior to (or at least in distinction with) the answers that Husserl also suggests. However, as Fink clearly admits, this risks an initial interpretation as to which questions one ought to begin with. In this way, the proper 'introduction' to Husserlian phenomenology is an *introduction to a set of questions* or to an *activity of questioning in general*. By leaving the specific question with which the Husserl scholar should begin open, it remains clear that a student of Husserl ought to begin *with questions* that reveal the problematicity of phenomena prior to considering the answers Husserl developed to resolve that problematicity. Although acquiring a clear grasp of Husserl's answers to phenomenological questions remains important, here we see the significance that Fink places on a genuine engagement with the very problematicity of the things themselves. Although Husserl rarely leaves his concepts and definitions at rest, what does remain consistent throughout his thought is the very activity of *investigation* (of phenomena, consciousness, etc.) and through this activity, the return to questions.

From this description, we can distinguish between the content of phenomenology and its correlate, i.e. the fluctuating experience of the phenomena themselves. Husserl suggests that we can question phenomena: the fleeting appearance of objects, both real and ideal, and acts of consciousness. In his work *Ideas I*, Husserl states that

> in phenomenology, as it begins, all concepts or terms have to remain in flux to a certain extent, always primed to be differentiated in keeping with the progress made in the analysis of consciousness and the recognition of new phenomenological layerings within what is first viewed as an undivided unity.
>
> (*Ideas I* 163)

In this way, then, we can initially understand 'phenomena' to be experience taken in the widest, richest and most encompassing sense as 'what appears to consciousness'. This becomes phenomenology when we try to give a scientific account of the very structures of experience, consciousness and phenomena. Maintaining this distinction between phenomenology and phenomena is also important for Husserl as he states that 'phenomenology presents itself in our expositions as a science *that is commencing*. Only the future can instruct us on how many of the results of the analyses attempted here [in *Ideas I*] are ultimately valid' (*Ideas I* 193). The distinction between *phenomenology as a science* and the *phenomena themselves* will help us to maintain the distinction between the collected questions of phenomenological investigation and their intended object: the phenomena themselves. Even though a phenomenological science aims to further develop a systematic understanding of consciousness and phenomena, it is equally important to maintain our questioning approach to phenomena in order to preserve the possibility that they may re-reveal themselves to us new ways. Maintaining a questioning stance towards the things themselves is emulated by Husserl's entire philosophical development. In *The Crisis of European Sciences and Transcendental Phenomenology* (henceforth *Crisis*), he writes that 'I seek not to instruct but only to lead, to point out and describe what I see. I claim no other right than that of speaking according to my best lights, principally before myself but in the same manner also before others, as one who has lived in all its seriousness the fate of a philosophical existence' (*Crisis* 18). Unto the very end, Husserl held that the role of a phenomenologist is to lead, point and describe and to examine not only what they see, but what is observable for any who are willing to make the effort to see for themselves.

For Husserl, phenomenology begins first with the renewed awakening to the world of phenomena and is followed by the process of trying to bring phenomena into focus without positing a theory about them. According to Fink, 'the interpretation of Husserl's phenomenology[,] on the basis of the fundamental problem which motivates it[,] must begin by attempting to characterize the way in which [...] wonder' forms the point of departure for phenomenology (Fink 1981 26). In effect, returning to a state of wonder about the things themselves is the attempt to bring about a state of receptivity for phenomena in such a way as to keep oneself from affecting phenomena in any 'pre-figurative' or 'theoretical' way. Fink states that

> if philosophy actually originates in wonder, then it never ascends merely to the small and limited peculiarity of this or that puzzling or noteworthy phenomenon, but, rather, ascends to the peculiarity of the existent as a whole. Worldly wisdom originates in universal wondering about the world.
>
> (Fink 1981 27)

This renewed attention to the original appearance of the world comprises Husserl's motto, 'to [wonder about] the things themselves'.

Although it may sound like an easy task to return to the wonder of experience, consciousness and the emergence of phenomena, the process of maintaining a state of unmodified receptivity to phenomena is actually incredibly difficult. That phenomena are fleeting, modifiable, lost or are easily covered up further suggests that the only way to 'keep them in view', as it were, is to maintain a *questioning attitude* towards them. As Husserl says in the 1920 foreword to the second edition of the *LI*: '[N]o amount of learning in the natural sciences or psychology or historical philosophies, will make it unnecessary to make these efforts in penetrating into phenomenology, or can do more than lighten them' (*LI* vol. II, 179). Not only is phenomenology initially difficult for the beginner, it remains so even for those who approach it with a great wealth of scientific and historical education. Later, in *Ideas I* section §87, Husserl states that

> [f]ar from being evident, [phenomenology] contains the most difficult problems of all, the sense of which is naturally hidden from all who still have no clue about the basic distinctions that set the standard for everything. In fact (if I may be allowed a judgement based on my own experience), it is a long and thorny path that leads from purely logical insights, from insights into the theory of meaning, from ontological and noetic insights, likewise from the usual normative and psychological epistemology to the apprehension of immanently psychological and then phenomenological givennesses in the genuine sense and leads finally to all the essential connections that render transcendental relations intelligible to us a priori. Something similar holds wherever we set out from objective insights in order to find the way to the phenomenological insights essentially pertaining to them.
>
> (*Ideas I* 172–3)

The whole process of finding a way into phenomenology is very arduous and can be summarized with Husserl's statement that 'everything [in phenomenology] is difficult; it requires painstaking concentration on the givennesses of the specifically phenomenological intuition of essences. There is no "royal path" into phenomenology, and so, too, there is none into philosophy' (*Ideas I* 193).[3] Just as philosophy begins when one starts to question their preconceived notions (of reality, self, ethics, meaning, etc.), phenomenology also begins when one questions one's own experience, consciousness and appearance. In both cases, it is to start with something incredibly familiar and make attempts to examine it, to make it more questionable.

In order to return to the matters themselves, one must first recognize just how difficult this call really is. According to Husserl, the difficulty of bringing phenomena into focus without posing a theory about them is due to the fact that we are constantly judging and taking a position towards the world in which we find ourselves. This difficulty holds not just for students, but also for the master. In his diary, which describes his encounter with Husserl on 8th May in 1928, the British philosopher and student of Husserl's W.R. Boyce Gibson stated that '[d]uring the last 15 years Husserl has published nothing. He told me they have been years of wandering through the jungle. In this jungle you meet wild beasts and bogs and he had been fighting wild beasts for the last 15 years, and he thought he had made some advances'.[4] Although second hand, this description of Husserl's slow advances reveals that part of the real work of phenomenology lies in genuinely struggling with its central questions as opposed to merely taking on its answers. If it was hard for Husserl, the original master, then recognizing and respecting this difficulty may in fact be not only something essential to the *practice* of phenomenology, but furthermore something that is easily overlooked when one simply jumps to phenomenology's hard-won answers. In his *Inaugural Lecture*, Husserl, after comparing pure phenomenology to the study of pure mathematics, argues that

> without troublesome work, no one can have any concrete, full idea of what pure mathematical research is like or of the profusion of insights that can be obtained from it. The same sort of penetrating work, for which no general characterization can adequately substitute, is required if one is to understand phenomenological science concretely.
>
> (*Inaugural Lecture* 132)

Thus, it is not enough to simply give mental assent to the answers that phenomenology proposes; a phenomenologist must further make real attempts to directly engage with the difficult work of returning to the things themselves. Phenomenology requires the reduction to bring phenomena into focus in a way that does not obfuscate them.

The phenomenological reduction is not an abstraction away from reality, one designed to obtain a more Platonic access to phenomena. Rather, the reduction moves in the 'opposite' direction, seeking to lead perception back to the original appearance of things as an experience that has first been glimpsed and then overlooked or modified. In this sense, phenomenology is a process of uncovering what has hitherto been covered up. If one says that phenomena are made into objects of study through the reduction, then phenomena can be understood as intentional objects constituted from the relationship between perceiver and the perceived. Phenomenology is always grounded in the demonstrative appeal that any other phenomenologist, at any stage in its development, may also *see for themselves* in order to validate another's claims. When maintained, this keeps phenomenology from becoming metaphysics (here defined pejoratively as a philosophical contrivance, conjectured without any genuine experiential content for its correlation and, therefore, experientially unverifiable). In light of the phenomenological reduction, becoming a phenomenologist always entails more than merely grasping the systems, definitions and distinctions of phenomenology; it also requires a laborious development of *phenomenological seeing* as an active and ongoing practice. Thus, it is never enough to merely understand what phenomenology claims (its definitions, concepts and methods); in order to be a phenomenologist, one must also be able to 'see' what is being *defined* and *conceptualized* in phenomenology and must be able to genuinely *practise* its methods and activities.

The *LI* is a major milestone in Husserl's development of phenomenology because it achieves two main tasks: (1) to introduce the reader to the activity of turning one's gaze towards viewing, retrieving and preserving phenomena themselves and (2) to give an accurate description of how phenomena genuinely appear *via* this activity. We can restate these two tasks using the structure of a question and say that the first task is accomplished when hitherto lost phenomena are retrieved through questioning the things themselves and the second task is accomplished when we answer these questions in the form of descriptions. However, in order to preserve the original questions, we must further maintain the realization that such descriptions will always fail to fully *exhaust* the phenomena they aim to describe. *There is no amount of phenomenological description that qualifies as sufficient to keep another phenomenologist from returning to the things themselves to verify what has hitherto been claimed.*

This interplay between questioning and answering is one of flux and stability. In this schema, Husserl suggests that our understanding of logic, meaning and number has become *too stable*. Instead of reviewing these stabilized ideas alongside their phenomenological character, thinkers merely take the ideas given to them by tradition for granted. Husserl's solution is to turn the thinker's gaze back to the original source of these traditional ideas: to return to the phenomenal flux of experience that correlates to every stabilized answer. In this way, what we previously believed to be a static and stabilized idea is further revealed to *also* be connected to a source of fluctuation: the phenomenon of what is being described. Turning our gaze towards the phenomenon is accomplished by questioning it. We shift from a perspective of questioning into one of answering as we move from phenomenologically perceiving phenomena towards describing them. The activity of questioning is one in which the multidirectional and dynamic flux of experience continually opens up our thinking, whereas the activity of answering is one in which the fluctuation of phenomena is stabilized. To be more specific, Husserl attempts to revive the original experiences that source our traditional and, therefore, stabilized ideas of logic, meaning and number.

Husserl's phenomenology, as it is presented in the *LI*, implements a radical questioning of logic, seeking to return to an original experience of how logic appears. This is accomplished by reviving the questions that elicit this original phenomenon. Thus, the *LI* reveals a way to conduct phenomenological research *via* a mode characterized by questions. In 1913, Husserl published *Ideas I*; this was a work that he felt advanced the whole project of phenomenology to a new level by providing answers to the questions raised by the *LI*. In comparison to the vibrant and dynamic vision of phenomena, as revealed in the *LI*, in *Ideas I* Husserl proposed a way to further stabilize phenomena into eidetic structures worthy of the auspicious title of science, one intended to be on par with that of mathematics. In *Ideas I*, Husserl states that 'science is only possible where the results of thinking can be preserved in the form of knowledge and can be applied for further thinking in the form of a system of assertions' (*Ideas I* 120). It is important to note that this systematicity, for the sake of science, is cultivated on the side of phenomenology and not necessarily on the side of phenomena. Although phenomenological descriptions pursue phenomena *in search of systematicity*, as the quotes from Husserl provided previously have suggested, phenomena also reflect a kind of radical flux for continual revelation and verification. Coming to understand this relationship between *systematic phenomenology* and its correlation with the *dynamic phenomena* it aims to describe reveals a greater connectivity between the philosophical concerns of Husserl and Heidegger.

The gravity of Husserl's discovery in *Ideas I* was powerful enough to cause him to begin re-drafting the *LI* into a 'higher' and 'better' form, one which introduced new readers to the genuine phenomenological work 'on the immediately envisaged and seized things themselves' (*LI* vol. I, 4). Husserl's hope was that the *LI* would open a thinker up to phenomena and prepare them for the presentation of the systematic discoveries awaiting them in *Ideas I*. Husserl states that

> the *Ideas* ought in effect to rest on the work of the *Logical Investigations*. If, through the latter, the reader has been brought openly to investigate and concern himself with a group of fundamental questions, then the *Ideas*, with their policy of illuminating method from ultimate sources […] could assist him to a further, independent advance.
>
> (*LI* vol. I, 4)

Thus, it seems fitting to describe the *LI* as a work designed to provoke phenomenological questioning and the *Ideas* as a work designed to systematically present the corresponding and updated method for this questioning in order to secure the results of phenomenological investigation as knowledge. In the *LI*, phenomenology was not a successful science for Husserl, given that it only tried to open a questioning way by which to rediscover and re-appreciate phenomena. According to Husserl, in order to raise phenomenology to the level of a science, it needed first to be further developed into eidetics. In order for phenomenology to become an eidetic science, fleeting phenomena need first to be stabilized to the same extent as mathematical objects are stable (thereby satisfying the requirement of stabilization *as knowledge* that any and all sciences necessitate by definition). What was occurring in this stabilization? If we view Husserl's development between the *LI* and *Ideas I* in terms of a movement from a presentation of questioning investigations to a presentation of answers that qualify as knowledge, then perhaps this might shed some light on why Heidegger parts ways with Husserl.

§4. Heidegger's return to and preservation of Husserl's phenomenological questioning

Before taking up the difficult task of trying to clarify the relationship between Husserl and Heidegger, it is important to first clarify just how perilous such an endeavour is. In his essay entitled 'On the Way to *Being and Time*'[5] scholar

Theodore Kisiel claims something interesting concerning the relationship between Husserl and Heidegger:

> What precisely does Heidegger take from Husserl? How does he depart from Husserl? At what precise point do these two phenomenologies part ways? The reader who carefully compares the two Parts [of *HCT*] will be rewarded by countless suggestions regarding these issues and will no doubt grasp in broad outline Heidegger's transposition of Husserl's themes ... and yet will find no definitive answer. There are a number of reasons for this. We have already found more than one occasion to remark on the fragmentary nature of Heidegger's retrieve of the Logical Investigations and to note how it might have been fleshed out more fully. Heidegger the teacher was no doubt in a hurry to finish an already protracted discussion of a difficult text. We are left to our own resources to fill in the detail.
>
> (Kisiel 1985 207)

Although Kisiel is specifically referring to the development between *HCT* and *BT* here, the same interpretation (one of general caution) may be extended to reading Heidegger as a whole against the backdrop of Husserl as a whole. Although it is difficult, as Kisiel claims, there are some illuminating comparisons to be made. That being said, it should be stated at the outset that this text does not aim to fully account for all of the differences and similarities between Husserl and Heidegger, nor could it given that such a project would take more than one large work. With that difficulty now having been clearly identified, I still attempt to find and trace a continuity regarding the activity of questioning from Husserl's phenomenology to Heidegger's reinterpretation of it.

As interpreting Heidegger in light of Husserl is always a precarious and complex endeavour, it is interesting to note that some scholars interpret Heidegger without comparing him to Husserl[6] while some, such as Theodore Kisiel, William J. Richardson and Thomas Sheehan, attempt a middle path and view Heidegger as remaining a phenomenologist through and through. In his essay 'What, After All, Was Heidegger about?' Sheehan claims that '[t]he premise of [his] essay is that Heidegger remained a phenomenologist from beginning to end and that phenomenology is exclusively about meaningfulness and its source' (Sheehan 2014 252).[7] Although I am arguing that Heidegger certainly remains concerned with phenomenology, at least within *BT*, I would hesitate to fully agree with Sheehan that Heidegger remained a 'phenomenologist from beginning to end', given that the so-called 'later Heidegger' takes on themes of *mythic* proportions.[8] Heidegger certainly takes up the unique power of questioning emulated by Husserl's phenomenology (again, perhaps more from the very practice of Husserl's phenomenology rather than from his written words); however, Heidegger certainly develops phenomenological questioning into something quite different from what Husserl would accept as strictly phenomenological. Although it remains outside of the scope of this text to *resolve* the relation between Husserl and Heidegger on the meaning of phenomenology, we can nonetheless focus upon their individual value and use of the activity of questioning.

What originally led Heidegger to Husserl's phenomenology, and what Heidegger later considered to be in danger of being overlooked, was the power of questioning as a means of phenomenological investigation that elicits the things themselves. In attempting to describe Husserl's leadership in a written speech for Husserl's seventieth birthday, Heidegger states that

> the essence of [Husserl's] leadership consists in […] the content and style of [his] *questioning* [that] should immediately force one into intense critical dialogue and should demand at each moment a readiness to reverse or even abandon one's position.
>
> (Heidegger 1929 475–6, my emphasis)

Here it is clear that Heidegger does not value Husserl's questions merely for the potentially novel answers they may or may not provide, but that such questions demand a unique kind of self-criticism that brings one into a state of radical openness to what appears, even when that appearance is contrary to what one initially believed. In response to Husserl's research, Heidegger sates that 'the works we present you are merely a witness to the fact that we *wanted* to follow your lead, not proof that we succeeded in becoming your disciples' (Heidegger 1929 476). The mark of Husserl's philosophical leadership prompted his students to think in a similar way as he had demonstrated through his practices, not merely to get them to agree with him. In trying to describe the scope of Husserl's accomplishments Heidegger rhetorically asks

> Is it not, rather, that first and foremost [Husserl's] research created an entirely new space for philosophical questioning, a space with new claims, transformed assessments, and a fresh regard for the hidden power of the great tradition of Western philosophy? Yes, it was precisely that. *The decisive element in your work has not been this or that answer to this or that question, but instead this breakthrough into a new dimension of philosophizing.* But this breakthrough is nothing less than the radicalizing [of how to do] philosophy.
>
> (Heidegger 1929 476, my emphasis)

In other words, Heidegger found Husserl's practices of *philosophizing* to be inspirational, an activity that revealed a new way to 'do' philosophy. Importantly, this new kind of philosophizing is not just another novel or supreme system or fixed method; rather, it is correlated with a genuine *experience of wonder*. Heidegger states:

> Whoever, by dint of research, has arrived at this self-understanding of philosophy is granted the basic experience of all philosophizing,[9] namely, that the more fully and originally [philosophical] research comes into its own, the more surely it is 'nothing but' the *transformation* of the same few simple questions. But those who wish to transform must bear within themselves the power of a fidelity that knows how to preserve. And no one will feel this power grow within him or her without being caught up in wonder.
>
> (Heidegger 1929 476–7)

The 'self-understanding' of philosophy is something one must see for themselves and has the power to transform even *via* simple questions when one is willing to preserve their experience of wonder. In other words, there is a kind of power in phenomenological questions to elicit wonder that Heidegger claims originates in Husserl's phenomenology.

In the 'Appendix B Husserl and Heidegger' of Kisiel and Sheehan's work *Becoming Heidegger: On the Trail of His Early Occasional Writings, 1910–1927* notes an introduction that Heidegger wrote for the publication of his speech for Husserl's birthday (*Akademische Mitteilung*). In the introduction for his speech, Heidegger states that

> [a]ny attempt to summarize Husserl's publications and philosophy is doomed to failure, and not merely because of the difficulty of the task. Such reports are by nature without life or effect and necessarily leave out the *single thing* that is worth knowing both now and in the future: that Husserl is among us as an active living force that enacts his true reality.
>
> (Kisiel & Sheehan 417)[10]

This certainly confirms that Heidegger found in Husserl a *force of philosophical questioning* that was felt well beyond the informational content that such questioning yielded, understood as a collection of detailed and sophisticated answers. However, this is importantly only one way to view Heidegger's speech.

Although these quotes provide some evidence that supports the claim that Heidegger found Husserl's questioning perhaps more influential than his answers, the issue remains far from conclusive. For the most part, I have interpreted Heidegger's words *positively*, but it should also be noted that these quotes can be interpreted in a more pejorative or acerbic way. Sheehan considers another way to read these passages and states that

> [o]ne thing that Husserl did not mention in his letter to Geiger was the speech Heidegger delivered before presenting the Festschrift – and there may have been good reasons for the omission. While heaping praise on Husserl for his many achievements over the last three decades, Heidegger also offered what he called 'sure points of reference for a true assessment of the value of your philosophical work,' and they were not necessarily the points Husserl would have chosen. For Heidegger those points of reference were not the founding of phenomenology, not the phenomenological method, not Husserl's painstaking reworking of problems, 'not this or that answer to this or that question,' but instead a 'breakthrough into a new dimension of philosophizing,' one that in the final analysis seemed to lie beyond Husserl's reach.
>
> (Kisiel & Sheehan 416)

Whether or not these interesting phrases connote a criticism of Husserl or indicate a legacy Heidegger genuinely saw in Husserl's work remains open for interpretation. Regarding the passage in which Heidegger states that they '*wanted* to follow' Husserl, Sheehan claims that 'Heidegger certainly had himself in mind' and that 'the speech became a self-advertisement for Heidegger's own work in contrast to Husserl's. […] And perhaps not without irony did Heidegger attribute to Husserl himself the insight "that we must always be ready to reverse or even abandon our positions"' (Kisiel & Sheehan 416–17). To what extent Heidegger was being genuine or not remains a problem for further consideration. However, given that the activity of questioning requires a genuine willingness to change one's own position, and Husserl's questioning certainly emulated such a conviction in light of his penchant for revision (to a much larger extent than Heidegger did), it is defensible to hold that Heidegger was not being cynical in his speech.[11] That being said, what Husserl thought of Heidegger and his work is quite clear.

It can be observed, from a few of Husserl's letters, that he had mixed feelings about Heidegger's work, specifically doubting the claim that it was a genuine follow-through of his own work. In his letter to Alexander Pfänder, dated 1 January 1931 Husserl wrote that 'Heidegger's phenomenology is something totally different from mine; rather than furthering the development of my scientific works, his university lectures as well as his book are, on the contrary, open or veiled attacks on my works' (Kisiel & Sheehan 402). As far as Husserl understood Heidegger's thought, whatever it was, it certainly was not the kind of phenomenology he had established. In the same letter, Husserl states that after devoting

> two months to studying *Being and Time* along with [Heidegger's] more recent writings [...] I arrived at the distressing conclusion that philosophically I have nothing to do with this Heideggerian profundity, with this brilliant but unscientific genius; that Heidegger's criticism, both open and veiled, is based on a gross misunderstanding; that he may be involved in the formation of a philosophical system of the kind which I have always considered it my life's work to render impossible forever.
>
> (Kisiel & Sheehan 403)

In another letter, dated seven days later to Dietrich Mahnke, Husserl makes an even stronger case against the idea that Heidegger is continuing his phenomenology. He states that after a 'repeated study of *Being and Time* I came to the conclusion that his "phenomenology" has not the least thing to do with my own, and I view its pseudo-scientific character as an obstacle to the development of philosophy' (Kisiel & Sheehan 405). In light of these comments, it is clear that Husserl himself did not see Heidegger's phenomenology as a continuation of his own. Thus, in order to show how one can view Heidegger's philosophy as a kind of phenomenological development in response to Husserl will require additional textual evidence and argumentation.

To begin setting up a way to show how one can read Heidegger's phenomenology as a continuation of Husserl's, one can turn to Heidegger's short essay 'My Way' given that it provides the first clue as to why he decides to part ways from Husserl. In the essay, Heidegger describes his own difficulties in trying to understand Husserl's phenomenology. He continually re-read Husserl's *LI* because he 'could not get over a main difficulty [that] concerned the simple question [of] how [...] "phenomenology" was to be carried out' ('My Way' 76). Enamoured with phenomenological questioning, Heidegger wanted more and says that 'the year 1913 brought an answer [in the form of Husserl's *Ideas I*]' (Heidegger 1972). According to Heidegger, *Ideas I* did more than provide answers to the questions of *LI*: '[I]n this universal project for a phenomenological philosophy, the *Logical Investigations*, too – which had so to speak remained philosophically neutral – could be assigned their systematic place. [Furthermore the investigations] had in the meantime undergone "profound revisions"' (Heidegger 1972 77). Here, Heidegger suggests that the structure and neutrality of the *LI* was changed to fit the programme of *Ideas I* and that, in doing so, something important in phenomenology was in danger of being lost.

According to Heidegger, a value for *questioning as such* turned out to be what was in danger of being lost. The powerful answer, in the form of an updated method of transcendental phenomenology presented in *Ideas I*, had the potential to cover up the *LI*'s accomplishments; put otherwise, Husserl's radical re-discovery of exploring phenomena through *the activity of questioning* was in jeopardy of being eclipsed by the power of eidetics as an 'excellent' answer. Heidegger states that even after *Ideas I* was published, he remained captivated by the magic of the *LI* ('My Way' 78). For Heidegger, the 'magic' of phenomenology is found not in its systematic descriptions, but in the very activity of phenomenological seeing [*phänomenologishchen Sehen*], of leading one back to re-question the matters themselves. It was this preservation of phenomena (first made visible in the *LI*) that captured Heidegger's attention. This is further confirmed in Heidegger's *Introduction to Phenomenological Research* (henceforth *IPR*) wherein he claims that

> [t]he *Logical Investigations* are not motivated by the ambition of working out anything like a new textbook in logic. Instead, the principal purpose is *to make the objects with which logic is preoccupied into the theme for once in such a way that research related to this is put into a position of being able actually to work on subject matters* – that the specific objects of this discipline are brought *to a specific intuition that identifies them.* 'Intuition' here means simply: to make present to oneself the object in itself, just as it presents itself.
>
> (*IPR* 37)

In other words, for Heidegger the *LI* did not present a new answer to be considered but the resurrection of the original question 'what is logic?' In this way, the *LI* aims to be preparatory, to return the reader to the original experience of logic itself and to see it as a correlate to the traditional definitions, concepts and descriptions developed in response to it. In a similar way that Reinach did for numbers (as discussed above), the *LI* for Heidegger represents an effort to re-question our experiences of logic and the objects of logic; its aim was to re-question the very experience of logic and its objects in such a way as to return a thinker to the original phenomena that are described, accounted for or conceptualized by tradition. Heidegger states that 'the *Logical Investigations* are intended to be the kind of preparatory labors that for once first seek to bring the objects of this discipline into view, just as if it appeared that sciences devoid of any object at all were being pursued' (*IPR* 39). Once the original source for, and perpetual appearance of, logic and its objects have been secured, we are then in a *phenomenological* position to consider how and to what extent our traditional concepts correlate to what they conceptualize. This effort is not simply done to enable us to see the shortcoming of traditional accounts of logic, but more so, to really see for ourselves how the original questioning into these phenomena are the source for such traditional answers. This is how things stand in relation to Husserl on the problems of logic, but Heidegger also identifies a power to question that he takes to be indicative of all phenomenology within this particular concern: Husserl's *LI* shows how phenomenological questions are still able to revitalize original experiences that reveal new discoveries, even after thousands of years of philosophical history concerning the issue of logic.[12] Although Husserl may have revitalized the original question of logic in the *LI* in order to present his own transcendental answer in *Ideas I*, Heidegger saw something much more powerful and encompassing in the very phenomenological means of revitalizing any question whatsoever.

While Heidegger wanted to participate in Husserl's impressive display of phenomenological questioning, he did not necessarily want to adopt Husserl's answers. Heidegger interprets Husserl's questioning as a means to return to experience itself in order to allow for phenomena themselves to appear to consciousness. Heidegger states that

> the distinctive feature of the *Logical Investigations* lies in the way in which a foundation for logic is sought, namely, by aiming to make present to oneself a fact of the matter in which all of logic's objects can be found and investigated, in such a way that logic would have a completely determinative milieu in which to move.
>
> (*IPR* 39–40)

In this way of questioning back to the things themselves then, does Heidegger actually attempt to take up the mantle of Husserl's phenomenology as depicted in the *LI* rather than that of *Ideas I*? This seems to be confirmed at the end of 'My Way' in which Heidegger states that

> in what is most its own[,] phenomenology is not a school. It is the possibility of thinking, at times changing and only thus persisting, of corresponding to the claim of what is to be thought. If phenomenology is thus experienced and retained, it can disappear as a designation in favor of the matter of thinking whose manifestness remains a mystery.
>
> ('My Way' 82)

It is the matters themselves, the flux of phenomena that correlate to phenomenological descriptions that claim to be thought. In other words, according to Heidegger it is the *possibility of thinking*, which enables one to return to the things themselves, that needs to be preserved over and against the incredible descriptions and concepts uncovered *via* the use of this possibility (the power of questioning needs to be preserved and distinguished from the results it enables). Heidegger added a supplement to 'My Way' in 1969 to further help clarify this statement, in which he recited his famous line of *Being and Time*: '[P]henomenology [has] shown that what is essential in it does not lie in its *actuality* as a philosophical [school or] "movement." Higher than actuality stands *possibility*. We can understand phenomenology only by seizing upon it as a possibility' (*BT* 63/38). How then does one grasp phenomenology as a possibility?

In a letter written to Fink, Heidegger enclosed a copy of the speech he gave for Fink on his sixtieth birthday which sheds some light on what he meant by the possibility of phenomenology. The speech, which is an account of how Heidegger came to know Fink as a student, states that

> [a]t that time you were already known as a recognized and privileged student of Husserl's. You now entered another, and yet the same school of phenomenology. Of course, we must understand this title correctly. It does not refer to a particular direction in philosophy. It names a possibility that continues to exist today, i.e., making it possible for thinking to attain the 'things themselves,' or to put it more clearly: to attain the matter of thinking.
>
> (*The Fundamental Concepts of Metaphysics. World, Finitude, Solitude* 367)

Here we see that Heidegger views his own 'school' of phenomenology in a strange relation to Husserl's, something similar but modified. Furthermore, Heidegger identifies phenomenology as not merely a collection of philosophical insights, but also a possibility to re-engage with the things themselves. Heidegger's target problem remains the same as Husserl's: the things themselves. However, although the target remains the same, Heidegger's response to this issue is quite different from that of Husserl's and this supports the claim that he viewed his own work as being indebted Husserl's. If Heidegger's suggests that one must grasp and understand phenomenology as a possibility, how then does one accomplish this?

Seizing upon phenomenology as a possibility encompasses two stages: first, to distinguish the science of phenomenological description from the experience of the multidirectional and dynamic flux of phenomena themselves and, second, to maintain the first distinction in order to preserve the openness of the phenomena alongside their powerful and sophisticated descriptions. It is the openness of experience that allows for any phenomenologist to verify any description posed and it is this possibility of verification that keeps phenomenology from falling into metaphysics (defined as a philosophical contrivance). For Heidegger, the value of phenomenology shifts when its systematic answers are presented in such a way as to eclipse its powerful ability to question and reveal their dynamic openness. In other words, when the results of phenomenological description begin to draw attention away from the *ability and activity to see* the phenomena themselves in their vibrancy, this threatens to conceal their fluctuation, thereby reducing phenomenology to just a list of propositions, definitions, concepts, etc.

For Heidegger, the problem in Husserl's development from the *LI* to *Ideas I* is that phenomenology, which was originally introduced as a way to think about and to view the world in a mode of vibrant and dynamic possibilities, had been shifted into a mode of static and stabilized eidetics. The unstable, fleeting and self-concealing nature of phenomena became overly stabilized in structures that are devoid of their original dynamism. The science of eidetics resolved the issue a little too neatly for Heidegger. Instead of a phenomenology that brought a hitherto missed dynamic aspect of phenomena into view, phenomenology, understood as eidetics, stabilized this dynamism into static ideal objects. In other words, the questioning power of phenomenology is valuable for Husserl because it led to establishing powerful answers; for Heidegger, this questioning power is valuable on its own in that it provides a way to view and perpetually re-engage with the flux of phenomena. However, while this is Heidegger's interpretation and judgement of Husserl, is it fair or even correct? After all, it was Husserl and not Heidegger who continually returned to *something* again and again that caused him to perpetually revise phenomenology.

In Husserl's defence, one might wonder if Heidegger maintained the distinction between descriptive phenomenology and the experience of phenomena themselves. Regarding Heidegger's famous statement that 'higher than actuality stands possibility' we can see that thirteen years prior to the publication of *BT*, Husserl says something very similar in *Ideas I*: 'As long as it is rightly understood and utilized in the right way, the old ontological doctrine *that the knowledge of "possibilities" must precede that of actualities* is, in my estimation, a great truth' (*Ideas I* 153). Elsewhere in *Ideas I*, Husserl speaks about the beginnings and progress that he hopes and expects students of phenomenology to undergo. Husserl states:

> At first [the phenomenological] procedure, *naively at work*, serves only to acclimate the researcher to the new domain, *to practice seeing* [*das Sehen*], apprehending, analyzing within it generally and to become a little acquainted

with the kinds of givenness in it. But then scientific reflection – reflection on the essence of the procedure itself, on the essence of the kinds of givenness at play in it [...] – *takes over the function of a general and logically rigorous justification of the method*. Consciously pursued, it then assumes the character and rank of scientific method that in a given case, through application of the rigorously formulated norms of the method, permits the practice of criticism that circumscribes and improves the endeavor.

(*Ideas I* 119, my emphasis)

In this quotation, we clearly see that phenomenology did not *begin as a science* even for Husserl, but that it would have to be developed into one (the scientific reflection required to raise phenomenology to a science would develop out of the initial naive starting point). The phrase 'to practice seeing' [*Sehen*] is a very informative one as it is the same phrase Heidegger uses in 'My Way'. It is also important to note that Husserl considers the systematicity of science as something that comes *after* the student has developed the ability to practise phenomenological seeing. If we recall that there is a distinction between the *science of* phenomenology and *the phenomena themselves* for Husserl, then we can perhaps respond to Heidegger's critique of Husserl and state that whereas Heidegger valued phenomenology for the possibility it provided to return to the experience of the things themselves, his analysis of Husserl's development from *LI* to *Ideas I* seems somewhat hasty. Even though it is flawed, the sentiment behind Heidegger's analysis might prove to be interesting in that it focuses attention on the activity of questioning.

With this analysis in view, we can perhaps temper Heidegger's critique of Husserl and in so doing we might show how the two thinkers are closer than they perhaps first appear historically. We can understand the *practice* of phenomenology as a *questioning way* to revive and return to experience itself and furthermore understand the results of that practice to be the answers derived from 'doing' it. In this sense, we might view *BT* as Heidegger's attempt to further develop Husserl's phenomenology as it was presented in the *LI*: taking the value of phenomenological questioning and maintaining the possibility of phenomena themselves over and against their scientific stabilizations. In this way we can interpret Heidegger's approach to phenomenological investigation as a way to continue Husserl's exploration of how lived experiences arise within consciousness in the first place. In order to accomplish this, Heidegger turns his gaze to the phenomenon of the questioner (Dasein) and reflects upon what structures of possibility are required for such an entity to be able to question in the first place. Heidegger is not alone in this pursuit of reinterpreting phenomenology in light of the activity of questioning, for another of Husserl's students (who is also a student of Heidegger's) continues to develop the central role of questioning in phenomenology.

§5. Patočka's undaunted phenomenology of the question 'what is history?'

The analysis of questioning is further developed in Patočka's work entitled *Heretical Essays* (henceforth *HE*) in which he considers the idea of participating in history as the preservation of the question 'what is history?' From an understanding of Patočka's phenomenology of history, we can trace the continual development of phenomenological questioning taken up by Husserl and reinterpreted by Heidegger. The preservation of questions alongside (or despite) their answers is how the phenomenologist remains open to the things themselves. This activity of remaining open in general is specifically accomplished when the flux of phenomena is kept in view and preserved alongside their descriptions.

Patočka's approach to phenomenological investigation seeks to explore the importance of participating in history. For Patočka, this participation extends beyond mere academic study and requires that one live their life in response to the question of history. Participating in history means asking and answering the question 'what is history?' without the guarantee of a pre-given meaning. This context of unsheltered life is not defined as a lack of traditional meaning, but rather as a weakening of its reliability or certitude (i.e. shaken meaning). In other words, the context of unsheltered life is one in which everything previously taken for granted is now open for re-investigation.[13] Although pre-given meaning remains available, it is never accepted *unreflectively*. By analysing Patočka's presentation of the question of history, the more general power of questioning becomes visible as a further development of the questioning kind of phenomenology evident in Husserl and Heidegger. From the way Patočka structures the question of history (as being preserved in contrast to, but alongside, its many 'excellent' answers), we can further expand these structures to any question whatsoever. Furthermore, from the way Patočka attempts a phenomenology of history using this structure of questioning, we can draw a formal approach to phenomenological questioning in general. In this way, then, we ascertain in Patočka a continuation of Husserl and Heidegger's work on the activity of phenomenological questioning as such. The relation between

Patočka's 'shaken meaning' and the possibility of phenomena preserved *via* phenomenological questioning further exemplifies how phenomenology can be understood as a rediscovery of the activity of questioning (its central place in philosophy and power to re-elicit the experiences of the things themselves).

In order to understand 'shaken meaning' we must first clarify how it is found in the context of unsheltered life. Patočka understands the development of history to be a movement from prehistory (characterized by absolute certainty in meaning) into history proper (characterized by problematicity). The shift from prehistory into history involves the development from a sheltered life into an unsheltered life. Life lived in prehistory is empowered by an absolute meaning that shelters those living within it from questions of nihilism, a total loss of meaning and the finality of death (finitude). This shelter takes shape in social, political and cultural organizations of meaning that provide a place for every individual and, in so doing, it provides them with absolute meaning for their life. In other words, sheltered life provides an *answer* to every philosophical question a thinker in prehistory may or may not ask.[14] What is the meaning of life in general? What is the meaning of my individual life? Why should I act in this or that way? All of these questions are softly quelled by absolute answers provided by sheltered life.

Sheltered life persists until prehistory becomes history, a time in which the traditional answers to these important questions lose some of their power (or lose their force of absolute resolution); the result is unsheltered life. It is the encounter with and effect of philosophy that moves prehistory into history proper:

> [P]hilosophy is the shaking of the ground which bears human familiarity with the existent [*Seiendem*], the shaking of the basis which forms the presupposition for the progressive augmentation of knowledge, the unsettling of the foundations of knowledge and the *questioning* of the existent *qua* existent and the nature of truth.
>
> (Fink 1981 23)

This can be understood as rhetorical questioning being exchanged for genuine philosophical questioning: in prehistory, questioning primarily focuses upon rhetorical issues in which the question only serves as a dogmatic path to an already-established answer and is asked merely, and therefore disingenuously, to restate an answer that has already been prefigured. In contrast to prehistory, history proper is characterized by questions that further problematize these 'already-established answers' and in so doing facilitate genuine or philosophical thinking. Such questions are asked without the absolute security that they will lead to anything specific, let alone a previously intended answer. In history proper, the *familiarity* of established answers no longer seems appealing however; on the contrary, those traditional answers that are perpetually re-confirmed by one's own responsible questioning become all the more valuable while those answers that do not become suspicious.

For Patočka, history only begins when absolute meaning becomes suspect and, therefore, when those living in the cave of sheltered life come out into the open world under the sun. No longer sheltered by traditional answers, thinkers are forced to face the original questions of philosophy and to genuinely wonder about what was previously taken for granted. In the preface to Patočka's *HE*, Paul Ricoeur states that 'in contrast to the warrior who is still sheltered from the danger he confronts by the stable grandeur for which he risks himself, in the case of the problematic human the goal is [freedom]' (*HE* xiii). Life lived in a controlled, predictable and systematic world, in which everyone and everything has a place, purpose and pre-given meaning, shifts into unsheltered life that is overtaken by a dynamic, uncontrolled and not always predictable world. Patočka states that warriors in prehistorical life 'find their support in a meaning woven into the immediacy of life, fighting for their home, family, for the continuum of life to which they belong – in them they have their support and goal, those provide them with the shelter from the danger they need' (*HE* 39). The fear that these warriors may perish is alleviated due to the fact that the meaning of their deaths will be preserved within the society for which they fight and die. This brings to mind the common phrase of 'living for something larger than yourself' that many recruiters use to urge individuals to enlist in the army. Patočka continues by stating that 'in contrast to [sheltered life] stands the goal of a *free* life as such, one's own or that of others; it is essentially, an unsheltered life' (*HE* 39). Specifically, Patočka defines unsheltered life as life that

> does not stand on the firm ground of generative continuity, it is not backed by the dark earth, but only by darkness, that is, it is ever *confronted* by its finitude and the permanent precariousness of life. Only by coming to terms with this threat, confronting it undaunted can free life as such unfold; [...] the freedom of the undaunted.
>
> (*HE* 38–9)

For Patočka, the human being is threatened or *daunted* by death. The prehistorical response to this threat is to build a society as a continuum: all who die in the service of the continuum are, therefore, preserved by its persistence over time. Being daunted by a fear of death seems to be a kind of existential browbeaten slavery, where humans live their lives out of, and in the service of avoiding, the fear of death. Here, Plato's idea that philosophy is the practice and preparation of dying, of shaking loose the fear of death, seems apt: those who accept the fear of death and face it directly, those who strive to be undaunted do so when they fully accept their freedom and the radical contingency of their lives. This is not to accept nihilism, but the fair recognition of the possibility of nihilism.

In unsheltered life, individuals take seriously the possibility of a total loss of meaning and in that recognition to strive to live for meaning all the more. Absolute meaning in sheltered life is tantamount to a frightened escape, denial or repression of the fear of death. In unsheltered life, absolute meaning is exchanged for *possible* meaning: it may or may not survive, persist or endure and in this sense only the possibility and not the *necessity* of nihilism is recognized. In the process of this recognition, the goal of working against nihilism also appears. Our proper pursuit of, and response to, *possible* meaning is questioning wherein we question it and after we think we have found it re-question it anew. Truth remains viable within possible meaning, but is now tempered through a perpetual reconfirmation by every individual; that is, truth becomes what everyone must see for themselves. If there are true answers that remain within unsheltered life, they are always preceded by their questions and, as such, their truth is revealed in the perpetual re-confirmation *via* one's questioning anew.

Whereas wisdom in the prehistorical world is a matter of knowing the correct answer to every question, wisdom in the historical world involves preserving the activity of questioning on its own alongside one's traditional answers. Importantly, however, traditional answers and ways of thinking are not discarded, but are instead preserved. Ricoeur states that 'the loss of "meaning" is not the descent into the "meaning-less", but [provides] an access to the quality of meaning implied in the search itself' (*HE* xiv). The meaning of sheltered life is not entirely lost, forsaken or discarded; instead, it merely loses its absolute efficacy (that is to say, its absolute power over thinkers weakens somewhat). Patočka states that

> nothing of the earlier life of acceptance remains in peace; all the pillars of the community, traditions, and myths, are equally shaken, as are all the answers that once preceded questions, the modest yet secure and soothing meaning, though not lost, is transformed. It becomes as enigmatic as all else.
>
> (*HE* 39–40)

The shift from the predictable sheltered life of prehistory into the more chaotic unsheltered life of history is not a total loss of tradition either: tradition remains, but becomes more enigmatic and, therefore, all the more questionable. It is important to note that the suspicion for traditional answers and their corresponding questions does not evoke distain, prejudice or rejection; instead, tradition, its answers and questions become all the more interesting and wondrous in the positive sense that they demand further study and more serious reflection and concern. Thus, the movement from sheltered life into unsheltered life increases the concern for tradition rather than merely undermining its efficacy. Ricoeur states that the 'meaning within the condition of problematicity is [...] a "proper meaning", a meaning neither too modest nor dogmatic, which gives courage for a life in the atmosphere of the problematic' (*HE* xiv). The atmosphere of the problematic is one in which original questions maintain their efficacy in propelling thinking further, despite the traditional answers already collected in response to these questions.

The renewal of questions does not displace answers entirely or suggest that the world is entirely relative and without truth. Instead, it preserves the traditional responses to philosophical questions, but maintains the dynamism that these questions originally possessed in addition to the well-developed answers of tradition. This dynamism is best understood as a special kind of possibility in thinking. Patočka writes that 'life unsheltered [...] itself opens up to the possibility for which it reaches [...]. [It] sees what life is and can be [...]. Such life does not seek to escape its contingency, but neither does it yield to it passively' (*HE* 39). The difficulty for thought in unsheltered life is specifically this creative tension between our pursuits of absolute truth and our inability to find it in every area of existence. That we do find absolute truth in some areas of existence (e.g. mathematics) seems to further tantalize prehistorical thinkers with the promise of finding absolute truth everywhere, if only it is sought out in the correct way. For the historical thinker, the pursuit of absolute truth is maintained alongside the mature awareness of what makes this prospect so tantalizing.

Patočka represents a very interesting synthesis of Husserl's and Heidegger's views: Husserl's pursuit of timeless truth persists alongside Heidegger's revelation that this timeless truth cannot always be attained in every domain of existence. Even though we know absolute truth will not be attained for all issues, we pursue it nonetheless. Were one to view the issue of truth merely from the perspective of answers, then they would be forced to take up an either/or position in response to the developmental differences between that Husserl and Heidegger. However, if one were to view the issue of truth from the perspective of the question 'what is truth?', then the either/or position reveals itself as an answer, that is as something *secondary* to the original question. A thinker is capable of thinking in questions as well as in terms of answers, and this reveals the 'requirement' of the either/or position to be limited to merely *thinking in answers*. The addition or renewed value of *thinking in questions*, therefore, expands our grasp of what is possible in thought and abolishes the 'absolute requirement' of either/or truth by showing that such a requirement only makes sense when one has restricted themselves to thinking in answers. This requirement maintains itself as valid within the domain of thinking in answers, but the limits of thinking in answers are revealed to be a smaller subset of thinking itself when one reconsiders the original power of a question. This interplay is the meaning of history for Patočka, as something that lies between a valued pursuit of timeless truth as answers and the realization that such a pursuit always remains worthy of further thought, that is questionable. In maintaining the value of the yet-to-be fully answered question 'what is history?', alongside its already-valued answers (e.g. progress, scientific posterity, democracy, etc.), we observe how the activity of questioning can keep the possibility for history open while simultaneously gathering and maintaining concern and thought for its traditional answers.

This scheme of shaken but undaunted philosophy is directly related to phenomenology in that it is phenomenology that returns the thinker to the place of questioning, wherein the world is re-infused with the possibility to reveal and/or conceal itself. In Fink's terms, phenomenology provides a way for the astonishment of anything from the most mundane everyday experiences to philosophy's most pressing matters. Fink defines astonishment as

> [a] forcing out: it forces man out of that fundamental way of life, one of laziness and metaphysical indolence, in which he has ceased to question the existent *qua* existent. Wonder dislodges man from the prejudice of everyday, publicly pregiven, traditional and worn out familiarity with the existent, drives him from the already authorized and expressly explicated interpretation of the sense of the world and into the creative poverty of not yet knowing what the existent is.
>
> (Fink 1981 24)

The power of phenomenological questioning revitalizes the givenness of the world through our dynamic and inexhaustible experience of questioning and re-questioning it and in so doing allow it to maintain a perpetual possibility to self-reveal anew. In this reinterpretation of phenomenology, Patočka preserves Husserl's charge that the philosopher must be resolved 'not to accept unquestioningly any pregiven opinion or tradition so that he can inquire, in respect to the whole traditionally pregiven universe, after what is true in itself, an ideality' (*Vienna Lecture* 286). Even though Patočka also acknowledges that there are areas of existence that seem to never yield absolute truth, no matter how long they are studied for, he nonetheless maintains that the primary value for research remains the search for truth. This distinguishes between a *search for truth* and the *possession of truth*. Fink states that 'in astonishment, the existent is manifested in a new, original way that interrupts the fixity of the established explication of being and commences the "hunt for the existent"' (Fink 1981 25). Even though previously held concepts have been shaken out of fixity, they are nonetheless still pursued with new attempts of re-conceptualization. Fink continues by stating that

> if the origin of a philosophical problem lies essentially in astonishment, then its emergence from astonishment is not a passive occurrence. Rather, the problem becomes actual by man's taking astonishment up voluntarily, by astonishment's being sustained and developed by the awakening force of conceptual cognition.
>
> (Fink 1981 25)

In this way, we can see how phenomenology's activity of re-questioning reinvigorates the possibility of phenomena to appear anew by raising and sustaining astonishment for how appearance arises out of experience. The accomplishment of Husserl's, in his many varying conceptualizations of method, is to bring a thinker into astonishment as an activity of questioning (investigation); such a feat can be distinguished from among Husserl's many attempts to clarify and to resolve this astonishment as an activity of answering (by way of description).

§6. The unique type of questioning employed by phenomenology

The three examples of Husserl, Heidegger and Patočka illustrate how the activity of questioning forms the basis of phenomenological investigation, although this is interpreted differently by each thinker. The activity of questioning may be used to help clarify the many differences and commonalities across individual movements of phenomenology in a unifying way that need not conflate or collapse their differences. In each case, special attention is paid to the phenomenon of *what* is under investigation alongside the *resulting descriptions* of its many appearances.

With this more encompassing definition of phenomenological questioning, which concerns something dynamic and constantly in flux as well as various stable descriptions of it, we have a way to view a continual unity in the thinking of Husserl to Heidegger and on to Patočka. This unity is composed of a curious doubling within phenomenology: it tracks the ability and activity to view and to think about unstable and dynamic phenomena alongside the scientific and philosophical attempts to describe their stable appearances. The instability of phenomena, and parenthetically our attempts to understand them, is what Husserl discovered and presented in the *LI* and, according to Heidegger, apparently lost or moved on from by the time he wrote *Ideas I*. It is this same instability that Patočka develops in his analysis of history and it is the very same instability that can still be uncovered and viewed by any thinker willing to question the things themselves. I think it is this instability of phenomena that Heidegger is referring to when he claims that 'higher than actuality stands *possibility*' (*BT* 63/38)[15] and if this is so, then phenomenology can be provisionally unified, at least regarding its central focus upon the activity of questioning, when understood[16] as thinking in a mode of possibility.[17]

The working and provisional definition of phenomenology understood as thinking in a mode of possibility is connected to the activity of questioning. In its requirement to strive to preserve the fluctuation of phenomena further to self-reveal additional appearances, phenomenology enables a thinker to recognize the fluid possibilities of existence alongside its stable actualities. Concerning the relationship phenomenological thinking has with experience, science and natural life, in his paper 'The Phenomenological Reduction: From Natural Life to Philosophical Thought', Bernet states that

> [p]henomenology changes how things look to us in natural life; it modifies their meaning. It mainly does so by opening, within natural life, the realm of *new possibilities*. These new possibilities phenomenology offers natural life come from philosophical thinking and concern *how natural life thinks about itself* [...]. What phenomenology can teach natural life is to think of its confirmed facts and constraints in terms of *mere possibilities*. This gives natural life the new freedom to *criticize* present or former ways of leading one's life and to *imagine* alternative ways of organizing one's life – both one's personal and social life. [...] Phenomenology changes natural life by awakening its hidden resources for an imaginative and creative mode of thinking.
>
> (Bernet 2016 332–3)

The kind of questioning that phenomenology employs when investigating phenomena, experience, science, life, etc., is done in a mode that, although *challenging* traditional and established views, theories, meanings and answers, as a mode of *possible thinking*, need not threaten a total relativism or pose a malicious critique. When we question a phenomenon (here remaining open to all of the multiple ways in which Husserl, Heidegger and Patočka define or remain open to appearances and their respective ways, insights and methods of doing so), we can bring a phenomenon's stability and instability into view. The stability of phenomena understood as concepts, definitions, structures, systems and truths appears alongside their instability, understood as *coming into or failing to be fully* conceptualized, defined, structured, systemized and found to be true or not. Alongside the discovery of answers in philosophy and science, we trace the thinking and investigating *mediation* through which such answers come to be or fail to be recognized, uncovered and identified as answers. By re-energizing the way phenomena emerge and fail to emerge, by tracing 'how instability becomes stabilized' and 'how stability becomes destabilized', we remain open to the novel and unknown ways in which phenomena can and may further self-reveal. In this way then, thinking in a mode that reveals the instability of phenomena in no way undermines thinking in a mode that reveals the stability of phenomena, but together make up the whole of phenomenological investigation.

By recollecting, considering and preserving the central questions of phenomenology, as identified and developed by Husserl, Heidegger and Patočka, I have introduced how we can trace and maintain a peculiar unity in phenomenology which correlates philosophical phenomenology alongside various individual phenomenologies as separate historical out-workings of Husserl's original questioning. In addition to this peculiar unity that does not conflate or collapse the differences of each individual phenomenology, it also, and at the same time, reveals how they all can and may be organized into a larger whole. This not only turns out to be a useful way to read the history of phenomenology, it also provides a way to anticipate future developments in phenomenology: rather than just viewing novel phenomenological research in light of how it adheres to or diverges from any individual or particular phenomenology *via* answers, we can also consider how it relates to phenomenology's central questions (in raising, answering, adding to or taking away from them).

We can apply Husserl's motto 'to the things themselves' to thinking by returning to, and thereby preserving for further thought, the *original questions* raised by individual thinkers alongside their powerful answers. When it comes to the power of perception, of what it can phenomenologically 'catch in its gaze' and, thus, to what we can continually return to again and again, we can consider whether or not the domain of thinking is larger than the domain of conceptual thinking. In his article 'The Limits of Conceptual Thinking', Bernet states:

> Husserl's view on conceptual thinking also has its limits [...]. For Husserl, pregiven concepts must have been formed, and the insight into the process of their formation is crucial for the rigorous determination of their meaning and of their use [...]. [T]here is no need for any internal intermediaries or mental screens in the relation between perceiver and perceived. Perception has an immediate grasp on reality [...]. Not only can a perceiver recognize something for which he has no name or concept, but he can also explore its qualities without making use of linguistic meanings.
>
> (Bernet 2014 228)

Here we see that the possibility we experience when we question may indeed be conceptualized in response to the question 'what is possibility?'; however, there is no limit to the number of excellent or powerful concepts that we could derive in response to this question that would fully account for or exhaust the experience it directs one to think about. Thus, no answer could or should bar another thinker from raising and asking this question anew. If this is the case, then whatever phenomenon we experience when we investigate the question 'what is x?', it is certainly always *more than* a concept and, furthermore, always *more than* whatever we make or describe of it, for we can always raise the question anew. In this sense, every phenomenological investigation ought to uphold the distinction between phenomenology (as a list of descriptions) and phenomena (the experience and perception of the things themselves self-revealing) and, in so doing, it will have to refrain from merely beginning with traditional list of concepts.

In *BT*, Heidegger encounters and resolves a similar problem regarding the traditional history of ontology in his plan to establish and revive the question of being. In §6 he contends:

> If the question of Being is to have its own history made transparent, then this hardened tradition must be loosened up, and the concealment which it has brought about must be dissolved. We understand this task as one in which by taking *the question of Being as our clue*, we are to *destroy* the traditional content of ancient ontology until we arrive at those primordial experiences in which we achieved our first ways of determining the nature of Being – the ways which have guided us ever since.
>
> (BT 44/22)

Heidegger's strategy of destruction has been a major point of contention in his work, but rather than getting sidetracked in that debate, I take his notion to be in line with Husserl's motto that in order to arrive at a genuine questioning of being itself, a thinker must first distance themselves from the 'gravity' of traditional answers already available to them. I say 'distance', whereas Heidegger says 'destruction' [*Destruktion*] and he defines it a few lines later stating that 'this destruction is just as far from having the *negative* sense of shaking off the ontological tradition. We must, on the contrary, stake out the positive possibilities of that tradition, and this always means keeping it within its *limits*' (*BT* 44/22).[18] In this sense, being able to destruct the traditional answers in such a way as to make room to revitalize original questions requires a thinker already understand the traditional link between these questions and the answers the act of destruction is intending to displace. This distancing is accomplished when we view tradition as a collection of answers to original questions. We must recognize the limitation of an answer and make sure that we do not begin our investigations merely with answers, but instead strive to revitalize the original experiences of the question to which such traditional answers respond to. In so doing we can construct a way to maintain what is valuable about *traditional answers* while simultaneously keeping these answers from undermining our *questioning investigation*. Importantly then, being able to successfully put distance (Heidegger's destruction) between traditional questions and their answers *requires a thorough grasp of that tradition*. This, in no way therefore, is a call to reject tradition wholesale, but to the contrary, throws a thinker back upon it.

The very fact that phenomenology has shown itself to be a special method of philosophy, one which makes attempts to remain open to the instability of the phenomena it describes, indicates that phenomenology does not aim to exhaust, but rather preserve, the experience of phenomena to perpetually self-reveal. To return to the words of the great phenomenologist Reinach:

> [t]o talk about phenomenology is the most idle thing in the world, so long as that is lacking which alone can give talk concrete fullness and intuitiveness, namely, the phenomenological *way of seeing* and the phenomenological *attitude*. For the essential point is this, that phenomenology is not a system of philosophical propositions and truths – a system of propositions in which all who call themselves phenomenologists must believe, and which I could prove to you – but rather it is a method of philosophizing which is required by the problems of philosophy.
>
> (Reinach 180)

It is certainly important for phenomenology to use and to present clear terms, definitions and concepts; however, it is *equally important* to take up and to *practise* the special way of seeing and not to confuse the former with the latter.[19]

To practise phenomenology and, therefore, to be a phenomenologist, one must learn its content in order to actualize what it enables: phenomenological seeing *via* the activity of questioning. Thus, alongside the difficulty of coming to a clear understanding of the content of phenomenology (its concepts, definitions and descriptions), there is the additional difficulty of taking up its *central questions* and *practise* the return to the things themselves in order to genuinely experience what correlates to this content. Taking up this practice means participating in the give and take of the things themselves. The give and take that lies in between the questions and their answers further reveals why Husserl's motto is so central: it allows for a phenomenologist to remain open to further questioning (the further investigation of dynamic and fluctuating phenomena) while at the same time keeping in view the important answers derived by this investigation (the stabilization of appearance, descriptions, concepts and structures).[20] The investigation takes on a role of active participation (questioning), whereas the results of these efforts compose the collection of insights (answers).

One of the powerful insights that phenomenology teaches, therefore, is to remain open to and to preserve questions, be they questions already answered very well by tradition, questions yet to be answered well or even questions that seem unanswerable. The value and power of answers are not undermined by this operation of question preservation; on the contrary, the re-affirmation of a powerful answer that is re-questioned and found to be the case again and again for the responsible thinker is just another valuable asset employed and demanded by phenomenology. What question preservation does overcome is the reduction of philosophy to a list of propositions, facts, theories or systems; this reduction concerns the very idea that philosophy could be 'mastered' as a collection of answers when one has memorized all of the data that has traditionally been collected, established and written in books. Contrary to this reduction of philosophy to a collection of answers, phenomenology teaches us to re-view this collection of answers alongside the paths that these thinkers originally took to find them, to *think about them in addition to knowing them*. To do so is to trace back beyond an answer to the original question that led thereto. If we want to engage with and participate in phenomenology by returning to the things themselves, then we need to include in this a return to the questions themselves.

2

Husserl's 'To the questions themselves'

§7. Chapter introduction

The aim of this chapter is to further clarify the central role questioning plays within Husserl's phenomenology. Indicated by Husserl's philosophical practices, we can observe how the activity of questioning takes shape, albeit in a concealed way, as an essential aspect fulfilling his phenomenological motto 'to the matters themselves' (*zu den Sachen selbst*). Specifically, questions are revealed to be the means by which a phenomenologist returns to re-experience the matters themselves, both to verify descriptions made previously and to develop new ones. Although Husserl's specific methods for phenomenology develop and change, his central concern to perpetually re-question the experience of the things themselves remains constant. The role that questioning plays in phenomenology is the very means by which one keeps the *flux of experience* in view in order to let it self-reveal. Phenomenological inquiry is not only initiated by questioning, it is also maintained by it.

In order to argue that keeping things in question occupies a central role within phenomenology for Husserl, in §8, I begin by making a distinction between Husserl's celebrated motto and his particular methods. This distinction reveals a tension in Husserl's philosophy between trying to figure out how to properly theorize phenomenological research (summarized by his motto) with the genuine attempts to work out and practise that theory (indicated by his variously developing methods). A comprehensive presentation and review of his methods is not attempted here, given that this text's purpose is to retrieve a richer understanding of Husserl's motto as a means of questioning.[1] In §9, I explore how phenomenology concerns the dynamism of experience, philosophy and history and how these issues characterize the centrality of questioning in phenomenology. In §10, I examine how Husserl raises and preserves the question 'what is the phenomenon?' in his *Inaugural Lecture*. When questioned anew, the direct experience of a phenomenon is enabled to perpetually self-reveal further appearances in different ways. In response to this preserved question, in §11, I present Husserl's distinctions of phenomena as pregnant Objects versus logical predicates, and in §12, I consider how phenomena can be further clarified as singular unities that elicit multiplicities of appearance. In §13, I explain why phenomenology is a systematic philosophy but may never be reduced to a mere system. Finally, in §14, I conclude that according to Husserl, phenomenological questions precede their answers. This priority reveals how a preserved question can be used to safeguard a dynamic phenomenon from being eclipsed by the stability of one of its appearances. Powerful answers remain significant for phenomenology, but under the caveat that no matter how excellent or clear any description, concept or account of an experience may be, they must be kept from eclipsing their origin in the flux experience.

As Husserl was inclined to revise his philosophy, it is difficult to frame his development. In order to begin clarifying what phenomenology means for him, one must first identify a period of his development, either temporally or textually. This chapter focuses on three of his early works: (1) his inaugural lecture at Freiburg in 1917 titled 'Pure Phenomenology, Its Method and Its Field of Investigation' (henceforth *Inaugural Lecture*), (2), *LI*, second edition, published in 1913, and (3) *Ideas I*, published in 1913. As is frequently referenced, Husserl describes his *LI* to be his '"break-through", not an end but rather a beginning [… wherein he] tried to give a fuller account of the meaning, the method and the philosophical scope of phenomenology' (*LI* 3). It is during this period of development of Husserl that the role of the activity of questioning in phenomenology can be observed; initially in how it develops into a way to re-elicit experience in the *LI* and later, in how it coalesces into a specific and powerful method of transcendental phenomenology in *Ideas I*.

My analysis focuses primarily on Husserl's *Inaugural Lecture* as it serves to be a focal point for the developmental differences between *LI* and *Ideas* regarding the role questioning is to play in phenomenology. In addition to being given in 1917, just a few years after the second edition of the *LI* and *Ideas I* were revised and published respectively, Husserl's *Inaugural Lecture* aims not only to introduce phenomenology but also to scope out its future plans. In his introduction to Husserl's *Inaugural Lecture*, Herman Van Breda states that '[i]n keeping with the academic traditions of such an august occasion, the newly appointed holder of the chair developed a far-reaching program of problems he intended to investigate in the following years. The text of this address speaks for itself' (Van Breda 3). Thus, in his *Inaugural Lecture*, Husserl gives a panorama of his phenomenological project, indicating both what it has accomplished thus far (in light of the *LI* and the *Ideas I*) and also demarcating where he intends phenomenology to go. Furthermore, Husserl's lecture provides a step-by-step demonstration of how one might use questioning for further research.

The role questioning plays within Husserl's phenomenological development is illustrated in his *Inaugural Lecture* through the particular phenomenological question 'what is the phenomenon?' Therein, this question is shown to be asked, preserved and re-asked in order to elicit many different appearances – each individual appearance capable of further clarifying the matter the question aims to investigate (e.g. the multifaceted meaning of the phenomenon itself). By using this question as a means to re-experience and to clarify how a phenomenon perpetually self-reveals, Husserl highlights various ways in which we can use questioning for phenomenological research. As a 'do-it-yourself' practice, Husserl's motto is best understood as a *charge* to do the same and this is why phenomenology has a motto that needs to be distinguished from its methods.

Provisionally, phenomenology is a collection of verifiable descriptions of experience that may be distinguished from the original phenomena with which they correlate. The process of initially deriving and later verifying these descriptions is enabled by *phenomenological seeing*; however, the original and dynamic appearance of phenomena is importantly not assumed or contrived in this activity of returning to the things themselves, but are instead allowed to emerge as they show themselves.[2] The activity of questioning is, therefore, revealed to be how the phenomenologist elicits the things themselves in order to re-experience them. Interwoven in Husserl's presentation and developments of phenomenology is a direct connection to the activity of questioning. Distinct from the many descriptions that comprise the *philosophical content* of phenomenology, Husserl's call to return to the things themselves can be further clarified as a *practice* of turning one's questioning gaze towards their own genuine experience. This *questioning practice* reveals that understanding phenomenology requires participation in an activity, a feat that is above and beyond the mere mental acquisition of conceptual data.

§8. Husserl's motto precedes his methods

Husserl spent his entire career trying to clarify and understand what phenomena are, how they appear to consciousness and what experience itself comprises. Even though this is a sign of dedication on his part, it also makes it rather difficult to find a good entry point into his phenomenology since he constantly revised and developed his ideas, methods and starting points. However, even before attempting to become a phenomenologist, the student can at least first observe that Husserl exemplifies his own motto: the genuine *return to* and *engagement with* the things themselves (*zu den Sachen selbst*). If this is so, then, this raises the important questions as to just what comprises this return, to what does Husserl return and how is this return to be practised?

Many of Husserl's published works and lectures were given the subtitle of 'introduction to phenomenology'. It is a running gag of sorts in Husserlian scholarship that Husserl was the perpetual, but edifying, beginner phenomenologist.[3] At many points of note in Husserl's work, his philosophy underwent significant changes, raising the interesting question as to what specifically kept prompting him to reformulate and to change his ideas. To what did Husserl continually return? What caused him to perpetually revise and remodel his philosophical descriptions, models, concepts, etc.?

As is visible from Husserl's writing, it was never enough to *just* have an excellent, interesting or powerful system of phenomenology; he rather always sought to *source*, *verify* and *correlate* his phenomenological descriptions within the genuine way that phenomena reveal themselves to consciousness. Additionally, he frequently suggests that his readers do the same and he certainly did not just want his students to take his word on some kind of authority. In this way, then, every phenomenological description, concept or distinction ought to correlate to a matter or to a thing (*die 'Sache'*) of experience that may be revived by any other phenomenologist in order to verify what has been claimed. Indeed, Husserl's penchant to revise his own findings reveals that in addition to a developing a system, he also maintained a pursuit of something *elusive* and *independent* from his philosophical writings that drove him back to the metaphorical drawing board again and again.

Husserl's perpetual attempt to write new introductions to phenomenology might appear suspicious and problematic (or at least frustrating) to some readers. It importantly testifies to the fact that, in addition to deriving a systematic account of how consciousness intends phenomena, Husserl genuinely and continually *returned* to the way phenomena revealed themselves, the way they originally appear to consciousness in the first place. In light of this genuine practice of returning to the various ways in which the things themselves self-reveal, Husserl's phenomenology is best understood as *not just* comprising a systematic account of consciousness, appearance and experience. In addition to these systematic descriptions, concepts and distinctions, Husserl's phenomenology also attempts to preserve the source correlates of genuine experience so that any other person may return to these sources whenever one raises a preserved phenomenological question for themselves. In this sense, phenomenology is not a philosophical invention or contrivance that merely rests on deduction or logical validity alone; additionally, Husserl's phenomenology should also be understood as requiring one to perpetually practise experiential verification. After all, it was this checking and re-checking of his own experience that testifies to what prompted Husserl to continually modify his own ideas.[4] Thus, instead of creating, modifying and developing phenomenology as a contrivance that is merely a conceptual, logical or constructive system, Husserl's perpetual revisions reveal that he continued to return to 'something' he hoped his phenomenology would both correspond to and account for. If this is so, then just what was this 'something' Husserl returned to again and again and by what means did he enact and *practise* this perpetual return?

The attempt to give a general overview of Husserl's many methodological or historical developments has been the subject of entire philosophical works.[5] Thus, a comprehensive review of Husserl's development is well beyond the capabilities and scope of this text; however, some general themes may be identified when phenomenology is viewed in light of the activity of questioning. This shows us that although he strove to be systematic, Husserl never simply wanted to formulate just a system. According to Husserl's final assistant Eugen Fink, we can view Husserl's general methodological development in three stages of *psychologism, descriptive phenomenology* and *transcendental phenomenology*.[6] Regarding the more technical specifics as to how Husserl's phenomenological epoché and reduction change and develop over his lifetime, Husserl scholars Rudolf Bernet, Iso Kern and Eduard Marbach (henceforth Bernet et al.) describe three main paths of Husserl's phenomenology in their work *An Introduction to Husserlian Phenomenology*: a Cartesian Path, an Ontological Path and a Path through Descriptive Intentional Psychology.[7] Bernet et al. add, in a footnote, a fourth Path by way of the History of Ideas.[8] In addition to the many possible ways one may divide Husserl's methodological changes, there is also the later shift in focus from a static versus genetic phenomenology.[9] In addition to Husserl's published texts there are also some 40,000–45,000 pages of his unpublished manuscripts or *Nachlass*.[10] In his work *Husserl's Phenomenology*, scholar Dan Zahavi contends that 'Husserl's output was enormous, making it unlikely that any one person has ever read everything he wrote. This fact not only makes Husserl research a relatively open affair […] it also complicates the attempt to write an exhaustive systematic account of his philosophy' (Zahavi 2–3).[11] In other words, one of the reasons why it is so difficult to systematize Husserl's achievements, to even give a general picture of how it occurred, is perhaps due to the fact that Husserl was not led by a project of system, but by a *practice* of following the problems themselves (*den Sachen selbst*).

Clearly Husserl is a prolific writer but interwoven within the magnitude of the projects he attempted to clarify one can trace a *practice* of following the problems wherever they led him. Rather than develop an over-encompassing frame that captures all of Husserl's work, his students would be better served to try and catch a glimpse of the individual issues he aimed to clarify one by one and this can be accomplished by collecting the primary questions Husserl endeavoured to raise, answer and repeat. In light of these many ways to characterize his development, it remains clear that something kept drawing Husserl back to revision and that 'something' was dynamic and problematic enough to reveal itself in the many different ways that his specific stages or paths indicate. In this sense, one may interpret this abundance as sourced in a response to the problems themselves, rather than in some desire to write for its own sake. In order to understand what his works *target* therefore requires one to re-elicit his original questions.

It is, therefore, clear that throughout his developing thought and work, Husserl's methods underwent many iterations and modifications; however, although saying something overarching about his development has proven difficult, we may still say that all of these changes resulted from Husserl's direct wrestling with the problems of experience itself. According to Moran, 'Husserl's development [...] is best seen as an ongoing clarification of the same set of initial problems, probed more and more deeply from different angles' (Moran 67). Thus, prior to and in a sense *alongside* the various developments of Husserl's methods, there is a more fundamental and general aim to keep the genuine questions of appearance and experience in view. Husserl confirms this in a letter dated 1 January 1905 in which he is describing his own work ethic by saying:

> Certainly I have not been an ambitious *Privatdozent* eagerly looking out for the public and for the government. Such a one will publish both much and frequently. He will let himself be influenced in his problems and methods by the fashion of the day, and he will in so doing lean as far as possible on the influential and famous ones (Wundt, Sigwart, Erdmann, etc.) and take special heed not to contradict them radically. I have done the exact opposite of all this, [...]. For nine years I have published practically nothing, and I have made enemies of almost all the influential people. The latter by the fact that I have chosen my problems myself and have gone my own ways: furthermore, in my criticism I have not allowed any other considerations to enter than those of the

subject matter (die '*Sache*'). Incidentally, I have acted this way not in order to be virtuous, but from a compelling necessity. The things themselves gained such power over me that I could not do otherwise [...].

(Spiegelberg 1960 89–90)

It is, therefore, fair to say that Husserl's methodological developments came about due to his perpetual return to the things themselves and in this way his motto precedes his methods.

Importantly, this is not to suggest that one may forgo the difficult task of learning and exploring Husserl's specific methods, his many distinctions and complex systems.[12] A teacher of mine once said 'there is no phenomenology without the reduction' and thus a great deal of serious study *must* be made upon the specifics of the various methods that Husserl undertook and developed in order to accomplish his motto of returning to the things themselves. However, as the beginner phenomenologist makes these attempts, it is also important for them to keep the following questions in mind: 'what was it that prompted Husserl to develop the idea of the reduction in the first place?', 'why did Husserl think he needed something like the reduction?' and, furthermore, 'to *what* specifically did Husserl *return to again and again* that subsequently prompted him to continually revise his work?' Interestingly, it is not a concept, system or specific kind of philosophy that prompted Husserl to revision; instead, it was the problematicity of *the things themselves*. Each time Husserl returned to experience, in order to double check and verify his current phenomenological descriptions, he frequently discovered that there was *more to be considered* and or that new problems emerged in light of his current clarifications and solutions. This reveals reciprocity between the questions he took to experience, and in response to those questions, the different answers that lead him back to his original questions.

The call to 'perpetually return to experience and appearance' may initially seem to only amount to a slogan in a pejorative or naive sense. However, when experience is questioned in a genuine way, what first appears to be simple can quickly become incredibly complex. As Husserl describes himself:

In any event, he who for decades did not speculate about a new Atlantis but instead actually journeyed in the trackless wilderness of a new continent and undertook the virgin cultivation of some of its areas will not allow himself to be deterred in any way by the rejection of geographers who judge his reports according to their habitual ways of experiencing and thinking and thereby excuse themselves from the pain of undertaking travels in the new land.

(*Ideas II* 422)

In order to follow Husserl's motto, we too are invited, as beginner phenomenologists, to leave the armchair of 'concept play philosophy' and journey to this 'new land' of experience itself, to see for ourselves and verify what Husserl claims to have discovered. However, that is only the *motto*, not yet a method. Even though one might cherish this 'experiential' aspect of Husserl's phenomenology, it is important to keep it in mind that he also says that

> as a matter of principle, phenomenology does not stand pat with any vague talk, with any obscure universalities; it demands systematically determined clarification, analysis, and description that penetrate into the essential connections and all the way to the last particularizations of them that lie within reach. It demands conclusive *work*.
>
> (*Ideas I* 301)[13]

The challenge then is to balance each aspect of phenomenological work with the other: on the one hand, the practice of returning to the *experience* of the things themselves and on the other, the conclusive and systematic work required in order to philosophically describe these experiences (to categorize and account for them). The former comprises the practice of *questioning* and *re-questioning* our experience of the world around us, whereas the latter comprises the systematic attempt to clarify how such experience operates (in the form of stabilized descriptions that are answers to such questioning). Thus, the activity of questioning begins to show its central role in phenomenological inquiry as *the way* we are able to return to, elicit and reflect on our own experience as we seek for the ever so coveted true answer.

When trying to clarify Husserl's philosophy we must distinguish between Husserl's motto and his varying methods. His methods demark different ways to accomplish and fulfil his motto. This is an important distinction because, as will be later explored in greater detail, the expertise gained by studying and mastering the 'conclusive work' of phenomenology (its content, definitions, systems, etc.) tends to eclipse the original experience such work correlates with and points back to (what the *motto* keeps in view). In other words, the better one gets at grasping the *methods* of phenomenology, the easier it becomes to overlook the *motto*: the experiences those methods elucidate, correlate with and return a thinker to reconsider. Indeed, this eclipse becomes total when one believes that there is no distinction between Husserl's motto and his various methods. In such a setting, phenomenology may even be reduced to a conceptual analysis that lacks any genuine correlate to experience itself; there, the idolatry of concept clarity and concept play stifles even the most interesting and radical ideas that Husserl put forth.

We must distinguish Husserl's motto from his methods in order to keep phenomenology from eclipsing the phenomena it is originally intended to bring a thinker back to re-experience, to reflect upon and to clarify. No matter how good or excellent Husserl's discovered answers were at any stage in his development, he always *returned* to re-question the things themselves to see if his current descriptions fit the way experience itself appears. When new appearances further complicated previously collected descriptions, revisions ensued. The central practice of phenomenology, therefore, begins in seeing the difference between the primary *questions* of phenomenology and the various *answers* such questioning yields. The original practice needs to be distinguished and preserved as this practice of returning to re-question experience again and again is always in danger of being eclipsed by the excellent answers it uncovers and clarifies.

§9. The experiential, philosophical and historical flux of phenomenology

Husserlian phenomenology emerges at the same historical time as science is generating a plethora of new disciplines and insights. Furthermore, what counts as scientific in the first place is also under profound reconsiderations in terms of its limit, scope and domain. Husserl states that 'in all the areas within which the intellectual life of humanity is at work, the historical epoch wherein fate has placed us is an epoch of stupendous happenings' (*Inaugural Lecture* 124). These 'stupendous happenings' are not developments that are limited to any one particular field or domain of science, but instead comprise the return to re-question the very meaning of science itself. Husserl claims that 'whatever previous generations cultivated by their toil and struggle into a harmonious whole, in every sphere of culture, whatever enduring style was deemed established as method and norm, is once more in flux' (*Inaugural Lecture* 124). This historical flux includes a way of viewing and valuing *past* scientific achievements and the proper way to imagine *future* potential endeavours.

The flux of scientific development is directed *backwards*, as a re-questioning of tradition, and *forwards*, as a re-questioning of what scientific posterity might entail. It is directed backwards, in the sense that what was previously taken for granted by tradition is now made *less than secure* in order to facilitate reconsideration and rediscovery. In this way, what was originally deemed stable is now destabilized by the activity of radical questioning. Husserl confirms this by stating that 'whatever enduring style was deemed established as method and norm [...] now seeks new forms whereby reason, as yet unsatisfied, may develop more freely' (*Inaugural Lecture* 124). This includes not only traditional answers, but also even the most cherished and valuable ways of traditional thinking. This flux is also directed forward into the future in the sense that what we hoped we would find through scientific progress also becomes opaque. The original picture of scientific posterity as developing truth upon truth has also become questionable. How science and culture develop in the future is also now viewed as being in flux.[14]

It seems that if there was some notion of the sacred in science – truth that was believed to be so secure and stable it could never be lost or reasonably criticized – then this adherence became destabilized in the late nineteenth and early twentieth centuries. Husserl states that this flux causes a renewed rational re-investigation 'in politics, in economic life, in technics, in the fine arts, and – by no means least of all – in the sciences' (*Inaugural Lecture* 124). Perhaps to the contemporary reader, Husserl speaking of flux in politics, in technology and in the fine arts is not so surprising, given that these areas rarely seem to exist without some kind of continual change or movement. However, attributing this flux to science, taken in its original meaning of truthful knowledge, does seem shocking because truth and knowledge are considered to be the most stable of all stable things. When this questioning is applied to the very idea of science itself, the paradigm in science that indicates the *worthwhileness* or *worthlessness* of a problem is also placed in flux. Thus, the flux of this development concerned not only the sciences themselves, but also their possibilities.

This flux of change is also not just a whim of new ideas and criticisms that were dropped as quickly as they were found; even very old and highly cherished ideas such as the structures of mathematics were being scrutinized. How this flux affects philosophy is precisely where phenomenology becomes significant. Husserl posits that

> philosophy, too, fits into this picture [of flux]. In philosophy, the forms whose energies were dissipated in the period following the overthrow of Hegelian philosophy were essentially those of a renaissance. They were forms that reclaimed past philosophies, and their methods as well as some of their essential content originated with great thinkers of the past.
>
> (*Inaugural Lecture* 124)

According to Husserl, in addition to a 'renaissance' kind of philosophy, genuine philosophy must also take up the original problems of tradition and *make them their own*. A scientist not only re-evaluates the methods and solutions provided by tradition but also its celebrated questions.[15] Of interest to Husserl was the notion that what needed to be revived is not another or novel paradigm, but the original means of questioning and answering: that which takes place within the construction, and evaluation of paradigms in the first place. It is in this situation that Husserl writes that there is a

> need for an utterly original philosophy [...] the need of a philosophy that – in contrast to the secondary productivity of renaissance philosophies – seeks by radically clarifying the sense and motifs of philosophical problems to penetrate to that primal ground on whose basis those problems must find whatever solution is genuinely scientific.
>
> (*Inaugural Lecture* 124)

The questioning Husserl uses is, therefore, *not just* one in search of 'productive' or 'secondary' answers from tradition, either lost or left somewhat underdeveloped, but in addition to a productive search, Husserl's approach is also fundamental. Making original questions our own entails investigating the answers provided by tradition and also seeking to revive the *original questions* which source these tradition answers. Thus, alongside the newer explaining power of a more advanced science, Husserl also preserves the openness and potentiality of these original questions.

The new science that Husserl proposes to address this flux is none other than pure phenomenology as 'a new fundamental science, [...] a thoroughly new type and endless [in] scope. It is inferior in methodological rigor to none of the modern sciences. [...] Philosophy is possible as a rigorous science at all only through pure phenomenology' (*Inaugural Lecture* 124). Husserl's project of pure phenomenology is a way for philosophy and science to preserve and explore the ongoing openness of questions while keeping such an infinite procedure in check with the establishment, clarification and the systematic presentation of answers.

Preserving original questions means maintaining questions that have yet to be answered and re-evoking original questions that have been *answered so well that they resist being revived*. Breathing new life into these ossified questions is what phenomenology aims to accomplish. Whereas this flux may be viewed as something miasmic to either 'conceptually clear' or 'systematically rigorous' philosophy, Husserl's phenomenology welcomes such flux. Husserl's rigour is one that *rigorously* struggles *with the problematicity* of experience rather than the kind of rigour-mortis that immunizes its own philosophical system from adequately dealing with genuine experience by demarking in advance just what experience is 'permitted' to be. Phenomenology shows itself to be flexible in the face of the flux of experience and the flux of historical change: rather than being a system that either simply works or does not, phenomenology is capable of relating to the dynamism perpetually challenging it while at the same time providing excellent answers. In phenomenology, a powerful explanatory system is sought for but it is also balanced by preserving the original questions that source such a system; in this way phenomenology is always more than just a system or list of answers because, by preserving its original questions, it also preserves the possibility to create a new set of answers and therefore a new explanatory system.

In order to clearly grasp what phenomenology studies and *describes*, i.e. phenomena, one must first understand the domain in which something like pure phenomenology operates. Husserl states that 'pure phenomenology claims to be the science of pure phenomena' (*Inaugural Lecture* 124). Husserl first outlines the horizon of phenomenology: experience and consciousness, stating that

> [w]e shall begin with the necessary correlation between object, truth, and cognition – using these words in their very broadest sense. To every object there correspond an ideally closed system of truths that are true of it and, on the other hand, an ideal system of possible cognitive processes by virtue of which the object and the truths about it would be given to any cognitive subject.
>
> (*Inaugural Lecture* 125)

This basic correlation between objects and the constituting means by which consciousness grasps them is another way to describe Husserl's technical idea of intentionality: *consciousness is always consciousness of something*. For Husserl, when we experience something, we intend it, and this avoids the problem of unnecessary object duplication (one in my mind and one in reality). Intentionality shows its elegance in that it does not matter what a thinker experiences through consciousness, whether they are experiencing ideal objects (e.g. numbers), spatiotemporal objects foreign to consciousness (e.g. tables), emotions, or the very acts of consciousness themselves through which such 'objects' are intended. Husserl's notion of intentionality accounts for all these many forms of conscious life. Phenomenologically speaking, intentionality is not really *designed* or *contrived* by Husserl, but is itself a description that correlates with the appearance of how consciousness encounters and experiences its own relation to objects. Furthermore, Husserl's description of intentionality can be verified and validated by anyone, by their own genuine return to the way their own consciousness appears to them. In this way, we can value intentionality in at least two different ways: (1) conceptually, it elegantly avoids many traditional problems that plague the study of consciousness and (2) objectivity, we can *see* for ourselves how our own experience verifies this description of intentionality.

Within the horizon of experience, consciousness is always consciousness of something which can be given to it wholly and originally. Just what this 'something' is is left in a sense ambiguous in order for us to see the correlation between consciousness and *its* intended correlate. Husserl states that 'at the lowest cognitive level, [the correlation between object, truth, and cognition are] processes of experiencing, or, to speak more generally, processes of intuiting that grasp the object in the original' (*Inaugural Lecture* 125). Thus, there are at least three things to clarify: (1) that the phenomenologist is always within a horizon of experience and consciousness; (2) that a phenomenologist is investigating consciousness, its cognitive processes and the 'something' to which it is always directed; and (3) that the 'something' which always correlates to a consciousness can be given to it in an original way. As is already observable, clarifying these issues proves quite difficult and obviously comprises an effort that goes well beyond a naive understanding or simple implementation of Husserl's motto.

More importantly, intentionality already suggests that whatever experience is, it is something *more than* concepts, descriptions and accounts of it can capture or delineate. This is the *flux* of experience, what initially calls for a project of phenomenology in the first place and what, even after a great deal of generational work, remains *inexhaustible*. Although the inexhaustibility of experience may seem to initially undermine any project of phenomenology (or science for that matter), unlike other sciences of experience, the very construction of phenomenology is designed and undertaken as a way to *engage with* the flux of experience, to describe and, if possible, account for it.

The inexhaustibility of experience is the flux that phenomenology aims to investigate, account for and describe without reducing it in any pejorative way. As a philosophy, phenomenology mirrors the flux of experience by adding to the already traditionally valued systematicity of philosophy, a dynamic practice of questioning: alongside excellently derived descriptions, concepts and systems understood as answers, phenomenology also preserves the original questions that source these answers. This preservation enables thinkers to verify what is claimed for themselves as well as remain open for new possibilities to emerge.

Now that the experiential, philosophical and historical context of flux has been established and the general scope of Husserl's phenomenology has been outlined, we can now consider examples that show this to be the case. One specific question Husserl uses in his *Inaugural Lecture* is 'what is the phenomenon?' In order to elicit an original experience of appearance itself, Husserl urges the listener to raise the question 'what is the phenomenon?' in order to 'see' and confirm for oneself what Husserl attributes to it. Although Husserl aims to provide answers for this question, he importantly also keeps this question preserved and in so doing keeps asking it again and again throughout the *Inaugural Lecture*. This reveals that phenomenological questions are capable of at least two functions: (1) a question may be used to elicit the originary experience of an appearance under investigation in order to verify a previously made description of it and (2) a question may be used to elicit new appearances that have yet to be described or fully accounted for. Thus, in addition to keeping watch for how Husserl conceptualizes the phenomenon, we must also pay attention to how Husserl uses the activity of questioning to elicit these conceptualizations. As an activity that *elicits*, questioning can be easily overlooked for what it brings to the fore, what it enables a phenomenologist to reflect upon. Thus, without diminishing the answers that Husserl derives through the activity of raising this question anew, it is still important to stress the very activity he practises that elicits these answers in the first place.

§10. What is the phenomenon for Husserl?

What is the *phenomenon* for Husserl? This question must first be distinguished from the similar-seeming question 'what is the *concept* of phenomenon for Husserl?' The issue of conceptualization properly belongs within one of Husserl's methods (as an *answer*), but the very activity of inquiring is itself something that properly belongs within his motto (as a *question*). This inquiry is understood as a philosophical activity distinct from any conceptualization, given that Husserl would have to first inquire into something (among *the things themselves*) in order to derive and conceptualize any particular notion of 'the phenomenon'. In other words, the original inquiry *via* questioning will precede any generation of answers. Any *concept* of the phenomenon, therefore, needs to be understood as properly belonging on the side of answering (limited to one of Husserl's methods), whereas the *original inquiry* belongs on the side of questioning: the genuine attempt to derive from the things themselves how one should understand the phenomenon.

It is possible for a student to merely understand the question 'what is the phenomenon?' in the specific form of 'what is the concept of phenomenon?' but to do so risks missing out on the real work of phenomenology: experiential verification. Understanding the varying ways Husserl conceptualizes the phenomenon through his different methods remains important, but these clarifying specifications also threaten to eclipse the original inquiry that is their source, namely, the experiential correlate of investigating the things themselves. This reveals that when we understand a concept only in terms of a clear and concise definition, we are only half way there. Additionally, we must raise Husserl's question and use it to elicit the same correlates (*die Sachen*) that enable proper phenomenological verification. In so doing we add to our technical understanding of concepts the phenomenological investigation that originally elicited and correlates to such concepts.

We can now return to our question 'what is the phenomenon for Husserl?' with the issue of conceptualization in brackets. As a question, it leads a thinker back to the flux of experience, but as an answer it yields a multi-layered concept which accounts for varying levels of appearance encapsulated by experience. Husserl's phenomenological developments reveal that the *question* 'what is the phenomenon?' is preserved as much as it is answered. As a preserved question, it remains an open and repeatable way to allow the very structures of what a phenomenon is to emerge and self-reveal.[16] As Husserl provides various answers to this question, each answer provides a stabilization of an appearance (e.g. a description or concept) that helps us to clarify our working and general understanding of appearance. Although the question remains open and preserved, Husserl's answers for what constitutes a phenomenon are not always compatible with each other.

In his attempt to clarify what the phenomenon means for phenomenology, Husserl maintains a questioning attitude that remains open for further clarification. It is always possible for an additional way to answer the question 'what is the phenomenon?' Alongside the various and interesting descriptions of what a phenomenon is (as stabilized answer), the beginner phenomenologist must also maintain the openness of how the very experience of the phenomenon itself appears (when it is re-questioned). One may return to the experience of appearance *via* the question 'what is the phenomenon?' with each answer proffered in order to see both how any particular answer is verifiable (or not) and how there are always more possible answers to be uncovered, considered or further reflected upon. In this sense, one is then able to see how all the possible stabilized answers relate to the original questions that comprise their source.

Phenomena can appear in many different ways, but *something* must first appear in order for us to say or even think anything at all. Husserl argues that 'if higher, theoretical cognition is to begin at all, objects belonging to the sphere in question must be intuited. Natural objects, for example, must be experienced before any theorizing about them can occur' (*Inaugural Lecture* 125). Husserl distinguishes between higher theoretical cognition and the experience of the appearance of phenomena themselves to consciousness. If phenomena do indeed appear to consciousness in a way that is pre-theoretical, then this original access to phenomena may be investigated. Thus, the starting consideration of the phenomenon is appearance but initially, the many different and distinct ways to distinguish appearance is left as a yet-to-be-clarified manifold.

Speaking of phenomena in any way also requires correlation to a consciousness. Husserl states that the concept '"phenomenon" signifies a certain content that intrinsically inhabits the intuitive consciousness [...] and is the substrate for its actuality valuation' (*Inaugural Lecture* 125). The phenomenon is what is evaluated to be either actual (outer 'objective' perception) or non-actual (inner 'subjective' perception); in both cases a phenomenon is still given: *something* appears to *a consciousness*. A phenomenon must be given to a consciousness, but it may be given in many different ways (original and pre-theoretical, in spatiotemporal perception, in imagination, phantasy and perhaps even more ways yet to be uncovered). Here it is visible that Husserl is making efforts to remain open to the many different ways a phenomenon may be given to consciousness before drawing distinctions. He does this because whereas the question 'what is appearance?' brings into experiential view all the many possible (or even impossible) ways appearance may emerge, any particular *answer* to this question can only bring into view what it specifically correlates with. Thus, we see that the correlating power of relating to experience is different within questions than it is within answers. Answers enable us to pick out and stabilize an appearance from the flux of experience, whereas questions enable us to bring this very flux, understood as a horizon, into view.

To return to the aforementioned question 'what is the phenomenon?' the first interesting thing we notice in response to this question is that appearances are capable of emerging in both possible and actual ways. Husserl remarks that 'even intuitions in phantasy [...] are intrinsically intuitions of objects and carry "objective phenomena" with them intrinsically, phenomena that are obviously not characterized as actualities' (*Inaugural Lecture* 125). When I perceive a table, I see a profile of an actual spatiotemporal object. Various actual profiles come into view and others go out of view as I change my perspective. What it means to call the actual object a table, to describe its 'objective phenomenon' seems to indicate what is common to all of the table's various possible profiles. What is interesting is that I can also phantasize about the table and modify its various aspects (e.g. its shape and colour). Thus, Husserl's initial clarification of a phenomenon includes both the actual and real perceptions of the table, in addition to the various possible and imagined phantasies about it. All count as appearances of the table regardless of whether they are real, ideal, actual, possible or phantasized.

In his essay 'Desiring to Know through Intuition' Bernet gives a clear description of how this process of returning to the phenomenon itself, to see how it appears to consciousness, brings into view something dynamic that requires careful consideration and precise unpacking. Therein, Bernet states that

> [f]or the phenomenology of the [*LI*], the phenomenon ultimately stands out on a horizon of originally interweaving different dimensions. Interwoven there are the dimensions of lived experience, the givenness of the things-themselves, and the mediation of their relation by linguistic significations. Despite their entanglement, these different points of view on the phenomenon are irreducible to one another.
>
> (Bernet 2003 153)

In attempting to grasp the meaning of the phenomenon, one must avoid reducing it to one of its emergent dimensions: lived experience, the givenness of the thing itself or its signification through language, and, furthermore, one must keep in mind that all three are entangled with each other. Bernet states that '[f]or the [*LI*], the phenomenon as it is conceived by phenomenology can be made to reside neither in consciousness nor in the world of empirical or ideal states of affairs nor in the meanings and expressions of language' (Bernet 2003 154). Restricting the phenomenon to one or the other turns out to be a major hurdle in clearly grasping what the phenomenon fully entails. However, when one allows the phenomenon to reveal itself by re-questioning the things themselves, a more comprehensive description of the phenomenon shows itself. Instead of merely reducing the phenomenon to one of the three dimensions it emerges entangled alongside (lived experience, givenness or signification), the question 'what is a phenomenon?' is able to bring about the whole appearance and further enables the phenomenologist to make distinctions between each dimension. Yet, this question yields more the more frequently it is raised genuinely. In this way, the question 'what is the phenomenon?' brings into view a horizon of possibilities that included the three Bernet has identified as the lived experience, givenness, signification but also more. As an answer, 'lived experience' provides an excellent response to the original question. Were the question not preserved, it could collapse into the stabilization of one of its possible answers. If so, then the other two possible answers could be overlooked or lost. The preservation of this question not only safeguards the other two possible answers, it furthermore preserves the possibility for more stabilizations to emerge to the fore.

§11. Phenomena understood as pregnant objects and logical predicates

That a phenomenon continues to reveal and re-reveal itself in new ways shows us that it is something dynamic. Husserl continues to further clarify the different aspects of the phenomenon by contrasting it with the idea of an Object [*Objekte*].[17] Husserl states that 'to characterize this [phenomenological] science more exactly we shall introduce a simple distinction between phenomena and Objects [*Objekte*] in the pregnant sense of the word' (*Inaugural Lecture* 127).[18] In order to follow the English translation, a few things need to be first clarified. I take the phrase 'pregnant sense of the word' [*prägnaten Wortsinn*] to indicate an *abundance* of some kind (i.e. of meaning), wherein something is given, albeit in a way that suggests there is *yet more* to be given (or perhaps more appropriately *yet more* to be seen). This can generally be interpreted in light of the English idiom *more than meets the eye* and the Gestalt theory idiom *more than the sum of its parts*. Both these idioms bring to mind that curious experience of encountering something that seems to fully reveal itself initially, only to later on *somehow* reveal more of itself. The interesting thing about abundances is that they are easily overlooked or reducible to one of their instantiations; thus, they must be considered with great care.

Husserl's Object [*Objekte*] is something given that has a kind of abundance 'within' it in that there is more to it than initially appears. This can be contrasted with the word object [*Gegenstand*], without a capital letter, which signifies a logical predicate without necessitating its real actuality, real possibility, its thing-like nature or its existence. Husserl states that 'in general logical parlance, any subject whatever of true predications is an object' (*Inaugural Lecture* 127). This means in reference to a statement of 'S is P', when restricting ourselves to a logical concern, any subject or thing that may be predicated of would, therefore, be an object in the logical sense. Such predication could refer to ideas, numbers, tables, chairs, beliefs, emotions or to anything else and Husserl concludes that 'in this sense, therefore, every phenomenon is also an object' in the logical sense of a predicate (*Inaugural Lecture* 127). Husserl posits that 'within this widest concept of object [as a predicate], and specifically within the concept of individual objects, *Objects* and *phenomena* stand in contrast with each other' (*Inaugural Lecture* 127). Thus, Husserl is using three ideas here: object as a (logical) predicate, Object in the pregnant sense of the word and phenomenon as *something that appears* (what the two have in common). Coming to a clear understanding of each of these ideas and how they relate to one another is essential to understanding what Husserl means by the phenomenon.

Husserl further clarifies Object by stating that 'all natural Objects, for example, are objects foreign to consciousness' (*Inaugural Lecture* 127). At this stage, we can further clarify that 'Object' refers to spatiotemporal things that are transcendent to consciousness. Husserl states that

> [c]onsciousness does, indeed, objectivate [Objects] and posit them as actual, yet the consciousness that experiences them and takes cognizance of them is so singularly astonishing that it bestows upon its own phenomena the sense of being appearances of Objects foreign to consciousness and knows these 'extrinsic' Objects through processes that take cognizance of their sense. Those objects that are neither conscious processes nor immanent constituents of conscious processes we therefore call Objects in the pregnant sense of the word.
> (*Inaugural Lecture* 127)

This further clarifies what is *excluded* by 'Object': any conscious process or immanent part of consciousness. A science of Objects would, therefore, concern a specific set of spatiotemporal things foreign to consciousness, whereas a science of (logical) objects could include Objective sciences, as well as those 'things' we can predicate *within* consciousness, parts of the very conscious acts that make up perception. For example, any study of plants (biology) or people (anthropology) would count as Objects in the pregnant sense, whereas a study of theorems or argumentative validity would be to study objects in the logical and predicative sense. What makes an Object, with a capital 'O', pregnant is that it already also includes the idea of a predicative object as well as something spatiotemporal and foreign to consciousness.

The point that Husserl is making in comparing objects as logical predicates and Objects as spatiotemporal things is that they both in fact *appear* to consciousness, but do so in different ways. As the empirical sciences deal with

Objects, and epistemology deals with objects, phenomenology would concern the different ways in which these 'things' appear to consciousness in different ways in the first place: *via phenomena*. Husserl further clarifies this by stating 'of these contrasted sciences there correspond two fundamentally different types of experience and of intuition generally: *immanent* experience and *Objective* experience, also called "external" or transcendent experience' (*Inaugural Lecture* 127). Thus, the distinction between objects and Objects, Husserl states that 'this places two separate sciences in the sharpest of contrasts: on the one hand, phenomenology, the science of consciousness as it is in itself; on the other, the "Objective" sciences as a totality' (*Inaugural Lecture* 127). With the appearance of 'immanent experience' we have the occasion to establish a new science that aims to deal with such experience with the same level of seriousness as empirical sciences do for transcendent experience. Husserl remarks that 'immanent experience consists in the mere viewing that takes place in reflection by which consciousness and that of which there is consciousness are grasped' (*Inaugural Lecture* 127). According to Husserl, the important aspect of immanent experience is that it is absolute and, therefore, apodictic (one may doubt it, but this doubt seems to make no sense). This is quite interesting for Husserl, just as when the one compares the appearance of immanent experience with transcendent experience, two different kinds of 'appearance' emerge that may be distinguished for further consideration. Husserl states:

> For example, a liking or a desiring that I am just now executing enters into my experience by way of a merely retrospective look and, by means of this look, is given absolutely. What 'absolutely' means here we can learn by contrast: we can experience any external thing only insofar as it presents itself to us sensuously through this or that adumbration [*Abschattung*]. A liking has no changing presentations; there are no changing perspectives on or views of it as if it might be seen from above or below, from near or far. It just is nothing foreign to consciousness at all that could present itself to consciousness through the mediation of phenomena different from the liking itself; to like is intrinsically to be conscious.
>
> (*Inaugural Lecture* 127–8)

The German word used is *Abschattung* which means 'shading' or 'nuance'. The translator uses the English word 'adumbration' which means to view something through various profiles, sides or angles. Experience of transcendent objects will always be given to consciousness through profiles that shift and change depending on perspective. Husserl discovers that to speak of profiles or perspectives within immanent experience has no place and, therefore, does not make sense when reflecting upon immanent conscious experience. When I love something, as opposed to perceive a spatiotemporal Object (e.g. a table) that is always given through profiles, this love is given to me *'without sides'*, that is, absolutely whereas the table may turn out to be a clever painting when further investigated. In this way, when we reflect on our own experience we find that there are aspects of our own consciousness that are given to us apodictically. Husserl writes that it is a fact that 'the existence of what is given to immanent reflection is indubitable while what is experienced through external experience always allows the possibility that it may prove to be an illusory Object in the course of further experiences' (*Inaugural Lecture* 128). We can always doubt that the spatiotemporal table could be a clever painting, illusion or hallucination, but we cannot doubt our liking or desiring. It is upon this indubitable aspect that a science of phenomenology may be based and developed. Securing how we get to and make use of immanent experience is addressed by Husserl in a shift from our natural attitude towards a phenomenological one.

What makes this difference between immanent and transcendent experience even more interesting is that although they are all both distinct, they are still related to each other. Husserl states that

> [i]mmanent and transcendent experience are nevertheless connected in a remarkable way: by a change in attitude, we can pass from the one to the other. In the natural attitude, we experience, among other things, processes in Nature; we are adverted to them, observe them, describe them, subsume them under concepts. While we do so, there occur in our experiencing and theorizing consciousness multiform conscious processes which have constantly changing immanent constituents.
>
> (*Inaugural Lecture* 128)

Thus, in the natural attitude we still make use of immanent aspects and it is not the case, therefore, that the natural attitude only deals with transcendent experience. In this sense, the phenomenological attitude seems to be a movement away from the natural attitude or what Husserl calls suspending the 'natural attitude'. Husserl states that a perceiving individual

> can convert his natural attentional focus into the phenomenologically reflective one; he can make the currently flowing consciousness and, thus, the infinitely multiform world of phenomena at large the theme of his fixating observations, descriptions, theoretical investigations – the investigations which, for short, we call 'phenomenological'.
>
> (*Inaugural Lecture* 128)

It is interesting that there seems to be a flux in both the natural and the phenomenological attitudes. In the natural attitude, 'the things involved present themselves through continuously flowing aspects; their shapes are perspectivally silhouetted in definitive ways; the data of the different senses are construed in definite ways' (*Inaugural Lecture* 128). When we move away from the natural attitude, and take on the phenomenological one, we still find a flux of a different sort, even though it is an apodictic one: we can use reflection to see *more* about the phenomenological structures of experience itself and in so doing we can always learn more about it. The phenomenologist has the ability to *discover new things* in the phenomenological attitude; making phenomenological discoveries is the whole point of phenomenology after all. The more we re-question the appearance of the phenomenon, the more we elicit ways to describe it. Thus, from the question 'what is the phenomenon?' Husserl has developed at least two clarifications: appearance by way of objects in the sense of logical predicates and appearance by way of Objects in the sense of spatiotemporal things; however, he is not yet done with this question. Husserl returns to once again ask and answer this question in order to further reveal more about the phenomenon.

§12. The multiplicity of singular unities: A phenomenon and its manifold

As Husserl continues to re-question how the phenomenon itself appears, this experience quickly becomes confounding, given that what counts as an appearance continues to expand. The complexity of the phenomenon is further revealed when we see its multiplicities revealed at various levels of consciousness. Husserl states that 'manifold intuitions [...] together make up the unity of one *continuous consciousness* of one and the same object' (*Inaugural Lecture* 125). Interestingly however, no matter how many multiplicities a phenomenon reveals of itself through perception, it nonetheless is *also* taken to be a unity. Husserl states that

> the manner in which the object is given within each of the single intuitions belonging to this continuous consciousness may vary constantly [...] may be forever new in the transition from one perception to continuously new perception. In spite of that, we have [... an] intuitive consciousness not of a changing multiplicity but rather of one and the same object that is variously presented.

(*Inaugural Lecture* 125)

For example, when we observe an Object on a table (e.g. a bottle), we are able to perceive it from various angles, left or right, higher or lower, but all the while through all of these multiplicities we perceive the very same Object as something continually revealing itself anew as the same unity in different ways. As we change our perspective view of the Object we do not then also think that new Objects are continually being revealed; instead, they are just new profiles of the same unity. For example, as I spin a bottle and perceive its different sides, I do not think that entire new bottles are being revealed with each new profile; rather, I intend the very same unity through its many manifold profiles. Husserl clarifies:

> To put it differently, within the pure immanence of such consciousness one unitary 'phenomenon' permeates all the manifolds of phenomenal presentation. It is the peculiar characteristic of such states of affairs which makes for a shift in the concept 'phenomenon.' Rather than just the thoroughgoing *unity* of intuition, the various changing modes in which the unity is presented, *e.g.*, the continuously changing perspectival looks of a real object, are also called 'phenomena'.
>
> (*Inaugural Lecture* 125)

Thus, in addition to the phenomenon of *the unity* which appears through its many different profiles, each of its specific profiles and different ways of showing itself are *also* to be understood and investigated as individual *phenomena of that specific unity*. Here things get complicated, but in a rich and edifying way. In the first moment, we have the same phenomenon as a unity that appears through many different profiles and in the second moment we may say that each of these different profiles can *also* be understood as individual phenomena.

As if the application of the concept of phenomenon was not complex or broad enough already, concerning how things reveal themselves to consciousness, how consciousness cognizes these varying phenomena as 'acts of consciousness' is also to be understood and investigated *as another kind or clarification of the phenomenon*. Husserl states that

> the extent of this concept is further broadened when we consider the higher cognitive functions: the multiform acts and coherency of referential, combinative, conceiving, theorizing cognition. Every single process of any of these sorts is, again, intrinsically consciousness of the object that is peculiar to it as a thought process of some particular sort or sorts.
>
> (*Inaugural Lecture* 125–6)

As we have observed previously, perceiving the same unity from different profiles complicated the way the phenomenon self-reveals, but the source of this complication came from the experience of the phenomenon itself in that it revealed *its* constancy as a unity through a multitude of profile appearances. Here, Husserl moves away from the 'object revealing itself' and focuses upon how 'consciousness *constitutes* the object' within perception. How the perceiver refers to the object, combines it with other perceptions, conceives of the object and theorizes about the object *are all themselves acts of consciousness*. Through reflection, these acts of consciousness can also be made into phenomena and thus, from the *perceiver's* side, these descriptions further broaden and complicate the way the phenomenon self-reveals.

Husserl remains open to the additional ways in which a phenomenon self-reveals to also account for modes of consciousness. He states that

> the concept 'phenomenon' carries over, furthermore, to the changing modes of being conscious of something – for example, the clear and the obscure, evident and blind modes – in which one and the same relation or connection, one and the same state-of-affairs, one and the same logical coherency, etc., can be given to consciousness.
>
> (*Inaugural Lecture* 126)

In the experiences of perceiving an object, we are able through reflection to make the very modes of conscious acts (characteristically obscure, clear, logical or illogical) into phenomena capable of being further investigated. In the example of a table and in response to the question 'what is the phenomenon?' we can identify at least four different ways to clarify appearance itself: (1) *the appearance of the unity of the table* as the same table viewed from different perspectives; (2) when the table is viewed from different perspectives this will also yield *the appearance of individual profiles* that relate to that unity; (3) in response to my reflection upon these individual perspectives, and how they relate to an original unity, yields *the appearance of an act of my consciousness*; and (4) finally through the recognition of my consciousness as clear, obscure, logical, etc., yields *the appearance of a mode of my consciousness*. Importantly, these different descriptions make up the various ways that Husserl can identify distinctions in appearance; as beginner phenomenologists we are encouraged to return to our own experiences of appearance itself and to see whether or not we can find the same kind of evidence for Husserl's descriptions. This return is accomplished by raising the question 'what is the phenomenon?' for ourselves, but in doing so the experience remains *open* for additional discoveries as it remains possible that more aspects of the phenomenon might be further revealed. In our own individual efforts to raise and to answer this question, to try and see the same experiential evidence Husserl is claiming he can see, it remains possible that we might see *something additional* to what Husserl has claimed. In this sense then, in addition to these four clarifications of the phenomenon (unity, profile, act and mode), we have a fifth that is also importantly their common source: the very question 'what is the phenomenon?' It thus remains open for future phenomenologists (i.e. Heidegger and Patočka) to participate in phenomenology by raising this question anew and, in so doing, they can potentially secure new and *additional descriptions*, thereby adding to the larger enterprise of Husserl's phenomenological work.

By re-questioning our own experience, Husserl claims that we can uncover, like Descartes already did long ago, the purely phenomenological sphere (*Inaugural Lecture* 129). In the cognition of an ideal object, a number for example, there are no sides or adumbrations to consider; it is given absolutely and as such it makes no sense to doubt it. Recall the example above of loving something: although it is possible to doubt the thing one may love or the reasons for loving it, the very act of loving itself is given to oneself apodictically. In the cognition of a spatiotemporal object, a table for example, there are sides that may be further explored as I shift my perception around the object. It is possible for the table to be further revealed as an illusion or a clever painting on a wall and not a real table at all. However, given the experience of perceiving a table and putting out of play its actuality, I may perform the phenomenological reduction and re-consider it merely as an appearance itself at which point I only concern the aspects of the experience that are given to me absolutely. According to Husserl, the

> *phenomenological reduction* can be effected by modifying Descartes's method, by carrying it through purely and consequentially while disregarding all Cartesian aims; phenomenological reduction is the method for effecting radical purification of the phenomenological field of consciousness from all obtrusions from Objective actualities and for keeping it pure of them.
>
> (*Inaugural Lecture* sic 129)

After applying the phenomenological reduction, we have a kind of experience that is indubitable. Although I may always doubt whether or not a spatiotemporal Object is what it appears to be, once I perform the reduction, its actuality is suspended and put out of play and only its appearance remains for further consideration. Husserl states:

> What is left over, once this radical methodological exclusion of all Objective actualities has been effected? The answer is clear. If we put every experienced

actuality out of action, we still have indubitably given every phenomenon of experience. This is true for the whole Objective world as well. We are forbidden to make use of the *actuality* of the Objective world: for us, the Objective world is as if it were placed in brackets. What remains to us is the totality of the phenomena of the world, the phenomena which are grasped by reflection as they are absolutely in themselves [*in ihrer absoluten Selbstheit*]. For, all of these constituents of conscious life remain intrinsically what they were; it is through them that the world is constituted.

(*Inaugural Lecture* 130)

The results of the reduction yield a new kind of phenomenological evidence that requires further thought and consideration. The more one reflects on such evidence, the more one uncovers the need for further reflection.

Interestingly, although after the reduction phenomenological evidence is apodictic, there are still uncharted possibilities to discover and in so doing to learn new things. In his work *Formal and Transcendental Logic* (henceforth *FTL*), Husserl famously states that '[e]ven an ostensibly apodictic evidence can become disclosed as deception and, in that event, presupposes a similar evidence by which it is "shattered"' (*FTL* 156). As each new example of evidence appears and problematizes previous understanding, it also provides a source for further reflection and consideration. In fact, even when phenomenology fulfils its highest aim and uncovers an *essence* – evidence that seems to perpetually confirm and re-confirm itself for everyone, all of the time – the *value* of this discovery is to be understood as an *active repetition* rather than a *singular proven true premise*. In other words, after the discovery of an essence, were a phenomenologist to forsake the original repetitive practices of questioning that yields it and simply, from that moment onwards, take it as a given truth no longer requiring further validation *via* questioning, they would cease to be a phenomenologist and effectively become a metaphysician (in the pejorative sense of basing their ideas on inventive contrivance, rather than on repetitive evidence). This is because the value and importance of evidence are not simply to build up a true system for phenomenology, but to use that evidence as a means to fulfil the *practice* of phenomenology (understood as a task of infinite repetition).

In Husserl's phenomenology, evidence is never left 'on the shelf' nor is it appealed to in the sense of an authority; rather, each and every phenomenologist is called to verify any claim based on evidence that everyone can return to and see for themselves. In *Conversations with Husserl and Fink*, Dorion Cairns claims that '[e]arlier in the conversation, when, in fact, I first spoke of evidence, Husserl spoke, as often before, of the importance of the phenomenon of

"*Fortgeltung*" < continuing acceptance, continuing validity >, that what I hold valid today, or this minute, continues in validity the next minute. Or can be returned to as valid' (Cairns 1976 41). The importance of validity for Husserl is not a 'coronation of truth' that simply later confirms authoritative claims, but is an experience in and of itself that one must participate in again and again. In this sense, evidence is best understood in the form of a question rather than as a true premise. It remains a 'collectible' but more in the sense of a *collected way to revive an original experience that confirms an essence*, rather than as a singular truth. The role of the activity of questioning in phenomenology not only shows itself as the means by which one may participate in the project of phenomenology, to gain insight, but furthermore is revealed as a collection of such questions which may be used to *perpetually practise* elicitation of original experiences that provide evidence for phenomenological claims. To be a phenomenologist, therefore, means to raise its preserved questions anew as well as striving to understand the excellent answers that are elicited in this process.

Husserl's *Inaugural Lecture* reveals how phenomenology enables us to return to a question again and again in order to further explore what it reveals in the asking. In the above case, this is done regarding the question 'what is the phenomenon?' or 'how does the phenomenon self-reveal to consciousness?' Husserl states that 'the first and most primitive concept of the phenomenon referred to the limited sphere of those sensuously given realities through which Nature is evinced in perceiving' (*Inaugural Lecture* 126). This primitive concept seems to be the traditional and empirical definition of an object. Husserl continues writing that

> [t]he concept was extended, without comment, to include every kind of sensuously meant or objectivated thing. It was then extended to include also the sphere of those synthetic objectivities that are given to consciousness through referential and connective conscious syntheses and to include these objects just the way they are given to consciousness. It thus includes all modes in which things are given to consciousness.
>
> (*Inaugural Lecture* 126)

The extension of the traditional concept of object, therefore, includes the way we think about phenomena, view and understand various connections between phenomena, and the various modes in which phenomena are given to consciousness. Husserl continues by stating that the concept of phenomenon 'was seen finally to include the whole realm of consciousness with *all* ways of being conscious of something and all the constituents that can be shown immanently to belong to them' (*Inaugural Lecture* 126). Thus, the widest sense of the phenomenon is something that 'includes *all* ways of being conscious of something means that it includes, as well, every sort of feeling, desiring, and willing with its immanent 'comportment' [*Verhalten*]' (*Inaugural Lecture* 126). Whatever *can* be counted as an appearance to consciousness can, therefore, also be understood as phenomena or be made into phenomena through reflection. It is clear from this quote that Husserl's project to clarify the phenomenon is also open and ongoing, tracing a preserved question through experience whilst developing, verifying and eliciting new answers in response to this questioning endeavour.

In this way, then, phenomenology is always a presentation of questions alongside a presentation of answers. Furthermore, these questions are genuine and alive; they are not rhetorically constructed paths that lead to already worked out answers; instead, they are invitations for further thinking and demonstrate participation in the development of phenomenology. It is, thus, possible that newer generations of phenomenologists may uncover hitherto concealed notions of the very idea of appearance and in so doing can further the work of Husserl by moving beyond him. When these new discoveries occur, they may be considered to be the result of following Husserl's questions, even when they may undermine Husserl's already-established answers. Participating in the project of phenomenology might have more to do with questioning that it does coming to a clear grasp of the answers derived from doing so; this, after all, is what Husserl perpetually did to his own discoveries and viewed them as conclusive works.

The study of these various ways of revealing, being consciousness of and describing distinctions of phenomena elucidates what phenomenology means in general. Husserl states that

> through this exposition of the concept 'phenomenon' we obtain a preliminary conception of a *general phenomenology*, viz., a science of objective phenomena of every kind, the science of every kind of object, an 'object' being taken purely as something having just those determinations with which it presents itself in consciousness and in just those changing modes through which it so presents itself.
>
> (*Inaugural Lecture* 126–5, my emphasis)

The process of eliciting a preliminary conception of general phenomenology entails a practice of questioning that Husserl emulates specifically (i.e. 'what is the phenomenon?') in his *Inaugural Lecture*. To participate in phenomenology, therefore, includes the collecting of primary questions that are used to elicit genuine experiences. Once elicited, the experience itself is used in tandem with any descriptions made of it. Husserl confirms this by stating that

> it would be the task of phenomenology, therefore, to investigate how something perceived, something remembered, something phantasied, something pictorially represented, something symbolized looks at such, *i.e.*, to investigate how it looks by virtue of that bestowal of sense and of characteristics which is carried out intrinsically by the perceiving, the remembering, the phantasying, the pictorial representing, etc., itself.
>
> (*Inaugural Lecture* 127)

By using the activity of questioning to elicit the genuine experiences of *perceiving*, *remembering*, *phantasying* and *pictorial representing*, we can then, in view of such experiences, phenomenologically describe and account for what perception, memory, phantasying and representation entail *via* activities. He continues by remarking that 'obviously, phenomenology would investigate in the same way how what is collected *looks in the collecting of it*; what is disjoined, *in the disjoining*; what is produced, *in the producing*; and, similarly, for *every* act of thinking, how it intrinsically "has" phenomenally in it what it thinks' (*Inaugural Lecture* 127, my emphasis). The activity of questioning is called upon to elicit, for the sake of investigation and clarification, the very experiences themselves. However, this only accounts for what the *practice* of phenomenology entails; what phenomenology aims to acquire in the performance of this practice is something else.

For Husserl, what phenomenology aims to uncover is an essential account of consciousness: a collection of universally valid structures for consciousness. Husserl posits that

> [w]hat phenomenology wants, in all these investigations, is to establish what admits of being stated with the universal validity of theory. In doing so, however, its investigations will, understandably, have to refer to the intrinsic nature of the perceiving itself, of remembering (or any other way of re-presenting) itself, and of thinking, valuing, willing, and doing themselves – these acts being taken just as they present themselves to immanently intuitive reflection.
>
> (*Inaugural Lecture* 127)

Thus, although phenomenology utilizes the activity of questioning in a powerful way to return to and elicit experiences, this is done with a higher goal in mind for Husserl: the true answers for such questions are indeed what Husserl's phenomenology is designed to unearth. As a project aiming to develop truthful answers, the role of system and systematicity emerges.

§13. Phenomenology as systematic but not merely a system

As long as phenomenology is a pursuit that scientifically studies experience itself, it can never just be a theoretical metaphysics or just another philosophical system. Theoretical metaphysics always suffers from *some kind* of speculative constructions or contrivances that cannot be verified. Although Husserl ascribes a deep value to logic and rationality, he maintains that the phenomena of experience must always reveal themselves prior to any descriptions thereof. In other words phenomenology, as a *science of* experience, will always strive to ground its findings and descriptions in genuine phenomenological experience; on this point, Husserl confirms that 'experience by itself is not science' (*Inaugural Lecture* 131). In this sense, the project of returning to experience in order to verify any scientific claim will always come before the project of stabilizing our verifications to the level of a science. Returning to his essay 'Concerning Phenomenology', Reinach confirms this by stating that phenomenological descriptions are certainly

> not to be blindly accepted, nor built upon a fabulous *consensus omnium* or vague necessities of thought. Nothing lies further from phenomenology than that. This derivative knowledge must rather be brought to luminosity, to the highest sort of intuitive givenness; and we precisely stress that for this purpose a special effort and methodology are required.
>
> (Reinach 192)

All of phenomenology's descriptions will be demonstrative in the sense that they are predicates of their correlates: the original phenomena of genuine experience. The ground that Husserlian phenomenology is to rest upon is experience itself, or more specifically on the 'soil of pure reflection upon experience', wherein those who desire to participate in its project must make great efforts to re-engage with experience itself, through questioning and re-questioning what goes on within experience in order to see what phenomenology describes.[19]

In his *Vienna Lecture*, Husserl states that the philosopher must be resolved 'not to accept unquestioningly any pregiven opinion or tradition so that he can inquire, in respect to the whole traditionally pregiven universe, after what is true in itself, an ideality' (*Vienna Lecture* 287). Similarly to how Husserl suggests that all traditional ideas need to be continually re-questioned, the same is true for the traditional *methods and practices of phenomenology* as well. In this sense, the radical re-questioning employed by phenomenology is never to be satisfied by deriving something merely theoretical *even after* these theories have been grounded upon some kind of phenomenological experience and, as such, this grounding will always include and preserve a return to the inexhaustibility of experience itself.

For Husserl, the primary motto of phenomenology is to *take nothing for granted – always return to the things themselves to see how they in fact self-reveal*. This does not comprise the naive claim to 'just look and see' but rather amounts to a respect for how complex, elusive and difficult it can be to reflect upon one's own experience. Furthermore, at each moment of discovery in the return to experience in order to verify our newly hypothesized knowledge claims, we find new problems emerge causing the entire process to begin anew. Nothing may be taken for granted in phenomenology, where even the most simple and obvious claim is still required to be grounded upon a repeatable experience that verifies it. Importantly, this needs to also be applied to the findings of phenomenology as well. In his epilogue to *Ideas II*, Husserl states:

> nothing [that is] held to be obvious, either predicatively or pre-predicatively, can pass, unquestioned, as a basis for knowledge. It is, I emphasize, an *idea,* which, as the further meditative interpretation will show, is to be realized only by way of relative and temporary validities and in an infinite historical process – but in this way it is, in fact, realizable.
>
> (*Ideas II* 406)[20]

Importantly, this stance of re-questioning everything is not understood pejoratively, just the opposite: it involves the responsibility of grounding one's own ideas, claims and philosophical pursuits upon the things themselves. Thus, as a form of ultimate responsibility, it places a central value on a thinker's ability to *question* prior to their ability to *answer*. It is this value that Husserl displays, encourages and builds phenomenology upon that made him so inspirational to his students. This is something that Heidegger will take up in *Being and Time* through his peculiar project to raise and legitimize a question, rather than to argue convincingly for a particular answer (*BT* 1/1) and what Jan Patočka will later describe as phenomenology's 'absolute responsibility' (*BCLW* 84).

It is this insight, to take nothing for granted, that proves to be most problematic for the traditional approach of philosophy, given the traditional idea that one must first clarify basic concepts and definitions before using them. Reinach states that 'in fact, we see that every definition essentially refers back to a knowing, from which alone it can receive its justification and verification' (Reinach 195). In this sense, every definition or concept is revealed to be based upon an 'already worked out' and therefore *stabilized flow of experience*. As such, it may be *de-stabilized* back into its original experiential flow. This would be one specific way to clarify what it means to question: to destabilize answers by reviving the original question for which it aims to provide a resolution. To phenomenologically understand a concept, therefore, comprises more than just giving mental assent to its meaning, but furthermore to see for oneself how that meaning emerges out of the flux of experience and may be stabilized into a definition. Thus, Husserl's radical insight is to reverse the traditional imperative of starting with clear concepts and then to compare and apply them to experience, to instead begin *first* with the experience of the phenomena themselves (with all the overwhelming, rich and abundance this entails) and *then* proceed to try and to figure out the conceptual framework dynamically at work in the acts of perceiving them.

Instead of exchanging one philosophical system for another, Husserl advocates for the revival of the activity that always precedes the development of any system whatsoever: the open re-questioning of *the things themselves*. This questioning is not arbitrary however, nor is it whimsical or without direction. It is *open* insofar as it remains attentive and willing to go 'wherever' the things themselves may lead, but under Husserl's project, it seeks to clarify what is essentially taking place for consciousness within any given experience. The work of phenomenology shifts depending on how one understands 'essence' and in light of which issue or problem of experience one wishes to clarify; however, experience comes first in every case. It is from the experience of the things themselves that phenomenological insights are drawn. Once collected, such insights may then be verified by another phenomenologist, and in so doing more of the original experience may yet reveal itself anew. This non-linear reciprocity is what comprises phenomenological investigation.

If Husserl continually stresses that phenomenology keep itself from being reduced to a system, then one must wonder why he concerns himself with systematic descriptions so significantly. The answer to this concern further reveals an important aspect of how phenomenology aims to, on the one hand, provide scientific insight into consciousness while, on the other hand, preserve the experiential sources of knowledge so that other phenomenologists may use those sources to see and ground insights for themselves. This is accomplished through a preservation of questions alongside their already-valued answers. From the analysis of Husserl's *Inaugural Lecture*, the precise role played by systems seems unclear. Although always striving for systematicity, Husserl's thought is nonetheless always developing and changing.[21] Phenomenology preserves the importance of experience itself and our access to it *via* reflection. At the end of his *Inaugural Lecture*, Husserl states that 'philosophers, as things now stand, are all too fond of offering criticism from on high instead of studying and understanding the things from within' (*Inaugural Lecture* 133). What Husserl has shown us not only *that* phenomenology can be used to re-elicit original and dynamic experiences that are stabilized into appearances, concepts and descriptions, but also how this is to be accomplished: generally, in light of his motto through the process of re-questioning experience, consciousness and the phenomena themselves, and specifically, instantiated *via* one of his particular methods. Husserl's phenomenology re-discovers the centrality of our questioning response to genuine and direct experience.

Although Husserl strives to be as systematic and as thorough as possible, he never presents phenomenology as just a system. In his new introduction to Husserl's *LI* from December 2000, Moran states that 'Husserl insisted [that the *LI*] was *not* a "systematic exposition of logic" (*eine systematische Darstellung der Logic*), but an effort at epistemological clarification and critique of the basic concepts of logical knowledge' (*LI* vol. I, xxi). In other words, the *LI* is Husserl's attempt to re-elicit the originary experiences of logic, the very experiences our epistemological concepts are properly to correlate with. To read the *LI* in this particular way will not give the reader merely another more coherent or specific system of logic, but rather bring into view what any and every logical system aims to correlate with: an experience of logic itself. Spiegelberg states that

> [a]t no stage of his career does Husserl present us with a philosophical system. Certainly he never aspired to develop his philosophy into a speculative synthesis. But this does not mean that he abandoned the goal of systematic philosophy in the sense of a philosophy which works patiently and painstakingly at the solution of limited though fundamental problems.
>
> (Spiegelberg 1960 75)

Also noted in his work *Doing Phenomenology*, Spiegelberg writes that despite 'all its aspirations to scientific rigor, Husserl's phenomenology never rigidified into an orthodox system. It grew and continued growing to the end, while becoming more radical in its demands' (Spiegelberg 1975 xxii). The difficulty in coming to understand the role of system and systematicity in Husserl's work is further clarified when one recognizes that the system can only be 'accomplished' on the side of answering; whereas the radical kind of questioning phenomenology equally concerns must remain 'outside' of any given system. Bernet et al. confirms this view by stating that

> Husserl's idea of philosophy is determined by the thought of a revival of the Socratic-Platonic idea of philosophy as absolute knowledge in its connection with self-knowledge. As such an idea, philosophy is only to be realized in Husserl's view in an infinite historical process, and not as the work of one man and his 'system'.
>
> (Bernet et al. 4)

The English translator of Husserl's *LI*, J.N. Findlay, describes Husserl's phenomenology as 'free from the extraneous trappings of a "system", and its dubious methodological and covertly metaphysical pretensions, and [is] simply one of the prime achievements of philosophy' (*LI* vol. I, lxxviii). Husserl gives a general introduction to phenomenology and knowledge in *LI*, after his famous section entitled 'Prolegomena to Pure Logic' but prior to his first investigation. Therein he importantly postulates that

> these investigations make no claim to be exhaustive. Their aim is *not to provide a logical system*, but to do the initial *spadework* for a philosophical logic which will derive clearness *from basic phenomenological sources*. The paths taken by such an analytic investigation will also naturally differ from those suitable to a final, systematic, logically ordered statement of established truth.
>
> (*LI* vol. I, 174, my emphasis)

The importance of phenomenological questions is to return a thinker to the sources of what phenomenological answers are hoping to truthfully describe. More importantly, the systematic clarification of phenomenology will, therefore, always come after one has already had the genuine experience of what that description aims to clarify. Husserl states that

> [s]ystematic clarification, whether in pure logic or any other discipline, would in itself seem to require a stepwise following out of the ordering of things, of the systematic interconnection in the science to be clarified. Our investigation can, however, only proceed securely, if it repeatedly breaks with such systematic sequence, if it removes conceptual obscurities which threaten the course of investigation *before* the natural sequence of subject-matters can lead up to such concepts. We search, as it were, in zig-zag fashion, a metaphor all the more apt since the close interdependence of our various epistemological concepts leads us back again and again to our original analyses, where the new confirms the old, and the old the new.
>
> (*LI* vol. I, 175)

Although the goal of providing a systematic account of phenomenology remains, Husserl clearly states here that a systematic step-by-step is undesirable since it might obfuscate the genuine experience that phenomenology seeks to clarify. Rather, Husserl seeks to re-create a path that leads back to the original experience that any insight (concept, logic, etc.) correlates with first, and to account for it systematically later. Husserl describes this process in the following way:

> [P]henomenology [...] lays bare the 'sources' from which the basic concepts and ideal laws of *pure* logic 'flow', and back to which they must once more be traced, so as to give them all the 'clearness and distinctness' needed for an understanding and for an epistemological critique, of pure logic.
>
> (*LI* vol. I, 166)

In this way then, the role of systematicity in Husserl's phenomenology is *secondary to phenomenological questioning*. Phenomenological investigation aims to enable one to re-enact or re-invigorate the correlation between an original experience and its phenomenological description.

Even if one agrees that Husserl does not present his phenomenology as a system, whether or not he eventually wanted it to become one remains unclear. In a letter responding to E. Parl Welch and in particular, responding to his question '[f]irst of all, do you conceive your system as organically connected with any philosophic predecessors?' (Spiegelberg 1973 171), Husserl responds by writing that

> [a]s to question 1: May I ask you not to call my philosophy a 'system'. For it is precisely its objective to make all 'systems' impossible once and for all. It wants to be rigorous science, which in an infinite progression systematically works its way toward its problems, methods and theories.
>
> (Spiegelberg 1973 179)

As this letter fragment suggests, Husserl did not want his phenomenology to become merely a system; like many of his ideas, this might not have always been the case for him. Spiegelberg states that

> one of the striking things is Husserl's emphatic denial of having developed a system and his claim that he wants to abolish all such systems once and for all. Actually this almost Nietzschean rejection of the will to a system is something that Husserl did not always maintain. From statements in some of his letters and fragments now found in his unpublished manuscripts it appears that Husserl cherishes the plan of condensing his final insights into something he himself called a system. Nevertheless, it remains true that he had no intention

of rivalling any of the great systems such as those of Aristotle or Hegel, and that he denied any substantial loans from them, claiming that he had reached their conclusions independently by his own method.

(Spiegelberg 1973 183)

Regardless of what side one may land on concerning the issue of system, it remains quite clear that Husserl greatly desired his phenomenology to be taken up as a practice – one that spurs reflection and wonder over and against correct memorization or mere mental assent.

Among the blurry contrast between systematic phenomenology and just another 'system' is the idea of rigour, but what exactly does rigour entail? To answer this question, we may turn to Husserl's somewhat infamous text 'Philosophy as a Rigorous Science' (henceforth *PRS*). Although it was not well received, according to Spiegelberg, Husserl remained nonetheless dedicated to this project.²² Husserl was certainly aware of this 'less than enthusiastic' reception to his ideas however, as he clearly states that '[p]hilosophy as science, as serious, rigorous, indeed apodictically rigorous, science – *the dream is over*' ('Denial of Scientific Philosophy' 389). However, to be fair to Husserl, he presents the idea of philosophy as a rigorous science as a *project yet to be done*, importantly saying that '[d]uring no period of its development has philosophy been capable of to this claim of being rigorous science [...]. It shows that even the proper sense of philosophical problems has not been made scientifically clear. [...] I do not say that philosophy is an imperfect science; I say simply [...] that as science it has not yet begun' (*PRS* 71–3). Interestingly, Husserl's claim that rigorous philosophy has yet to begin does not entail the displacement or rejection of the tradition with something new (Husserl's own type of rigorous philosophy), but importantly, it begins with a re-examination of earlier historical attempts to do so. In particular, Husserl credits 'the Kantian system [as] the first attempt, and one carried out with impressive scientific seriousness, at a truly universal transcendental philosophy meant to be a *rigorous science* in a sense of scientific rigor which has only now been discovered and which is the only genuine sense' (*Crisis* 99). Thus, whatever 'rigorous science' and 'system' will mean for Husserl's phenomenology, the meanings will be grounded in a reflection upon earlier traditional attempts to do the same. This practice of Husserl's foreshadows what Patočka will develop into a theme of its own, namely a heretical way to philosophize by keeping what one criticizes in view while simultaneously moving away from it.

Husserl raises the question of system by asking 'what meaning should be given to the "system" for which we yearn, which is supposed to gleam as an ideal before us in the lowlands where we are doing our investigated work?' (*PRS* 75). Regardless of how it will 'look', Husserl is quite clear on *how* it should be built up, as something that 'really begins from the ground up with a foundation *free of doubt* and rises up like any skill construction, wherein stone is set upon stone, each as solid as the other, *in accord with directive insights*' (*PRS* 76, my emphasis). Thus, it is clear that merely having a list of propositions or a system of insights will not be enough unless they are of the kind that begin from the ground-up, emerge in a way that is free of doubt and are given directly. This idea of 'rigour' for Husserl, therefore, has more to do with the means through which one obtains an insight than it does with one's ability to systematize it or not. For Husserl, rigour means to rigorously struggle with the things themselves. However, the notion of system remains in view as an ideal goal the phenomenologist continually strives for, albeit at a distance.

The ideal notion of systematic rigour is informed for Husserl by the mathematical sciences. Spiegelberg states that 'for Husserl scientific rigor was primarily the rigor of the deductive sciences familiar to the mathematician, rather than that of the inductive natural sciences' (Spiegelberg 1960 77). The mathematical sense of rigour brings to mind a 'perfect' system and the acquisition of such a system through the building up, one true proposition at a time axiomatically. Considering this idea, Buckley considers two ways to interpret the idea of rigour: axiomatic and responsible. Regarding axiomatic rigour, Buckley writes that at 'first glance, the word "rigour"[23] seems to be based on inspiration drawn from the deductive, axiomatic sciences. That is, to be rigorous as a science is to be based on a few fundamental propositions or axioms [... and on] this basis, one can move deductively and methodically [...] and thereby build a system of certain knowledge' (Buckley 21). Such a mathematical system, however appealing it may appear due to its *internally perfect systematicity*, can for this very reason also become unappealing as it is quite possible to contrive a perfect system that correlates to nothing, perhaps even signifies nothing.[24] In other words, a formally coherent and internally perfect system is not enough to achieve the level of rigorous philosophy Husserl is aiming for and this is another reason why phenomenology ought never to be understood as *merely* a system.

If phenomenology is not to be rigorous in an axiomatic or mathematical sense, then in what sense does Husserl mean 'rigour'? Regarding responsible rigour, Buckley writes that 'Husserl has something more substantial in mind with the idea of rigour. Rigour for Husserl is not just a matter of proceeding, of making progress – but understanding *how* that progress has been made and for what purpose. Rigour is not just a matter of continuing forward with certainty, but also recalling and understanding where one *began*' (Buckley 22). Where does phenomenology begin, if not in experience as such? Experience, with all its messiness, complications, confusions, dynamisms, fluctuating moments, rich and robust content that requires perpetual unpacking – it is all this that phenomenology rigorously embraces and wrestles with.[25] Buckley states that '[a]nother way of defining rigour is to say that to be rigorous is to be *responsible*, to be able to justify each and every position taken, to be willing to provide the evidence for one's beliefs' (Buckley 22). As an effort to keep that which one aims to correlate descriptions within view, the term 'responsible' seems apt. Such a responsible approach can never be merely a system because it keeps in view that which phenomenology always remains a *response to*: experience. If phenomenology is properly understood as a perpetual *response* to experience, then the dynamic instability of experience itself will also be perpetually kept in view. However, the results of this approach are still nonetheless formulated systematically, even though it keeps something dynamic preserved and in view.

Although Husserl seems to be placing great limitations upon the use, power and value of rigour, the idea of system and systematicity remains highly important for the project of phenomenology. Without it, phenomenology would not be able to become a science. Husserl returns to this same idea again in the introduction to Investigation III in *LI*, stating that

> [h]ere again we cannot allow our analytic investigation to wait on the systematic development of our subject matter. Difficult notions employed by us in our clarificatory study of knowledge, and made to work rather in the manner of a lever, cannot be left unexamined, till they spontaneously emerge in the systematic fabric of the logical realm. For we are not here engaged on a systematic exposition of logic, but on an epistemological clarification, as well as on the prolegomena to any future exposition of logic.
>
> (*LI* vol. II, 3)

Also, recall that Husserl claims that 'science is only possible where the results of thinking can be preserved in the form of knowledge and can be applied for further thinking in the form of a system of assertions' (*Ideas I* 120). Thus, we can see that systematicity remains highly valued by Husserl, but that he also recognizes that its power as a tool can also cause problems when one wants to begin with a *system of* logic (*via* answers) as opposed to the *experience of* logic (*via* questioning).

Thus, in light of the distinction of phenomenological questioning (used to return to elicit the experiences themselves) and phenomenological answering (wherein phenomenology is able to attain the level of a science), it also becomes clear what may be salvaged in phenomenology were one to consider its strictly scientific project to be a bust. Those who wish to criticize Husserl for intellectualism, Platonism, esotericism or of falling back into psychologism should further consider that *even if such charges were true*, Husserl's rediscovery, development and use of the activity of questioning would remain a separate worthwhile activity to further develop phenomenology. Indeed, this is precisely what Husserl himself continued to do to his own stabilized results: return to his own experience with them in order to see whether or not experience validated them again and again. In each instance, this questioning yielded additional 'things' to be considered and this began the question-answer-question activity all over again.

§14. Chapter conclusion: Phenomenological questions precede their answers

We find not a method, assumption or answer at the very heart of Husserl's work, but rather a motto: *to the things themselves!* Although this charge to return to experience in no way undermines nor lessens the great value of his collected and clarifies answers, how his entire work and thought stem from and embody a questioning reflection on experience itself is clearly visible. If such a description is fair, or at least defensible, then this would shed a very different light upon Heidegger's reinterpretations of phenomenology. However, if one thing remains clear about Husserl's phenomenology, it is that there is no such thing as only *one kind, type or singular definition*. However, this failure to find 'one phenomenology' in Husserl's work might be more of a failure in how one approaches it. As Husserl perpetually returned to experience itself to see how well or poorly his current rendering of phenomenology correlated to it, we might completely abandon the idea of whether or not there is a strictly Husserlian phenomenology for any of his flowers to 'properly pay homage to' in the first place. Considering the 'violence' nearly all of his students did to his phenomenology, were any of them as violent as Husserl was to himself? Alternatively, it might be argued that the violence done to Husserl's phenomenology by any of his followers may indeed be the proper 'phenomenological' homage to be paid in the wake of what Husserl's own *practices* displayed.

When it comes to the phenomenological project of clarifying the phenomenon, we see that alongside the various descriptions we attribute to appearance, the original question 'what is a phenomenon?' remains a separate worthwhile avenue for further research even now in light of 122 years of phenomenological research conducted. By maintaining this question as a worthwhile issue to re-raise again and again, phenomenological inquiry maintains a value for the activity of questioning alongside verifiable descriptions that prove to be the same each time a subsequent phenomenologist raises and answers the question. In addition to essential confirmation, the question also reveals additional aspects of the phenomenon. The more Husserl questions the phenomenon, the more ways it reveals itself.

A phenomenon is, therefore, a synthesis of possible and actual appearances given to consciousness through experience. Bringing about a full appreciation and clear understanding of what a phenomenon fully entails turns out to be an infinite task. It is certainly not a case of merely defining what the concept of phenomenon means in advance, and then looking for experiential evidence to back it up, but just the opposite: to try and allow the emergence of the phenomenon to self-reveal and then conform our concepts to it. The many different descriptions or concepts of the phenomenon are, therefore, developed in response to their emergence within experience and not the other way around. Thus, woven into the very operation of every phenomenological inquiry is a kind of edifying repetition that seeks to confirm and reconfirm what previous descriptions have claimed, whilst also enabling new appearances to come to the fore for further reflection and consideration. This very process of questioning, answering and re-questioning lies at the heart of Husserl's penchant for revision and embodies his motto 'to the [questions] themselves!'

3

Heidegger's 'possibility' of phenomenology

§15. Chapter introduction

This chapter continues to follow the development of phenomenology as Husserl's philosophical position is reinterpreted by Heidegger. Specifically, Heidegger's *BT* is interpreted as a text that further develops Husserl's motto into a philosophy that develops transparent questioning as its central theme. In §16, I argue that although Heidegger's *BT* moves against the direction of Husserl's *Ideas*, it nonetheless aims to follow what Heidegger takes to be Husserl's great accomplishments in the *LI*. In §17, I explore how Heidegger further develops Husserl's questioning practice in *BT* to include the attempt to clarify, make transparent and explicitly formulate a question (instantiated specifically in his presentation of the question of being). In §18, I clarify how *BT* can be understood as an introduction to a 'questioning philosophy'. In §19, I execute a textual analysis of how *BT* reinterprets Husserlian phenomenology and in §20, I specifically consider how Heidegger uses the question 'what is the phenomenon?' to further clarify the ideas of phenomenon, semblance, appearance and mere appearance. Lastly, in §21, I reconsider how Heidegger's idea of logos changes the way in which he understands the activity of phenomenology. I then conclude in §22 by summarizing that this development of phenomenology uncovers the power to preserve a question for Heidegger.

According to Heidegger, phenomenology is not really a school of thought or a particular discipline but is best understood as a way to do research. In *BT*,[1] he confirms this by saying 'the expression "phenomenology" signifies primarily a *methodological conception*. This expression does not characterize the *what* [...] of philosophical research [...], but rather the *how* of that research' (M&R *BT* 50/27). Qualifying his approach, he states that phenomenology is far removed from 'what we call "technical devices", though there are many such devices even in the theoretical disciplines' (M&R *BT* 50/27). I take these comments to be a way for Heidegger to attempt to remain within Husserl's phenomenology while at the same time criticizing Husserl's *apparent* preference for seeking to systematize phenomenological description.² This is further validated when Heidegger goes on to repeat Husserl's motto, stating that 'the term 'phenomenology' expresses a maxim which can be formulated as "To the things themselves!"' (M&R *BT* 50/28). By contrasting Husserl's motto with a critique of 'technical devices' (itself something that may be taken as a veiled attack on Husserl), Heidegger reveals a nuanced interpretation of phenomenology that seems to celebrate the *practice* of Husserl's phenomenology while also being critical to one of Husserl's methods. In *BT*, Heidegger reinterprets phenomenology as ontology by applying Husserl's motto to the question: 'what is being?' However, in his attempt to derive an 'earlier' starting point, Heidegger attempts to establish *the meaning of* the question of being, prior to actually trying to answer it.³

§16. Heidegger moves away from Husserl

According to Heidegger in *LI*, Husserl was in a searching mode that sought to raise various phenomenological questions, rather than one wherein he attempted to give a detailed, systematic and scientific exposition of how to ground phenomenology, as he does in *Ideas I*. Based on this interpretation we can reconsider Heidegger's approach to phenomenology to be less of a radical shift away from Husserl and more of an attempt to stay true to what he believed was Husserl's original impetus for phenomenology (at least as it was developed in the *LI*). However, Heidegger's interpretation of Husserl is not always reliable, convincing, or fair and as such needs to be viewed critically. That said, although Heidegger's critique of Husserl is suspicious, it nonetheless reveals an interesting development of how the activity of questioning is taken up and used within his own interpretation of phenomenological investigation.

In his short essay 'My Way', Heidegger describes why and where his phenomenology parts ways from Husserl's. As a young student, Heidegger found himself repeatedly drawn back to Husserl's *LI*. His captivation revolved around one unresolved issue concerning 'the simple question how thinking's manner of procedure which called itself "phenomenology" was to be carried out. What worried [Heidegger] about this question came from the ambiguity which Husserl's work showed at first glance' ('My Way' 76). As Heidegger continued to read and re-read the *LI*, Husserl continued to develop his own research and published *Ideas I*. In response to his own developments of phenomenology, Husserl subsequently began to revise the second edition of the *LI*, making it more in tune with the new discoveries and design of the *Ideas*. It seems that for Husserl, the *Ideas* did not represent just another development of his phenomenology, but one that he felt required him to revise his previous work in light of the new.

Heidegger claims that Husserl's revisions threatened to cover up the significant shift in Husserl's thought from *LI* to *Ideas I*. As the news of a new philosophy called phenomenology gained momentum, Heidegger claims that 'such historical calculation did not comprehend what had happened in virtue of "phenomenology", that is, [as observable] already within the *Logical Investigations*' ('My Way' 77). Just what was this already valuable 'thing' accomplished in the *LI* that was potentially being covered up in the *Ideas*? According to Heidegger, where the *LI* inquires into phenomena in a *questioning* way that seeks to retrieve the instability of phenomena, *Ideas I* alternatively inquires into phenomena in an *answering* way that seeks to stabilize phenomena too much in its attempt to provide phenomenology with a systematic method in order to establish it as a science. For Heidegger, the significant difference between Husserl's two texts is a shift from a presentation of the *central phenomenological questions* in the *LI*, towards the successful development of a *scientific and methodological foundation* for phenomenology in *Ideas I*. Thus, instead of reading the development between *LI* and *Ideas I* in a linear fashion (as Husserl claims and as Heidegger critiques), we may view *LI*, *Ideas I* and *BT* as different but related non-linear instantiations (i.e. methods) of Husserl's motto at work.

This often-overlooked shift between the two works fostered a misinterpretation that phenomenology's main accomplishment dealt primarily within the means of systematic thought. Heidegger confirms this by saying that 'Husserl's own programmatical explanations and methodological presentations rather strengthened the misunderstanding that through 'phenomenology' a beginning of philosophy was claimed which denied all previous thinking' ('My Way' 78). This misinterpretation is importantly not attributed to Husserl himself, but rather to the general misunderstanding of phenomenology as a systematic accomplishment. The systematic approach of *Ideas I* posed to eclipse the equally important display of phenomenological questioning already present in the *LI*. For Heidegger, the essential and beneficial core of phenomenology is not the powerful or interesting phenomenological *descriptions* it provides *via* its various methods; instead, what appealed to Heidegger was the novel and profound openness and receptivity to how entities reveal themselves in response to the activity of questioning. As Husserl's questioning methods developed a power to derive better and better answers, earlier versions of phenomenology (e.g. the *LI*) were reconsidered and subsequently revised in light of these more recent achievements (e.g. the *Ideas I*). In other words, Heidegger considered that the certain achievements of phenomenology, already obtained and visible within the *LI*, were in danger of being concealed by the newer and perhaps more powerful achievements of the *Ideas*. This Husserl was not only aware of, but also planned for, as in the second edition foreword to the *LI* he writes that he had

> originally cherished the hope that, after discovering and exploring the radical problems of pure phenomenology and phenomenological philosophy, [he] should be able to present a series of systematic expositions that would render a reprinting of the old work unnecessary.
>
> (*LI* vol. I, 3)

It seems that both Husserl and Heidegger viewed the *LI* as valuable, but where Husserl saw it as a work *on the way* to something better that might even be expendable once that higher level is achieved (e.g. *Ideas*), Heidegger viewed the two works separately and that their divergent value was in danger of collapsing. That Husserl believed the presentation of systematic expositions could make the *LI* unnecessary for the project of phenomenology reveals that he may have in fact viewed his development from *LI* to *Ideas* in a linear fashion. From this quote we can see that the ideal of 'systematic expositions' may have in fact remained a goal that Husserl was working towards, at least in the sense that Husserl thought it would be possible to develop beyond the *LI* to make it obsolete. However, once Husserl began to revise the *LI* in order to fit it to the new approach presented in *Ideas I*, he found that this was only possible for the first five of the six logical investigations.[4] Given that Husserl always wanted to develop his project of phenomenology into a proper science, we need not fault him for perhaps letting this desire eclipse some of the already-available accomplishments of his project thus far (e.g. the *LI*). That said, we may perhaps further temper the implications of Heidegger's critique of Husserl to be one that is less undermining of Husserl's general project and one that is more oriented to the attempt of salvaging something valuable that was in danger of being overlooked.

As Husserl worked on his revisions, Heidegger grew more and more focused upon what he believed was being covering up: the power of questions to re-elicit original experiences and phenomena. Although *Ideas I* provided excellent phenomenological answers, Heidegger considered these answers to distract phenomenologists from the power of questioning to enable a thinker to see, return to and revive original experiences.[5] Rather than using phenomenological questioning to derive a system of indubitable descriptions regarding consciousness (that is, a set of answers), the real heart of Husserl's phenomenology is the perpetual practice of using questions to re-elicit experiences of phenomena. Heidegger writes that as he himself

> practiced phenomenological seeing, teaching and learning in Husserl's proximity after 1919 and at the same time tried out a transformed understanding of Aristotle in a seminar, [his] interest leaned anew toward *Logical Investigations*, above all the sixth investigation in the first edition. [...] For this reason we – the friends and pupils – begged the master again and again to republish the sixth investigation which was then difficult to obtain.
>
> ('My Way' 78)

Regardless of Husserl's revisions, Heidegger held fast to the conviction that a return to the things themselves *via* questioning composed the essential core of phenomenology and it was this difference that would begin to drive the student from the master.[6]

According to Heidegger, this division on how to value phenomenology concerned the issue of system. Whereas Heidegger valued phenomenology for its ability to retrieve the fluctuation of phenomena, he subsequently viewed Husserl's concern for system to be a potential impediment to fully utilizing that value. Before considering how to respond to this claim, it is important to consider whether or not Heidegger's interpretation of Husserl was fair and correct. After all, and as already discussed above, the precise relationship between system and systematic descriptions is ambiguous in Husserl.[7] Heidegger's concern can at least be somewhat confirmed from Husserl's statements in the foreword to the second edition of the *LI*, in which he contends that his 'new teaching activity at Freiburg favored a direction of [his] interest to dominant generalities and to system. Only very recently have these systematic studies led [him] back into the territories where [his] phenomenological researches originated' (*LI* vol. II, 177). This supports Heidegger's claim that the shift in Husserl's phenomenological thinking between the *LI* and *Ideas I* changed from a project based on raising questions into a project dedicated to systematically laying out a scientific method to studying the structures of consciousness. Furthermore, Husserl also writes in the second-edition foreword that 'the *Logical Investigations* would be republished, and that in a better form, adapted to the standpoint of the *Ideas*' (*LI* vol. I, 4). Just what was it about the standpoint of the *Ideas* that made it 'better' or on a 'higher level' for Husserl?[8]

That Husserl wished to revise the *LI* and/or to keep it from being made available suggests that whatever change in his thinking had occurred regarding phenomenology was significant. Heidegger remarks that in the end and 'true to his dedication to the cause of phenomenology, the publisher Niemeyer published the last chapter of the *LI* again in 1922' ('My Way' 78–9). For Heidegger, this is significant because it attests to Husserl's resistance and Husserl confirms this by noting in the second-edition foreword of the *LI* that 'as things stand, I had to give in to the wishes of the friends of this work and decide to make its last chapter available again in its old form' (*LI* vol. II, 177). Interestingly in response to this, Heidegger states that 'with the phrase "the friends of this work", Husserl also wanted to say that he himself could not quite get close to the *LI* after the publication of *Ideas*' ('My Way' 78–9). Whether or not this claim is true, it certainly attests to how Heidegger viewed Husserl's philosophical development at that time. Thus, it was not only clear that Heidegger's phenomenological research was moving in a different direction than that of Husserl, but furthermore that Husserl was no longer interested or able to conceptually agree with his previous method of phenomenology. Although their thought was moving in different directions, Heidegger states that 'Husserl watched me in a generous fashion, but at the bottom in disagreement, as I worked on the *LI*' ('My Way' 79). This suggests that the awareness of their diverging paths was possibly mutual and that working in phenomenology at that time was perhaps a relatively open affair.

It is important to note that during these early years, Husserlian phenomenology was doing more to inspire young students than it was establishing a clear and concise philosophy with which one had to either agree or disagree. The list of Husserl's students reads like the 'who's who of 20th Century Philosophy'. In the Göttingen years (1901–16), Husserl inspired Theodor Conrad, Hedwig Conrad-Martius, Jean Héring, Fritz Kaufmann, Winthrop Bell, Roman Ingarden, Alexandre Koyré and Edith Stein. In Munich, Husserl inspired Johannes Daubert, Alexander Pfänder, Adolf Reinach and Max Scheler. Later on in the Freiburg years (1916–38), Husserl inspired Dorion Cairns, Marvin Farber, Karl Löwith, Aron Gurwitsch, Hans-Georg Gadamer, Günther Stern, Herbert Marcuse, Eugen Fink, Ludwig Landgrebe, Alfred Schütz, Rudolf Carnap and many others.[9] We can see that phenomenology was reawakening creative thinking in its students more than it was garnering dogmatic followers to a particular doctrine of phenomenology.[10] Even though Heidegger's position to take up and focus upon one of the many paths already pioneered by Husserl may appear as 'traitorous' from our perspective, in fact, when viewed in light of how phenomenological research was being conducted at that time it may have been more in line with the inspirational wake of Husserl's influence. As Husserl perpetually criticized and revised his own work, and in so doing continually opened up new ways to reinterpret and develop phenomenology, it is reasonable that such practices also influenced Husserl's students to act accordingly.

As Husserl continued to work on the systematic and methodological foundation for a scientific phenomenology in *Ideas I*, Heidegger continued to develop the path he believed was found and abandoned by Husserl in the *LI*. From his research, Heidegger claims that he learned at least one thing:

> What occurs for the phenomenology of the acts of consciousness as the self-manifestations of phenomena is thought more originally by Aristotle and in all Greek thinking and existence as aletheia, as the unconcealedness of what-is present, its being revealed, its showing itself.
>
> ('My Way' 79)

The centrality of Husserl's motto to perpetually question experiences in order to elicit the self-showing of phenomena and use such experiences to further verify and to develop phenomenological descriptions certainly supports the interpretation that Heidegger found the practice of phenomenological questioning more captivating than the various results gathered *via* this activity.

After Heidegger had spent a few years working on his own path of phenomenology, he continued to struggle to understand Husserl's motto. This struggle is visible within his own lecture series '*Geschichte des Zeitbegriffs*' later translated into English as *History of the Concept of Time* (henceforth *HCT*).[11] In this lecture series, Heidegger further develops his critique of the attempt to raise phenomenology to the level of a science by comparing it to the similar problem faced by the science of history: should history be studied historiologically or by some other approach?[12] For Heidegger, although phenomenological questions can be useful for scientific projects, the attempt to fully transpose phenomenology into a science, or to reduce it entirely to the apparatus of a system, robs it of its most impressive and core power. Importantly, this is not a problem with phenomenology or science, but with the assumption that a 'scientific phenomenology' is a superior form of both.[13] In the opening of *HCT*, Heidegger states that it remains unclear

> whether historiological knowledge of historical reality ever enables us to see history in its historicity. It might well be that something essential necessarily remains closed to the potentially scientific way of disclosing a particular field of subject matter; indeed, must remain closed if the science wishes to perform its proper function.
>
> (*HCT* 1)

This is not a criticism of science, but rather a clarification of its limits. As science demands a certain kind of stabilization of its results (in order to fulfil the requirements of attaining a science), Heidegger wonders whether or not all issues can or even should meet this requirement. It is possible that there are certain aspects of experience that are impoverished when restricted to such a rubric. However, this is not a problem with the scientific method; it only becomes a problem when it is considered to be 'the' *only* and *proper* means to do research.[14] It is important to clarify that although both Husserl and Heidegger may at first appear to sound anti-scientific, when you look closer you see a concern for science rather than a vulgar anti-scientific sentiment.[15] To be fair, one may indeed be able to develop phenomenology into a science and I do not think Heidegger would necessarily have a problem with such a project; however, to consider a scientific construction as the *only* or *highest* rendition of phenomenology is to apply an unnecessary restriction that undermines its greater potential (not to mention, threatens to eclipse the very 'phenomenological means' by which such a science originally is generated by and emerges from). Recall that for Husserl, the notion of science remains important for phenomenology, but must always come second to it.

As we have already discussed in the previous chapter, any scientific collection of appearances will always have to come after, and in response, to its original source phenomena. Heidegger clarifies this insight by addressing the problem of history in order to show how and why the phenomenology of history will always be prior to the science of history. Heidegger claims that a 'phenomenology of history and nature promises to disclose reality precisely as it shows itself *before* scientific inquiry, as the reality which is already given to it' (*HCT* 2). This is a clear call back to Husserl's phenomenology that seeks to revitalize the original source experiences of any topic or problem in order to compare such dynamic experiences with their traditionally stabilized descriptions (and is one way to describe what Husserl's *LI* aims to do for the topic of logic). The same is true for a consideration of science itself. Heidegger states that 'hence, phenomenology has the task of making the domain of the subject matter comprehensible *before* its scientific treatment' (*HCT* 2). Here we can provisionally interpret the 'phenomenological work' as the effort to elicit from experience the unstable phenomena *via* questioning that is then taken to be the 'material' *worked upon* by the 'scientific work' of stabilizing that material *via* answering. Heidegger highlights the power of phenomenology in this schema to enable a kind of pre-scientific work for the sake of clarifying the meaning of science. Such work is accomplished by 'bringing the subject matters under investigation to an original experience, before their concealment by a particular scientific inquiry' (HCT 3). We can further understand 'concealment' as a kind of stabilization, wherein the claims of science may be understood as stabilized answers for previously eclipsed questions. In this way, phenomenology does not oppose scientific answers, but it certainly should not be wholly restricted to a scientific method or framework either. Phenomenology can provide a means to re-elicit the original experiences that correlate with the scientific study of a subject matter. Were the pre-scientific aspects of phenomenology subsumed under a new scientific programmatical structure, or worse jettisoned entirely and forgotten in light of only accepting and allowing for so-called 'scientific phenomenology', then something essential and valuable would be lost. Here we see that Heidegger is clearly remaining within Husserl's motto over and against any particular method (Husserl's or otherwise). That said, to be fair to Husserl, we can also interpret Heidegger to be making room for his own method in contradistinction to Husserl. If this is so, then the force behind Heidegger's critique of Husserl's methods may be somewhat lessened.

Heidegger suggests that by taking up a genuine phenomenological question, we are able to re-elicit an original experience and that this form of research is not only different from scientific inquiry; it rightfully precedes it. Heidegger writes:

> [I]f [...] the basic question of philosophical research [...] compels us to enter into an original arena of research which *precedes* the traditional partition of philosophical work into historiological and systematic knowledge, then the *prolegomena* to the investigation of entities in their being are to be won only by way of *history*. This amounts to saying that the manner of research is *neither* historiological *nor* systematic, but instead *phenomenological*. One of the goals of this lecture course is to demonstrate the necessity and the sense of such a fundamental form of research.
>
> (HCT 7)

Here it is clear that this 'fundamental form of research' is Heidegger's reinterpretation of Husserl's motto for phenomenology. Interestingly, not only does phenomenology precede historiological knowledge but *systematic* knowledge as well. Heidegger confirms this a few lines later when he states that 'this original mode of research which *precedes* the historiological mode and the so-called systematic mode we shall come to understand as the *phenomenological mode*' (HCT 7).[16] Heidegger distinguishes phenomenological from scientific research, clearly stating that the former precedes the latter. If Heidegger views an intrinsic opposition between phenomenological research and systematic research, then this will perhaps shed some light on what he is concerned about regarding the developmental shift between Husserl's *LI* and *Ideas I*. If Husserl's

LI is appropriately considered to be a 'theory of knowledge', then according to Heidegger 'calling it a theory is still a covert form of naturalism, for which any theory is a deductive system whose goal is to explain given facts. Husserl expressly rejects this customary sense of a theory of knowledge' (*HCT* 26). Instead of a theory of knowledge, Heidegger considers Husserl's *LI* to be a work that

> calls for a step-by-step, expressly intuitive envisaging of the matters at issue and a verifying demonstration of them. Accordingly, one cannot, without subverting the entire sense of the investigations, simply pull out results and integrate them into a system. Rather, the whole thrust of the work serves to implicate the reader into pressing further and working through the matters under investigation.
>
> (*HCT* 26)

As a demonstrative activity, phenomenological research (*via* questioning) for Heidegger must always be distinguished from the results of that activity (i.e. *answers*). The further distinction between phenomenological and systematic research is visible for Heidegger in that

> the essence of phenomenological investigations […] cannot be reviewed summarily but must in each case be rehearsed and *repeated* anew. Any further synopsis which merely summarizes the contents of [the *LI*] would thus be, phenomenologically speaking, a misunderstanding.
>
> (*HCT* 26)[17]

Here it is helpful to add the distinction between Husserl's motto and his various methods as Heidegger's critique ultimately amounts to rejecting their collapse: for instance, when one of Husserl's methods is taken as the starting point and the original motto is eclipsed or jettisoned. As phenomenological research is properly understood as a perpetually practised activity, it rightfully cannot be reduced to a set of ideas or method; the reduction of the practice of phenomenology to systematic schemata effectively threatens to conceal Husserl's motto. Although Heidegger does not specifically claim so in the *HCT*, we can observe it at play behind Heidegger's concern regarding the shift between Husserl's *LI* and *Ideas I*: that the *LI* represents for him an effort to bring the original problems of phenomenology into view, for open consideration while *Ideas I* represents an effort to secure a method for phenomenology that raises it to the status of a scientific project.

Heidegger's concern for the development between Husserl's *LI* and *Ideas* is made clearer when reviewed through the lens of instability (the activity of questioning) and stability (the activity of answering). According to Heidegger, the *LI* represents a work that aims to revive and elicit the instability of logic, as a phenomenological experience that correlates with any concept of logic (as found in the tradition). Husserl's genius in the *LI* was to take the stability of the traditional concepts of logic and destabilize them with the phenomenological question 'what is logic?' As a work that sought to de-stabilize traditional concepts, in order to revive the original experiences such concepts were intended to correlate with, revealed the power of phenomenological questions for Heidegger: they turn out to be a powerful means to relate to experience and, when used in this way, can elicit genuine experiences that completely change the way we view and understand whatever it is we investigate. In the specific case of Husserl's *LI*, questioning does this for the traditional concepts of logic (as stable answers) and how they correlate to a genuine experience of logic (themselves elicited by phenomenological questions that destabilize). Now, when *Ideas* emerges as 'the even better way to stabilize phenomenological investigation' it seems that for Heidegger, this originary power to de-stabilize is becoming threatened. In this way *Ideas* represents for Heidegger a shift from thinking phenomenologically through the activity of questioning towards thinking phenomenologically through the activity of answering. In *Ideas I*, Husserl moves away from establishing questions about phenomena towards building a systematic and, therefore, scientific method for their description. Although this development in Husserl's thinking is not without value, these systematic descriptions began to eclipse the original power of phenomenological seeing and the new 'version' began to rewrite and cover up old accomplishments of phenomenology. Heidegger's response to *Ideas I* was that the power of phenomenological questions to elicit original experiences was in danger of being covered up and lost in the face of this new and powerful method. Heidegger's response to this situation is to present a phenomenology understood as a possibility: one that develops the phenomenological power of questioning into a theme of its own. However, this power of questioning is not presented on its own as a way to philosophize, but only indirectly and partially through Heidegger's presentation of the question of being in *BT*.

§17. Heidegger on the structures of an explicitly formulated question

Having parted ways with Husserl methods, Heidegger's *BT* attempts to set up a phenomenological way to clarify the meaning of the question of being. According to some scholars (William J. Richardson[18] and Robert Sokolowski[19]), this question remains Heidegger's focus throughout his entire life and work. There is something significantly different in the way Heidegger begins *BT*: he does not simply begin with a question that he intends to answer but instead first seeks to *raise the meaning of a question* throughout the course of an entire philosophical text (the whole of *BT*).

For Heidegger, how we approach a question, whether or not it is transparent to us and how our thinking functions *within* a question – all prior to defining, debating or even conceptualizing *answers* for it – needs to be clarified in order to genuinely raise a question in the first place. Regarding his central concern for the question of being, Heidegger proceeds to free up this question from the traditional answers that traditionally threaten to eclipse it.

The question 'what is being?' has already been answered in at least three traditional ways: being is the *most universal concept*, it is an *indefinable concept* and it is the *most self-evident concept* (M&R *BT* 23/4). According to Heidegger, it is the power of these answers that restricts us from fully engaging with the *question of being itself* as they obscure our thinking by pre-emptively covering up what this question aims to return a thinker to reconsider (i.e. its source-phenomenon in experience itself). Thus, in order to free up this question, Heidegger first shows how these traditional answers merely eclipse the question instead of genuinely answering it.[20] Heidegger indicates that we not only have insufficient answers for the question of being, but more importantly that the question itself needs to be reformulated, developed and made transparent.

The activity of raising, thinking about and answering questions, for Heidegger, entails more complexity than it initially sounds. In the activity of questioning, how we *arrive* at a question, from *whence* we ask it and *what* we seek or do not seek in the very asking of it, all considerably affect how things appear to us *via* this activity. In order to clarify this complexity, Heidegger briefly discusses 'what belongs to any question whatsoever' (M&R *BT* 24/5). According to Heidegger:

> Every questioning is a seeking. Every seeking takes its lead beforehand from what is sought. Questioning is a knowing search for beings in their thatness and whatness. The knowing search can become an 'investigation,' as the revealing determination of what the question aims at. As questioning about ... questioning has *what it asks about* [*Gefragtes*]. All asking about ... is in some way an inquiring of ... Besides what is asked, what is *interrogated* [*Befragtes*] also belongs to questioning. What is questioned is to be defined and conceptualized in the investigating, that is, the specifically theoretical, question. As what is really intended, what is to be *ascertained* [*Erfragtes*] lies in what is questioned; here questioning arrives at its goal.

(JS *BT* 4/5)

From the starting point of a question to the arrival of its goal, Heidegger greatly expands the process of 'asking and answering a question'. Heidegger contrasts three structures of questioning: (1) *Gefragtes*, which is 'what a question asks about', (2) *Befragtes*, which is 'what a question interrogates' and (3) *Erfragtes*, which is 'what a question ascertains'. These three structures represent major moments of a questioning endeavour. After this, Heidegger adds:

> As an attitude adopted by a being [*Seienden*], the questioner, questioning has its own character of being [*Sein*]. Questioning can come about as 'just asking around' or as an explicitly formulated question. What is peculiar to the latter is the fact that questioning first becomes lucid in advance with regard to all the above-named constitutive characteristics of the question.
>
> (JS *BT* 4/5)

Heidegger suggests that there are initially at least two ways to question: in a *casual* or *explicitly formulated* way. Both seem to be immediately available for thinking, but Heidegger stresses that the latter can only be achieved after all three of the structures of the *Gefragtes*, *Befragtes* and *Erfragtes* of a question have been clarified. The casual way to question sounds similar to colloquial questioning (highlighted in the introduction of this text), wherein we question in a simple and straightforward way that simply attempts to get information. When we find that our traditional answers to a question interfere with our ability to genuinely raise and engage with it (as the three traditional answers do for the question of being), then we experience how contemplative questioning can be reduced to colloquial questioning; in other words, when our philosophical questioning is reduced to 'just asking around' for information. When this occurs, we find that our research is pre-emptively stifled and can only amount to a request for information (the empty taking on of traditional answers without understanding the questions that they are originally aiming to respond to). The solution to this stifling of our questioning is to re-develop a casual question into an explicitly formulated one and this is precisely what Heidegger attempts to do for the question of being.

An explicitly formulated question is one in which each of the three structures or moments of inquiry (*Gefragtes*, *Befragtes*, and *Erfragtes*) has been fully clarified. Heidegger describes an explicitly formulated question as '*selbst durchsichtig*'.[21] What is entailed in an *explicitly formulated question* understood as 'lucid in advance' or 'transparent to itself' exactly? Heidegger states that 'the question to be *formulated* [for the project of *BT*] is about the meaning of being. Thus, we are confronted with the necessity of explicated the question of being with regard to the structural moments cited' (JS *BT* 4/5.). In order to *explicitly formulate the question* 'what is being?' we must secure its three structures of *Gefragtes, Befragtes* and *Erfragtes*, which is to say that we must first clarify 'what the question of being asks about' [*Gefragtes*], 'what the question of being interrogates' [*Befragtes*] and 'what the question of being will ascertain' [*Erfragtes*].[22] Only after all three structures of the question of being have been made transparent, will we be able to ask 'what is being?' in an explicitly formulated way. How then would one go about clarifying the three structures of *Gefragtes, Befragtes* and *Erfragtes* within the question of being?

The *Gefragtes* of the question of being, *what we ask about*, turns out to be an additional hurdle in the way of even *initially* formulating it. Heidegger states that

> [a]s a seeking, questioning needs prior guidance from what it seeks. The meaning of being must therefore already be available to us in a certain way. We intimated that we are always already involved in an understanding of being [… and even though] we do not even know the horizon upon which we are supposed to grasp and pin down the meaning [of being] *this average and vague understanding of being is a fact.*
>
> (JS *BT* 4/5; translation modified)

Although accounting for and explaining exactly what this 'average and vague yet factual understanding of being' entails will be a separate problem, its role as the *Gefragtes* for the question of being is confirmed where Heidegger states that 'what *is asked about* in the question to be elaborated is being, that which determines [entities as entities], that in which [entities] have always been understood no matter how they are discussed' (JS *BT* 4–5/6). As if things were not truncated and complicated enough, Heidegger adds a further stipulation here by stating that the 'being of [an entity] "is" itself not [an entity]. The first philosophical step in understanding the problem of being consists in avoiding [… the assumption that] being has the character of a [*Seienden*]' (JS *BT* 5/6). Leaving the issue of the ontological difference aside, we can at least see that for Heidegger, the *Gefragtes* of the question of being is our own average and vague understanding of being and that this understanding appears to us phenomenologically through our always already relatedness to the world around us. So, when we raise the question of being, what we more specifically do is ask about the fact that we already seem to know something vague about it.

Now in the strategy of *BT*, the purpose of the *Gefragtes* of the question of being has a very clear and helpful design: we will turn to ourselves, to our own average and vague understanding of being in order to develop the question of being into an explicit formulation. This is strikingly phenomenological in at least two senses: (1) the weight and importance of *BT* will depend less on Heidegger's skill to craft an argument and more on his description of experience and phenomena in such a way that *we are to see in our own experience what Heidegger claims he sees in his own experience* and (2) the validity of Heidegger's claims will, therefore, not be taken up authoritatively or because it fits in a particular system; instead, it demands that we return to the matter itself: we return to *our own* average yet vague understanding of being. We do this in order to find out if we can in fact *see* what Heidegger claims he sees. Thus, the *Gefragtes* of the question of being is not found in any history or tradition (history of philosophy, ontology or metaphysics, etc.) but in a turning to our own lived experience wherein we find and recognize that we always already have some vague sense of the being of entities.

The *Befragtes* of the question of being, *what we interrogate*, is also an entity but one that shows it priority among all entities: ourselves understood as Dasein (specifically, our ability as Dasein to relate to ourselves and other entities we find ourselves surrounded by). We already vaguely understand entities through our ability to use, manipulate and to navigate them (something Heidegger will even suggest occurs pre-theoretically). Heidegger states that 'insofar as being constitutes what is asked about, and insofar as being means the being of [entities], [entities] themselves turn out to be what is interrogated with regard to their being' (JS *BT* 5/6). This is all well and good, but is complicated by the fact that 'we call many things "existent" ["*seiend*"], and in different senses. Everything we talk about, mean, and are related to is existent [*seiend*] in one way or another. What and how we ourselves are is also existent' (JS *BT* 5/7). However saturated our experience is with the existent, there is one particular entity that shows a priority among other entities: 'this [entity], which we ourselves in each case are and which includes inquiry among the possibilities of its being, we formulate terminologically as *Dasein*' (JS *BT* 7/7). The introduction of the idea of Dasein shows the connection between the *Befragtes* (entities, of which Dasein shows a priority of sorts) with the *Gefragtes* (our average and vague understanding of being) of the question of being; however, what about the *Erfragtes*?

Heidegger does not seem to fully clarify what the *Erfragtes* of the question of being is. He states that 'what is to be *ascertained*, the meaning of being, will require its own conceptualization, which again is essentially distinct from the concepts in which [entities] receive their determination of meaning' (JS *BT* 5/6). After this, he returns to further discuss the relationship between the *Gefragtes* and the *Befragtes*. Is Heidegger's description of the *Erfragtes* of the question of being sufficient to match his earlier claim that all three structures of the question must be made transparent? If we find something unclear within the question of being then, does this conflict with Heidegger's claim that the question of being must be made '*selbst durchsichtig*' of which we have two translations: 'transparent to itself' (Macquarrie & Robinson) and/or 'lucid in advance' (Stambaugh)? Perhaps, but we must be careful here as Heidegger has already claimed that 'the question of the meaning of being must be *formulated*' (JS *BT* 24/5). As such, Heidegger is not simply giving an already-worked-out schema of the question of being, but is genuinely trying to set it up as a question.[23]

The very aim of *BT* is to *explicitly formulate* this question of being for the reader and this, in fact, turns out to be necessary before efforts to properly answer it may be attempted. Recall that Heidegger writes that 'the aim of the following treatise is to work out the question of the meaning of "being" ["*Sein*"] and to do so concretely. The provisional aim is the interpretation of *time* as the possible horizon for any understanding whatsoever of being' (JS *BT* 1/1). In light of this, it seems more reasonable to view *BT* as a project that is aiming more to raise and *explicitly formulate* the question of being before making efforts to *answer it*. If this is so, then the *Erfragtes* of the question of being is only partially conceptualized and done so both positively and negatively: positively, Heidegger anticipates that the meaning of being will be clarified on the horizon of temporality; negatively, in whatever way being [*Sein*] itself is clarified, it will not be understood as an entity [*Seienden*].[24] From the standpoint of a question, as a means to figure something out, it might be beneficial that the *Erfragtes* of the question of being is left open.

What exactly the *Erfragtes* means for the question of being is perhaps further complicated by the fact that Heidegger's work of *BT* is unfinished; however, for those who perhaps decide too quickly that this makes *BT* a failure (Heidegger's own disparaging remarks of the text notwithstanding), we should recall that he also states in the preface to the seventh German edition in 1953 that 'the designation "First Half", which previous editions bore, has been deleted. After a quarter century, the second half could no longer be added without the first being presented anew. Nonetheless, its path still remains a necessary one even today, if the question of being is to move our Dasein' (JS *BT* xxvii). Thus, even in light of the incompleteness of *BT* to succeed at its aim, incompleteness might not necessarily equate to failure. Furthermore, as the very *aim* of *BT* is to formulate a question, such a failure would more appropriately be understood as a failure to *formulate* and to *make explicit* the question of being, rather than a failure to sufficiently answer it or not. As is also already somewhat clear, a failure to answer a question can sometimes make an original question all the more enigmatic and worthy of further thought. In this sense, the 'failure' of *BT* could in fact be a boon for further thought as opposed to being a reason to wholly ignore it. Furthermore, if it is true that Heidegger remains preoccupied with this question, then perhaps the 'failure' of *BT* is one that simply spurred Heidegger onwards, to redouble his efforts in subsequent texts to clarify the question of being in new and different ways? If so, then the failure of *BT* would be a kind of invitation for the reader to try it for themselves, rather than something that confirms in advance that they should not bother.

Heidegger's strategy in *BT* involves highlighting that the question of being must already have within it something we recognize in order for the question to be possible in the first place. In other words, in order to question after the meaning of being, we must first already have some kind of working understanding for being beforehand. He clarifies this by saying, '[W]e do not *know* what "being" means. But even if we ask, What *is* "being"?, we keep within an understanding of the "is", though we are unable to fix conceptionally what that "is" signifies' (M&R *BT* 25/6). At this point it is clear that we are not simply working within the strict binaries of knowing something or not; Heidegger is clearly trying to expand on this binary approach of knowledge in an edifying way here. He goes on to further complicate this situation by saying that 'we do not even know the horizon in terms of which that meaning is to be grasped and fixed. *But this vague average understanding of being is still a Fact*' (M&R *BT* 25/6). We can therefore see that although every act of questioning requires some kind of knowledge of what is sought, this knowledge can be vague, underdeveloped or confused. Indeed, for when we uncover the appearance of something vague and feel as if we do not yet fully understand something or believe ourselves to be confused about an idea is when we genuinely question in the first place. In the same way, it is because our understanding of being is vague, underdeveloped and confused that Heidegger requires that the *question* (significantly *not* an answer) must first be formulated prior to being asked and answered. If we are to understand what Heidegger has to offer, through his lengthy attendance to the topic of being, we must first begin to question in a different way.

§18. Heidegger's *BT* as an introduction to phenomenology as possibility

According to Heidegger, understanding the central role questioning is to play in phenomenology is to grasp it as a *possibility*. In a supplement to 'My Way' in 1969, Heidegger quotes himself and states that one can already read in *Being and Time* (1927) pp. 62–63 [*SZ* 38]: its (phenomenology's) essential character does not consist in being actual as a philosophical school. Higher than actuality stands possibility. The comprehension of phenomenology consists solely in grasping it as a possibility.

('My Way' 82)

Seizing upon phenomenology as a possibility involves two stages: first, to distinguish the science of *phenomenological description* (understood as stabilized appearances) from the multidirectional and dynamic flux of the *phenomena themselves*; and second, to maintain the first distinction in order to preserve the flux of phenomena to perpetually generate additional appearances. It is this flux that allows for any phenomenologist to verify any other description and it is this possibility of verification that keeps phenomenology from becoming metaphysics (understood as a philosophical contrivance). For Heidegger, the value of phenomenology shifts when its systematic answers are presented in such a way that eclipses its equally powerful ability to re-elicit original phenomena. In other words, when phenomenological *descriptions* begin to draw attention away from the *ability and activity to see* phenomena in their vibrancy, this endangers the flux of phenomena to be covered up or stabilized in a pejorative sense. Phenomenology is not just valuable for the scientific descriptions it provides, it is also valuable for the renewed attention it gives to how phenomena are given to consciousness in the first place.

Whereas Heidegger's work is confined to the philosophical questioning of the meaning of being, I believe that there is evidence of a modality of thought woven into his unique approach that values and preserves Husserl's power of questioning (the very core of his motto). One can trace this power of questioning as a way to preserve the possibility of perception, experience and philosophy within Heidegger's definition, understanding and use of phenomenology.

In order to understand what is important about the activity of questioning within phenomenology, it is helpful to first view Heidegger's position as a modified version of Husserl's motto 'to the things themselves'. In outlining his phenomenological method in *BT* §7, Heidegger states something curious:

> When, moreover, we use the term 'ontology', we are not talking about some definitive philosophical discipline standing in interconnection with the others. Here one does not have to measure up to the tasks of some discipline that has been presented beforehand; on the contrary, only in terms of the objective necessities of definitive questions and the kind of treatment which the 'things themselves' require, can one develop such a discipline.

(M&R *BT* 49/27)

In other words, just as Husserl claims that descriptions must always come after and in light of the phenomena themselves, Heidegger claims that disciplines must always come after and in response to the efforts of questioning. I believe that Heidegger is doing two subtle things within the above quote: on the one hand, he is intentionally using Husserl's motto to distance and subtly criticize Husserl's methods of phenomenology while also salvaging a modification thereof on the other. The kind of ontology that Heidegger is aiming to establish is of a questioning kind. Here Heidegger distinguishes between the phenomena (*things themselves*) and *their descriptions*. For example, we can ask questions about a water bottle in many ways: we can ask an engineering question about the material substance of the object and consider what it is made of, or we might ask an anthropological question and consider what the bottle's purpose, meaning, or use is and so on. In each of these cases, the original phenomenon of the bottle remains the same, but this very same phenomenon provides very different appearances that emerge in response to different inquiries. If one were to collapse the distinction between a phenomenon and its many possible appearances, one may mistake one of those appearances for the phenomenon itself, thereby losing access to the many other *possible* appearances. This is precisely what occurs when a question is eclipsed by an answer: the question no longer provides a possibility to elicit further thought, but merely becomes a singular path to a pre-determined answer (as observable when a genuine philosophical question is reduced to a rhetorical formation).

When it comes to the term 'ontology', Heidegger is trying to revive the distance between the question 'what is ontology?' and its traditional answers. Such a revival is accomplished when we return to a phenomenon and ask 'how does something originally appear?' or 'what about its being?' These kinds of 'ontological' questions are not simply confined to a discipline but make up the fundamental activity of relating to how we experience the world around us, how phenomena appear to our consciousness. Collecting the various descriptions generated from such questioning is what comprises the 'discipline' of ontology. Just like the example of the bottle, to confuse a definition of ontology with the question 'what is ontology?' is to lose the possibility for further ontological inquiry.

Excellent and powerful answers have a way of exacting a particular kind of gravity in thinking that can warp and undermine further questioning. The renewal of ontology is, therefore, accomplished when we retrieve its source experience: the questioning of the being of entities. This activity purports the many possible descriptions that tradition has already codified, but tradition is only half the story; without the original wellspring of questioning that originally provided the source of these answers, traditional questioning can be reduced to rhetorical questioning. The point is to recognize that since we have traditional answers, we must also have traditional questions; if we have traditional questions then they must be sourced in response to some genuine experience, that is, to some phenomenon. Once these traditional questions are retrieved and revived, we may then use them to elicit that original experience and in so doing can begin to participate in the problems that tradition is ultimately founded upon. However, as easy as this may sound, what is already quite clear is just how difficult such phenomenological work in fact turns out to be.

At this point it is important to point out that Heidegger's interesting take on the power of genuine questioning is not really his invention, but is the very thing that he initially attributes to Husserl's *LI*. However, this power of questioning of Husserl's is not necessarily outlined philosophically, but is instead implicitly *exemplified* in the *LI*. Husserl's questioning of logic, knowledge, meaning, expression, consciousness and experience all have the hallmarks of overcoming the over-stabilization of traditional answers. The means by which Husserl overcomes this stabilization is to revive the things themselves and begin re-questioning everything, only accepting what may be directly verified by one's own experience. This kind of phenomenology is one that is commencing and is *something that remains in action* as an infinite task. In Heidegger's view, Husserl's practice to think in questions is an excellent starting point for phenomenology, but Husserl's desire for apodictic results proves to be unnecessarily restrictive.[25] Heidegger praises Husserl's *LI* for its attempt to bring about a questioning approach to being, but he is wary of how Husserl's strategy in *Ideas* too quickly exchanges traditional stability with a newly minted transcendental-phenomenological kind of stability. The same issue of 'solidification' of phenomena results when one applies a systematic and scientific account. In light of this, we can view how Heidegger intended *BT* to be the 'proper' continuation of the path believed began in the *LI*:

> With the question of the meaning of being, our investigation comes up against the fundamental question of philosophy. This is one that must be treated *phenomenologically*. Thus our treatise does not subscribe to a 'stand point' or represent any special 'direction'; for phenomenology is nothing of either sort, nor can it become[,] so as long as it understands itself.
>
> (M&R *BT* 49–50/27)

Heidegger intends *BT* to be a work that did not just analyse and list the various answers *for* the question of being, but one that genuinely brings the reader into a clarified and transparent view of it *as a question* that enables them to genuinely engage with the 'phenomenon' of being itself. Although *BT* is dedicated to clarifying the meaning of the question of being, its use of the activity of questioning is not so much ontological as it is phenomenological, in that it aims to enable the reader to approach and 'see' being for themselves. In this way we can reconsider Heidegger's *BT* and reinterpret it as a continuation of Husserl's philosophical practice: the establishment, preservation and participation in the problematicity of questions.

§19. What does phenomenology mean for Heidegger?

The following analysis of *BT* will expand upon what phenomenology means for Heidegger through a close textual examination of §7 of *BT*. Following Heidegger's lead, I will first consider the relationship between phenomenology and ontology, followed by an etymological analysis of the ancient Greek terms of 'phenomenon' and 'logos'. Then the concept of phenomenon will be further developed into four variations: *phenomenon, semblance [Schein], appearance [Erscheinung]* and *mere appearance [bloße Erscheinung]*. The important relationship between phenomenon and the two kinds of appearance will be illustrated by using Kant's transcendental philosophy. The concept of logos will then be examined, followed by an analysis of how the ideas of phenomenon and logos fit together. I will then conclude with a discussion of what phenomenology means for Heidegger in light of both these insights and various developments in Husserl's work.

In §7 of *BT*, entitled 'The Phenomenological Method of Investigation', Heidegger thanks Husserl, stating that 'the following investigations would not have been possible without the foundation laid by Edmund Husserl; with his *Logical Investigations* phenomenology achieved a breakthrough' (JS *BT* 36/38). In the Macquarrie and Robinson edition of *BT*, there is a lengthier version of this dedication in an endnote:

> If the following investigation has taken any steps forward in disclosing the 'things themselves', the author must first of all thank E. Husserl, who, by providing his own incisive personal guidance and by freely turning over his unpublished investigations, familiarized the author with the most diverse areas of phenomenological research during his student years at Freiburg.
>
> (M&R *BT* 489)

This passage confirms that *BT* is designed by Heidegger to be a follow-through of Husserl's elucidation of questioning the 'things themselves'. In his lecture course entitled *Towards the Definition of Philosophy*, Heidegger states that '*questioning* in phenomenology is not constructive, conceptually deductive and dialectical, but springs from and aims at the what, the *quale* of the phenomena; no free-floating, unfolded *conceptual questions!*' (*Towards the Definition of Philosophy* 97). The things themselves (the phenomena that correlate with phenomenological description) are matters that the phenomenologist may return to again and again *via* questioning.

In order to understand what phenomenology means for Heidegger, one must first clarify the role played by ontology. Heidegger states that '[w]ith the preliminary characterization of the thematic object of the investigation (the being of [entities], or the meaning of being in general) its method too would appear to be already prescribed. The task of ontology is to set in relief the being of [entities] and to explicate being itself' (JS *BT* 26/27). The most reasonable starting point for this project would be to consult traditional ontology in order to find a point of departure. This would be unproblematic except for the fact that Heidegger states that 'the method of ontology remains questionable in the highest degree as long as we wish merely to consult historically transmitted ontologies or similar efforts' (JS *BT* 26/27). Thus, Heidegger rules out the option of consulting traditional ontology. If we cannot trust the traditional ontology already available to us, then the next reasonable step would be to critically consult the history of its method and hope to either derive a grounded method or discover a new method that avoids all of the criticism of which the traditional method is guilty. However, Heidegger anticipates this move and states that 'since the term "ontology" is used in this investigation in a sense which is formally broad, any attempt to clarify the method of ontology by tracing its history is automatically ruled out' (M&R *BT* 49/27). Reconsidering the idea of ontology, Heidegger states that 'it should not at all be our task to satisfy the demands of any established discipline. On the contrary, such a discipline can be developed only from the objective necessity of particular questions and procedures demanded by the "things themselves"' (JS *BT* 26/27). Thus, the ontological task of allowing the being of an entity to reveal itself is not a task done *within* or in light of a particular discipline, but is in fact initially required prior to having a proper discipline of ontology in the first place. Left without a method, discipline, tradition or history, Heidegger suggests that one must return to the original impetus or questioning investigation for these very things. In this sense, philosophical work begins with a question rather than an answer (or with a set of answers).

§20. The four terms of *phenomenon, semblance, appearance* and *mere appearance*

If what Heidegger is going to investigate is something that is *self-evident*, and we are going to try and see it for ourselves to let it self-reveal to us, then why must he outline a method if we already have access to it? Heidegger's response is that 'the issue here is a kind of "self-evidence" which we should like to bring closer to us, so far as it is important to do so in casting light upon the procedure of our treatise' (M&R *BT* 50/28). Strangely, it seems that we are not only going to begin with and examine something *self-evident* according to Heidegger, but that we will try to make it even *more* self-evident than when we first found it. Thus, we can see that such an undertaking will certainly require a detailed explanation of what Heidegger has in mind and in order to do so he writes that 'we shall explicate only the preliminary concept of phenomenology' (JS *BT* 26/28). Heidegger performs an etymological analysis of the words 'phenomena' and 'logos' and considers what is gained by their combination in order to establish this preliminary concept.

Heidegger first considers the Greek origins of the word 'phenomenon' which comes from the verb *phainesthai* to show itself, what shows itself, the self-showing, the manifest. Heidegger states that '*phainesthai* itself is a "middle voice" construction of *phaino*, to bring into daylight, to place in brightness. *Phaino* belongs to the root *pha-*, like *phos*, light or brightness, that is, that within which something can become manifest, visible in itself' (JS *BT* 27/28). The application of this idea of phenomenon deals directly with an attempt to make what is manifest visible from itself. Whatever counts as a phenomenon is, therefore, visible on its own without the need for any kind of intermediary or authority. Heidegger states that 'the meaning of the expression "phenomenon" is *established as what shows itself in itself*, what is manifest. The "phenomena", are thus the totality of what lies in the light of day or can be brought to light' (JS *BT* 27/28). Although this is applicable to any and all manifestations of entities, this general meaning of phenomenon is also related to how and in what way they are uncovered. Heidegger states that 'beings can show themselves from themselves in various ways, depending on the mode of access to them' (JS *BT* 27/28).[26] Thus, the various modes of access also need to be explored and clarified in order to gain a comprehensive understanding of what the phenomenon full means.

Heidegger suggests that the concept of phenomenon is not as simple as it might sound. The complexity of just what counts as a phenomenon has already been clearly established from the perspective of Husserl. Following the master, the passages of *BT* in which Heidegger further develops the concept of phenomenon are likewise quite dense. In a footnote given by Macquarrie and Robinson, the English translators of the 1962 edition of *BT*, it states that 'the passage shows some signs of hasty construction' (M&R *BT* 52). In this footnote, the translators trace three definitions of phenomenon; the first and the third definitions are further subdivided. Although this footnote is helpful, I think it is clearer to begin with the four terms Heidegger uses a few pages later when he states that

> the bewildering multiplicity of 'phenomena' designated by the words 'phenomenon,' 'semblance' [*Schein*], 'appearance' [*Erscheinung*], [and] 'mere appearance' [*bloße Erscheinung*], cannot be disentangled unless the concept of the phenomenon is understood from the beginning as that which shows itself in itself.
>
> (M&R *BT* 54/31)

I have decided to focus on these four terms given by Heidegger instead of the schema given by Macquarrie and Robinson. As a note for further research, *HCT* is a text based on Heidegger's lecture notes delivered in Marburg University in the summer semester of 1925 (*HCT* xiii). Theodore Kisiel, the translator of *HCT*, describes it 'as a text that is clearly in transition towards *Being and Time*' (*HCT* xv). Interestingly, it provides a more detailed deliberation on the topic of phenomenology, even though it was written two years prior to *BT*. Section nine of *HCT*, entitled the *Clarification of the name "phenomenology"*, also focuses on these four terms primarily: phenomenon, semblance [*Schein*], appearance [*Erscheinung*] and mere appearance [*bloße Erscheinung*]. For these reasons, focusing on these four terms is a good place to begin to try to clearly and comprehensively understand just what Heidegger fully means by phenomenon.

It should be noted that the following analysis for the rest of this chapter uses certain regular English words (e.g. 'semblance', 'appearance' and 'mere appearance') in the special technical ways Heidegger has outlined in German ('*Schein*', '*Erscheinung*' and '*bloße Erscheinung*' respectively; to help keep this clear, when using Heidegger's ideas I provide the German in square brackets). Thus, in order to follow Heidegger's thought, the reader is cautioned to keep his technical clarifications in mind after they have been established.[27] Heidegger uses these four qualifications regarding the concept of 'phenomenon' in order to explore at least four different ways entities may be revealed: (1) an entity can be revealed as *phenomenon* when *x* shows itself as it is; (2) an entity can be revealed as a *semblance* [*Schein*] when *x* shows itself as pseudo-*x*, that is, as something it is not; (3) an entity can be revealed as an *appearance* [*Erscheinung*] when *y* announces itself in the place of *x* where *x* shows itself as it is; finally; (4) an entity can be revealed as *mere appearance* [*bloße Erscheinung*] when *y* announces itself in the place of *x* but *x* does not show itself as it is. The general point of Heidegger's presentation is to show the interrelatedness of these four ways an entity can be revealed; thus, it is important to view them alongside one another:

Mere appearance [*bloße Erscheinung*]	.... *y* as *y*
Appearance [*Erscheinung*]	*x* as *x* as *y*
Phenomenon	*x* as *x*
Semblance [*Schein*]	*x* as *pseudo-x*

As the structure of mere appearance [*bloße Erscheinung*] and the phenomenon are formally similar ('... *y* as *y*' compared with '*x* as *x*'), it is important to keep in mind that for Heidegger, mere appearances always have an underlying phenomenon that is concealed (hence the use of ellipses to indicate the lurking concealment) whereas phenomena show themselves from themselves. Regarding the theme of stability versus flux, appearances and mere appearances are also to be understood as *stabilizations of* phenomena, whereas the phenomena themselves remain in a dynamic flux. We can picture the relation between the structures as follows:

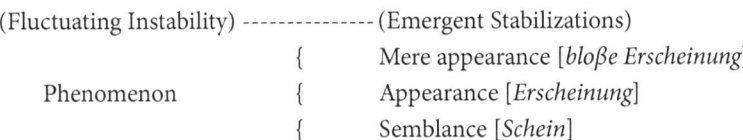

On the issue of whether or not a deeper analysis is possible 'beyond' the phenomenon, Heidegger claims that '"[b]ehind" the phenomena of phenomenology there is essentially nothing else; on the other hand, what is to become a phenomenon can be hidden. And just because the phenomena are proximally and for the most part *not* given, there is need for phenomenology' (M&R *BT* 60/36). That said, as the phenomenon is a dynamic flux, capable of generating further stabilizations, it remains possible that more aspects of the phenomenon may emerge. If we keep the very question 'what is the phenomenon?' preserved alongside our already-stabilized answers, then we remain open to the emergence of additional appearances. In this sense, although nothing is deeper than the phenomenon, when properly understood as something in flux, questioning a phenomenon and letting it perpetually show itself turn out to be an infinite and non-linear task. Each time we raise for ourselves the genuine question 'what is the phenomenon?' it remains possible that something new and hitherto concealed may emerge. This is why one of the main practices of phenomenology, according to Heidegger, is to collect mere appearances and appearances and to try to develop their underlying and concealed phenomena. This is accomplished when we take an answer and try to develop its original question (exemplified in Heidegger's *BT* as the effort to do this for question of being).[28]

The ideas of phenomenon and semblance [*Schein*] are somewhat straightforward, but Heidegger's unique take on 'appearance' [*Erscheinung*] and 'mere appearance' [*bloße Erscheinung*] requires more clarification. Clearly, understanding how *appearance* [*Erscheinung*] is always related to and requires an underlying phenomenon is crucial to Heidegger's project for uncovering the phenomena of being as it appears through entities. A phenomenon is always more than the sum of its appearances because as an appearance, y makes itself known, that is, it *announces* itself in the place of x where x may or may not show itself. This means that appearances [*Erscheinungen*] will always be based upon an underlying phenomenon. When one develops an appearance back into a phenomenon that reveals itself from itself, then this 'develops' the situation that enables one to see the correlation between the particular appearance [*Erscheinung*] and its underlying phenomenon by showing the connection between the two. This is significant, because as we will see later, this is what Heidegger thinks the phenomenologist's main task is: to bring what only vaguely 'announces' itself in mere appearance [*bloße Erscheinung*] into focus as an appearance [*Erscheinung*] further based on an underlying phenomenon that finally shows itself from itself. Heidegger states that

> although 'appearing' is never a self-showing in the sense of phenomenon, appearing is possible only *on the basis* of a *self-showing* of something. But this, the self-showing that makes appearing possible, is not appearing itself. Appearing is an *announcing* of itself through something that shows itself.
>
> (JS *BT* 28/29)

Heidegger's illustration for this relationship between a 'self-showing' and an 'announcing' is similar to the relationship between a disease and its symptom. The disease does not reveal itself from itself (the infection revealed as a virus, bacteria, parasites, fungi, etc.) but rather only *appears* through a symptom. The symptom *directly* shows itself from itself (coughing, fever, weight loss, pain, etc.) but it also *indirectly* announces the underlying disease.[29] Heidegger states that 'phenomena are *never* appearances [*Erscheinungen*], but every appearance

[*Erscheinung*] is dependent upon phenomena' (JS *BT* 28/30). Thus, it seems that Heidegger's tentative conclusion is that appearance [*Erscheinung*] is not on par with phenomenon as a self-showing but instead always requires an underlying phenomenon in order to be an appearance [*Erscheinung*] in the first place.

An entity can be revealed as a *mere appearance* [*bloße Erscheinung*] when *y* announces itself in the place of *x* but *x* does not show itself as it is. Heidegger states that

> [i]f one understands that which does the announcing – that which in its self-showing indicates the nonmanifest – as what comes to the fore in the nonmanifest itself, and radiates from it in such a way that[,] what is nonmanifest is thought of as what is essentially *never* manifest, if this is so, then appearance is tantamount to [a bringing-forth] [...]. However, this does not constitute the real being of [bringing-forth], but is rather appearance in the sense of 'mere appearance'.
>
> (JS *BT* 28–9/30)

In the case of mere appearance [*bloße Erscheinung*], since the underlying phenomenon is never manifested and remains concealed, this amounts to a kind of hollow 'revealing' where what is heralded is implied but never actually comes into view. To return to the analogy of symptom and disease, we can illustrate mere appearance [*bloße Erscheinung*] as occurring when one has many symptoms but no clear sense of the underlying disease (of what all the symptoms have in common). A symptom *merely appears* to announce the presence of an underlying disease that does not in fact show itself at all. Heidegger states that 'what does the announcing and is brought forward indeed shows itself in such a way that, as the emanation of what it announces, it precisely and continually veils what it is in itself' (JS *BT* 29/30). As the work of a good doctor is to identify symptoms, their patient is suffering from (initially as they merely appear) and then diagnose the underlying disease (thereby developing the mere appearance into an appearance that identifies its underlying phenomenon), a similar kind of work is undertaken by the phenomenologist. Phenomenologists, like doctors, collect mere appearances and appearances and try to ascertain their underlying phenomenon.

What seems important about mere appearance [*bloße Erscheinung*] is that it conceals its own underlying phenomenon. Heidegger is quick to add that 'then again, this not-showing which veils is not semblance' (JS *BT* 29/30). The danger of confusing mere appearance [*bloße Erscheinung*] with semblance [*Schein*] is precisely what Heidegger wants to clarify in order to avoid a misunderstanding: if a thinker only has the ideas of phenomenon and semblance [*Schein*], then what is covered up and veiled through mere appearance [*bloße Erscheinung*] would be lost forever. Speaking of recollecting something veiled would be impossible unless what is retrievable still shows itself in a very un-thematic and/or vague way. Locating these un-thematic and vague mere appearances [*bloße Erscheinung*] and thematizing them into appearances in order to enable their underlying phenomenon to reveal itself from itself turn out to be the main task of the phenomenologist. To demonstrate this Heidegger cites Kant's work on the forms of intuition as an example of this process.

In order to illustrate the difference and relationship between mere appearance [*bloße Erscheinung*], appearance [*Erscheinung*] and their underlying phenomenon, Heidegger turns to Kant's *CPR* stating that 'Kant uses the term "appearance" in this twofold way' (JS *BT* 29/30). Heidegger suggests that in Kant's philosophy, the objects of empirical intuition appear for us, but through their appearing, these objects also *announce* the 'forms of intuition'. Heidegger states that

> on the one hand, appearances [*Erscheinungen*] are for [Kant] the 'objects of empirical intuition,' that which shows itself in intuition. This self-showing (phenomenon in the genuine, original sense) is, on the other hand, 'appearance' [*Erscheinung*] as the emanation of something that makes itself known but *conceals* itself in the appearance [*Erscheinung*].
>
> (JS *BT* 29/30)

For Kant, objects of empirical intuition appear to us and announce something they conceal, namely the forms of intuition. The forms of intuition are, therefore, *announced* to us but only in a concealed and un-thematic way. In order for the forms of intuition to be developed into a theme of their own, and therefore to be explicated, something like Kant's transcendental philosophy needs to be undertaken. Thus, Heidegger reinterprets Kant's transcendental philosophy phenomenologically, as the attempt to thematize the very forms of intuition, that is, to bring them into focus as phenomena and to try and allow the forms of intuition to reveal themselves from themselves. Heidegger's reinterpretation of Kant allows us to take another look at the history between Hume and Kant.

In short, we can hastily summarize Hume's problem by using Heidegger's language. Hume states that we cannot observe the necessary connexion of causality and this (amongst other important ideas) interrupted Kant's dogmatic slumber.[30] If we view Kant's *CPR* as a response to Hume, then we can ask whether Kant proves Hume right or wrong. Of course, the situation is much more complicated than that, but following Heidegger's illustration, rather than refuting Hume, Kant's *CPR* proves Hume's claim to be indeed correct.[31] In Heidegger's language, Hume and Kant agree that objects of empirical intuition reveal themselves to us but the causality they *announce* only appears [*Erscheinung*] and, therefore, does not actually show itself from itself (as a phenomenon). The necessary connexion of causality remains announced but veiled. Hume picked up on this vague announcement and his response to it is to claim that we must recognize that our beliefs of causality cannot be philosophically grounded *a priori*, whereas Kant's response to the same situation is to appeal to transcendental philosophy: if we cannot observe the structures of experience itself, perhaps we can ask the question 'what are the conditions of possibility for experience in the first place?' In the *CPR*, Kant states, 'I call cognition transcendental that is occupied not so much with objects but rather with our mode of cognition of objects insofar as this is to be possible *a priori*' (*CPR* A11/B25). Thus for Heidegger, Kant's transcendental discovery is to agree with Hume that even though objects of empirical intuition do indeed reveal themselves, the causality they announce only appears (i.e. causality has not yet been developed into a phenomenon that shows itself from itself but only amounts to an *announcement*; it shows itself as an appearance [*Erscheinung*]). A transcendental account of empirical intuition will therefore be required in order to philosophically ground causality *a priori*, given that announcement is a mode of vague and un-thematic givenness. The whole project of transcendental philosophy, according to Heidegger on Kant, is therefore to bring the forms of intuition into focus as phenomena, to try and bring what is merely announced and therefore veiled (i.e. the forms of intuition) to the fore so that they may reveal themselves from themselves and therefore become phenomena.

Whether this interpretation of Kant is convincing or not, it is important to remember that Heidegger is only trying to demonstrate within this historical example how an appearance (or mere appearance) may be developed into a phenomenon proper. At this point, Heidegger claims that this only amounts to a clarification of the *formal concept of phenomenon* and thus Heidegger wants to de-formalize it into the *phenomenological concept* of phenomenon. Heidegger states that

> if in the way we grasp the concept of phenomenon we leave undetermined which beings are to be addressed as phenomena, and if we leave altogether open whether the self-showing is actually a particular [entity] or a characteristic of the being of [entities], then we are dealing solely with the *formal* concept of phenomenon.

(JS *BT* 29/31)

As the being of entities is itself not an entity, the formal concept of phenomenon must be de-formalized into a phenomenological concept. Heidegger states that

> [i]f by 'that which shows itself' we understand those entities which are accessible through the empirical 'intuition' in, let us say, Kant's sense, then the formal conception of 'phenomenon' will indeed be legitimately employed. In this usage 'phenomenon' has the signification of the *ordinary* [*vulgären*] conception of phenomenon. But this ordinary conception is not the phenomenological conception. If we keep within the horizon of the Kantian problematic, we can give an illustration of what is conceived phenomenologically as a 'phenomenon', with reservations as to the other differences.
>
> (M&R *BT* 54/31)

Here Heidegger is saying that once Kant's forms of intuition are revealed to be announced through the appearances of empirical objects, we can then understand Kant's transcendental philosophy as the means to develop such appearances into phenomena. Once we understand Kant in this way, then we are able to see for ourselves that the forms of intuition reveal themselves from themselves. Thus, Heidegger understands and interprets Kant phenomenologically as a philosopher who develops a particular appearance into phenomena (e.g. in the case of causality).

For Heidegger, what makes Kant's *CPR* such an excellent illustration for phenomenology in action is not located in its success or failure (i.e. grounding metaphysics once and for all), but in *what it does*: to develop the appearance of causality (in light of Hume) into a phenomenon that self-reveals. In other words, for Heidegger, Kant's *CPR* is significant for what it *shows philosophy is capable of doing*, not just in whether or not Kant is correct or not. To use Heidegger's conceptual language, we could say that the *CPR* is important for *what it brings into view* rather than for *what it specifically says*. However, in order to understand what Heidegger means here we must clarify the idea of logos.

§21. The concepts of logos and aletheia within the activity of phenomenology

Heidegger's concept of logos is the explanation as to how a phenomenologist is able to develop appearances and mere appearances into phenomena.[32] For Heidegger, phenomenology begins when one collects various 'riddles' of experience that emerge as problematic and therefore require some kind of exploration and explanation. A few examples of such problematic issues in phenomenology are 'what is experience?', 'what is perception?' and 'what is a number?' Of course, we already 'know' what experience, perception and numbers 'are' in the general sense that we have already encountered and are familiar with our use of such things. However, the more we investigate these things the more confounding they can become. When a phenomenological question successfully 'captures' an issue with all of its problematicity, it may be used to raise for oneself the unresolved quality of the issue. Thinking through a question entails mulling it over, either in search of some kind of resolution, or just for the sake of further exploration. When a phenomenological description successfully clarifies an issue or at least develops it for the sake of additional thinking, then something like logos has occurred.

In *BT* Heidegger considers the translation of logos as 'discourse' to be an acceptable translation so long as one further clarifies the inauthentic versus authentic ways in which discourse can be understood. Understanding logos as discourse is acceptable as long as one furthermore distinguishes 'what is brought into view' (authentic discourse) *via* 'what is specifically said' (inauthentic discourse). Heidegger states that

> if we say that the basic meaning of logos is discourse, this literal translation becomes valid only when we define what discourse itself means. The later history of the word logos and especially the manifold and arbitrary interpretations of subsequent philosophy, constantly conceal the authentic meaning of discourse.
>
> (JS *BT* 30/32)[33]

Provisionally we can understand inauthentic discourse as occurring when one restricts the possibility of meaning to the specifics of what in fact is said or written, whereas authentic discourse includes an awareness of the specifics but allows the specifics to bring something additional into view. A pejorative example of this is observable when someone is quoted out of context in order to manipulate the way a quote 'sounds' inauthentically, well beyond the original situation that authentically contextualizes its intended meaning.[34] Another example of this that is more positive can be observed in a riddle, which can be understood on at least two levels: (1) a riddle can be inauthentically understood for merely what it specifically says and (2) a riddle can be authentically understood for what its solution brings into view.[35]

The importance of logos understood as discourse for Heidegger is this additional aspect that 'brings something into view'. Heidegger defines authentic logos as the attempt

> to make manifest 'what is being talked about' in discourse [...] logos, lets something be seen (*phainesthai*), namely what is being talked about [...]

> Discourse 'lets us see' *apo* … from itself, what is being talked about. In discourse (*apophansis*), insofar as it is genuine, *what* is said should be derived *from* what is being talked about.
>
> (JS *BT* 30–1/32)

In other words, what is specifically said within discourse can be distinguished from what such talk brings into view, what it manifests.[36] Phenomenological work is accomplished when one describes an issue in such a way as to facilitate logos: to elicit the thing itself in all of its problematicity as something that manifests.[37] The danger to avoid is the reduction of 'the manifest' to 'the described'. For Heidegger, this is not only true for science and philosophy at large; it is also certainly a danger for phenomenology.

Heidegger seems to be aware of just how difficult it is to convey the idea of logos for he also tries to phenomenologically *show* his newly developed sense of 'the phenomenon' by illustrating it through another reconsideration of Kant's *CPR*.[38] Although this has been re-created in the previous section, we can return to the demonstration of Kant, and apply the idea of logos and in so doing we can distinguish between what the text *specifically says* versus what it is capable of *bringing into view*. Those who memorize the *CPR* and understand it as a project unto itself would properly 'understand what the *CPR* says' (they would effectively be an expert in what the text specifically says) but those who allow the text to elicit for themselves a genuine experience of the vague appearance of causality and is then developed into a phenomenon of causality that self-reveals, then the *CPR* is used for more than just a collection of 'information' in that it becomes a phenomenological source for the very problem of causality itself. Importantly, the development of an inauthentic reading into an authentic one is not linear as it remains possible for someone to be an expert in the specifics of the *CPR* without experiencing its potential as logos. Furthermore, it would be possible for someone to already experience the phenomenon of causality, in its full problematicity, without understanding the specifics of the *CPR*. I think Heidegger's point is that there are many texts in the history of philosophy that have been properly understood for their specifics (or for what is written in a text) but remain to be utilized for the untapped logos they also possess as a possibility. The logos of Kant's *CPR* can, therefore, become a source of experiential manifestation of the issue of causality.

The logos of a text concern its ability to 'bring-forth' something that may or may not occur in response to reading it. As the activity of 'letting something be revealed', logos is an experience of truth for Heidegger.[39] He states that furthermore, because logos lets something be seen, it can *therefore* be true or false. But everything depends on staying clear of any concept of truth construed in the sense of 'correspondence' or 'accordance' [*"Übereinstimmung"*]. This idea [of correspondence] is by no means the primary one in the concept of *aletheia*.

(JS *BT* 31/33)

Here it seems that Heidegger is considering the relationship between correspondence and something being revealed in a similar way to how he understands phenomenon and appearance [*Erscheinung*]. In the same way that we can only have a stable appearance [*Erscheinung*] on the basis of an underlying emergent phenomenon, Heidegger suggests that we first need the emergence of an entity to be revealed in order for a belief to correspond to it.[40] Thus, it seems that one may have truth, understood as *aletheia*, without necessarily also having truth as correspondence but not the other way around. In other words, we cannot have a truth claim that corresponds to something unless we first have a *something* for it to correspond to.

To again return to the illustration of Kant's *CPR*, we can further clarify Heidegger's distinction between truth as correspondence when compared with truth as *aletheia*. The original phenomenon that must first appear in order to have an appearance at all is the very phenomenon of causality (with all its problematicity). This phenomenon lies on the side of experience which means it is already an emergent issue for any consciousness to encounter it. This phenomenon appeared differently to both Kant and Hume; their individual responses to this phenomenon are recorded in their texts (*CPR* and *Enquiry* respectively). For us students, when we read one of these texts, we initially encounter the texts as a mere appearance [*bloße Erscheinung*]. As we come to understand what is specifically posited in the text we develop our understanding from a mere appearance into a proper appearance [*Erscheinung*], in that we now understand the text *as a particular stabilization* of a deeper fluctuating problem (i.e. an underlying phenomenon). At this point, if we were to stop our efforts we could properly make claims about the text (the specifics of the *CPR* states 'such and such') and this would count as truth as correspondence; however, if we take the step beyond the concern of *what is specifically said* in the text towards *what do the specifics manifest?*, then we would effectively let the text elicit the underlying phenomenon: *to elicit the originary experience of how causality appears in a vague way*. The vagueness of how causality appears is precisely what both Hume and Kant have also experienced and is part of why they wrote their works (*Enquiry* and *CPR* respectively). In this sense, we could say that Hume's *Enquiry* successfully established the vagueness of causality as mere appearance [*bloße Erscheinung*], but Kant's *CPR* develops causality into an appearance [*Erscheinung*] with Husserl and Heidegger following suit and showing how causality can be fully developed into a phenomenon that self-reveals. For us students, we can use these texts to bring the very experience of causality itself into view for ourselves. With this experience in view, we could then properly say that the phenomenon of causality has emerged for us in a truthful way as *aletheia* when, in addition to being able to say Hume or Kant properly say 'such and such', we are also able to say honestly and genuinely *that we can see the very issue they have in mind for ourselves.*

This also helps to clarify why Heidegger suggests that truth as aletheia is a more fundamental type of truth than truth as correspondence: as the experience of the phenomenon of causality stabilizes and therefore appears in many ways (e.g. as visible when one compares the different ways it stabilizes between Kant and Hume), it only makes sense to make claims *via* correspondence with a stable appearance. What remains in flux, the original phenomenon of causality, is shown to be the source of both appearances. However, as 'something' that can at least appear in two ways, the phenomenon of causality is also shown to be unstable; it can only properly be questioned, whereas our answers to this questioning yield stabilizations of it (i.e. appearances of the experience of causality in the form of what Kant and Hume claim thereof). Now, what happens if, for instance, the reader only allows Kant's *CPR* to emerge as a mere appearance? In this case, the underlying phenomenon of the genuine experience of causality as vague remains concealed. In this sense we can already see how the activity of questioning is at work within any phenomenological project: when a text is understood as something that aims to answer a question, we can use it as an answer to return to its originary question and subsequently use that *question* to phenomenologically re-elicit for ourselves the experience it aims to discuss.[41] This effort of trying to bring something out of concealment into unconcealment is logos.

The difference between phenomena and semblance [*Schein*] is further developed in logos using concealment and unconcealment. Heidegger states that

> [t]he 'being true' of logos as *aletheuein* means: to take beings that are being talked *about* in *legein* as *apophainesthai* out of their concealment; to let them be seen as something unconcealed (*alethes*); to *discover* them. Similarly 'being false', *pseudesthai*, is tantamount to deceiving in the sense of covering up; putting something in front of something else (by way of letting it be seen) and thereby passing it off *as* something it is *not*.
>
> (JS *BT* 31/33)

Concealed entities can be unconcealed and they can also be masked. Thus, regarding truth as *aletheia*, Heidegger states that 'perception is always true [in the sense of *aletheia*]. This means that looking always discovers colors, hearing always discovers tones' (JS *BT* 32/33). Experience will always comprise phenomena, but when we make descriptive claims of these phenomena, our descriptions may be distinguishable as stabilizations of their original fluctuating correlate in experience. Truth understood as correspondence is located on the side of descriptive claims, whereas truth understood as *aletheia* is located on the side of experience itself. In this sense then, truth as *aletheia* suggests that there is a possibility of further covering up in every uncovering. This claim explains why the phenomenologist must always be suspicious of statements that are taken to be 'timelessly true', statements given by tradition or authority, or any statement taken unreflectively. Instead of viewing the activity of questioning as merely a means to find what we desire, we can instead see it as a valuable method for further thought. Rather than the traditional view that truth is something we no longer need to question, truth is precisely what we should properly and continually question in Heidegger's phenomenological schema.[42]

Now that Heidegger has developed the formal concept of phenomenology into the phenomenological concept of phenomenology, he asks the reader what novelty comes into view for the first time. He asks, '[W]hat is it that phenomenology is to "let us see?" What is it that must be called a "phenomenon" in a distinctive sense? What is it that by its very essence is *necessarily* the theme whenever we exhibit something *explicitly*?' (M&R *BT* 59/35). The answer to this question is yet another question, albeit a peculiar one:

> Manifestly, it is something that proximally and for the most part does *not* show itself at all: it is something that lies *hidden*, in contrast to that which proximally and for the most part does show itself; but at the same time it is something that belongs to what thus shows itself, and it belongs to it so essentially as to constitute its meaning and its ground. Yet that which remains *hidden* in an egregious sense, or which relapses and gets *covered up* again, or which shows itself only '*in disguise*', is not just this entity or that, but rather the *Being* of entities, as our previous observations have shown.
>
> (M&R *BT* 59/35)

In this way, Heidegger's attempt to explain the meaning of both phenomenon and logos has led to the very problem *BT* is pursuing: revising the establishing the question of being. As the being of entities is itself not a thing because it remains in flux, and unstable, and as such it may only properly be questioned. However, we can now also see that establishing the meaning of the question of being takes shape as a phenomenological source for further thinking and is clearly not just another ontological description. Certainly, such stable descriptions are also made in *BT* but their clarification is aimed to allow something else to come into view (as a bringing-forth): the dynamic manifestation of being itself.

The main work of phenomenology for Heidegger is to allow being to show itself from itself and this requires 'restoring' the question of being so that it may be used as a means to re-elicit the phenomenon of being itself. In so doing, 'phenomenology has taken into its "grasp" thematically as its object that which, in terms of its ownmost content, demands that it become a phenomenon in a distinct sense' (JS *BT* 33/35). This phenomenological work is required because the being of entities is perpetually concealing itself through the unconcealment of entities, that is, through the stabilization of appearances. The process of uncovering, the need for uncovering and the way to properly uncover phenomena are revealed to be the central themes of phenomenology for Heidegger. Heidegger states that 'it is precisely because phenomena are initially and for the most part *not* given that phenomenology is needed. Being covered up is the counter-concept to "phenomenon"' (JS *BT* 34/36). Thus, the phenomenologist must not only pursue the uncovering and stabilization of phenomena, but must also guard against their fleeting back into concealment or the loss of their underlying dynamism as fluctuations in the weave of experience.

The situation a thinker of traditional ontology finds themselves within, according to Heidegger, is one in which the original phenomenological source of being has been concealed by the stabilizations of traditional ontology (here understood as a list of answers). In this state, the original question of being cannot even be asked, due to its having been eclipsed by already-ready answers that induce forgetfulness. By reconsidering what Heidegger has outlined, regarding the various ways a phenomenon can (or may not) reveal itself, Heidegger aims to bring the issue of being from a state of mere appearance [*bloße Erscheinung*] into one of appearance [*Erscheinung*]. Importantly, this state of appearance [*Erscheinung*] is not yet a phenomenon (a self-showing, where *x* reveals itself as it is). This furthermore supports the fact that *BT*, as a work, aims *only* to raise and make transparent the question of being as a question and does not yet propose an answer *per se*.

Heidegger suggests that there is always a danger of losing what has been uncovered back into concealment. He states that

> [t]he covering up itself, whether it be understood in the sense of concealment, being submerged, or disguised, has in turn a twofold possibility [...]. It is possible

for every phenomenological concept and proposition drawn from genuine origins to degenerate when communicated as a statement. It gets circulated in a vacuous fashion, loses its autochthony, and becomes a freefloating thesis. Even in the concrete work of phenomenology itself there lurks the possibility of a calcification and of the inability to grasp what was originally 'grasped.' And the difficulty of this research consists precisely in making it self-critical in a positive sense.

(JS *BT* 34/36)

It is significant that Heidegger includes phenomenology as one of the possible places in which our genuine insight can fall into a mere repetition without genuine content. Even in phenomenology, there is a danger that our genuine insights can become concealed within their repetitive use as slogans or as popular mottos. This certainly applies to Husserl's motto 'to the things themselves' when it is reduced to a vacuous or as a naive slogan. Importantly, this quotation further emphasizes that having the correct descriptions memorized by rote is not enough for a phenomenologist; what is furthermore needed is a direct engagement with the phenomena described, to perpetually make attempts to re-elicit originary experiences that correlate and ground their descriptions. One of the primary ways to remain vigilant, through maintaining a direct engagement with phenomena, is to keep one's own thoughts, ideas, methods and answers in *question*. Thus, we can see that a phenomenologist must always keep themselves and the things themselves in question in order to avoid this danger (just as Husserl exhibited through his practices and instructs his students to do the same).

The meaning of phenomenology for Heidegger is not only initiated by the activity of questioning, it is also sustained by and, therefore, continually requires it. Heidegger argues that

[t]he way of encountering being and the structures of being in the mode of phenomenon must first be *wrested* from the objects of phenomenology. Thus the *point of departure* of the analysis, the *access* to the phenomenon, and *passage through* the prevalent coverings must secure their own method. The idea of an 'originary' and 'intuitive' grasp and explication of phenomena must be opposed to the naiveté of an accidental, 'immediate' and unreflective 'beholding'.

(JS *BT* 34/36–7)

Thus, every phenomenological investigation will first be required to establish itself phenomenologically before moving ahead. As a rubric, this requirement immediately resists any claims to undemonstrated or accidental discovery.

In this way phenomenology is, therefore, only allowed to stand on what it demonstrates *via* experience for itself, where every claim posed is and ought to be verified by other phenomenologists before agreement (which is to say that all claims need to be seen for oneself). In other words, it is perhaps best to avoid talking about the 'accomplishments' of phenomenology and more accurate to speak of its currently collected demonstrable claims that may be taken up and self-verified by all who desire to do so. To participate in phenomenology then clearly means to take up its central practice of questioning and to demonstrate for oneself all of the claims put forth by phenomenology (as opposed to merely giving mental assent to the various descriptions, concepts and distinctions it claims). This would further clarify the difference between thinking or accidentally being correct in one's claims with knowing why one is correct because they have seen *why* they are correct for themselves (the evidence for any claim viewed alongside it).

Thus, Heidegger is able to conclude on the goal, content and method of phenomenology. The goal is to elucidate the being of an entity, to let it show itself from itself. Heidegger states that

> [b]ecause phenomena, as understood phenomenologically, are never anything but what goes to make up Being, while Being is in every case the Being of some entity, we must first bring forward the entities themselves if it is our aim that Being should be laid bare [...]. These entities must likewise show themselves with the kind of access which genuinely belongs to them. And in this way the ordinary [*vulgäre*] conception of phenomenon becomes phenomenologically relevant.
>
> (M&R *BT* 61/37)

Thus, the goal of phenomenology for Heidegger is to elucidate the being of entities in a clear and thematic way, to take what is only announced and to bring it forth in a way that allows it to reveal itself from itself.

The content of phenomenology is certainly phenomena, but now it is more richly defined as the various ways entities reveal themselves in many different ways (phenomenon, semblance [*Schein*], appearance [*Erscheinung*] and mere appearance [*bloße Erscheinung*]). Heidegger claims that

> as far as content goes, phenomenology is the science of the being of [entities] – ontology. In our elucidation of the task of ontology the necessity arose from a fundamental ontology which would have as its theme that being which is ontologically and ontically distinctive, namely, Dasein.
>
> (JS *BT* 35/37)

The entity Heidegger will begin with is Dasein, through which something like being is announced but in an un-thematic way; however, the existential analytic of Dasein proves to be just one way to develop a path into phenomenology even though it is a 'path of questioning [that] became longer than [Heidegger first] suspected [demanding] many stops, detours and wrong paths' ('My Way' 80). Although wrought with difficulties, this path remains a phenomenological one.

§22. Chapter conclusion: The uncovered power of question preservation

What has Heidegger accomplished in his particular interpretation of Husserl's phenomenology regarding the issue of being? On the whole, he has taken a forgotten question and has not only revived it for additional inquiry, but has also preserved it for further investigation. As unconcealed phenomena can and may always fall back into concealment, the phenomenologist is tasked with a double duty: the gathering up and collecting of various distinctions and even systematically organizing their many different structures, but also and perhaps more importantly, to persistently keep the things themselves in *question* in order to preserve them from falling back into concealment. This second duty does not comprise a collection of information but is an existential activity, a vigilance to return to experience anew that is itself always threatened by the interesting, powerful and novel answers that are always being uncovered by this very activity. It is clear that Heidegger has done something philosophically unique regarding the question of being independent of his positing of phenomenology as ontology. Heidegger has shown the power and centrality of questioning within phenomenology. His aim is certainly to revive ontology and to further develop Husserl's phenomenology as presented in the *LI* in a new way. However, apart from these accomplishments, separate from his peculiar approach to ontology, there is this revival of the activity of questioning.

Although this strategy of question preservation initially seems to be very original and wholly Heidegger's invention, upon further reflection it is also revealed to be thoroughly indebted to Husserl. Although Husserl does not explicitly outline a 'questioning strategy' in his written works (perhaps in an unpublished manuscript?), his penchant for revision certainly embodies such a strategy through his philosophical practice. If Heidegger is correct that something was overlooked or lost in Husserl's transition from the *LI* to *Ideas I*, then this likely has to deal directly with this idea of question revival and question preservation. If the *LI* is designed by Husserl to be a work that revives the phenomenological sources of our experience of logic, that once re-elicited is then to be used as an experiential correlate to any and every stable claim we want to make of logic, then we may now see how and why Heidegger's *BT* aims to follow this path by crafting a work that revives the phenomenological source of the being of entities.[43] Whether or not we agree or disagree with Heidegger's criticism or interpretation of Husserl, it is certainly clear that Heidegger's efforts to further develop the activity of questioning have proven to be a valuable addition to phenomenology.

Similarly to Husserl, Heidegger does not fully clarify or explicitly map out his peculiar questioning strategy (although he does have a lot to say about questions and wonder which will be covered in Chapter 5). However, his insights and developmental path remain visible within his effort to raise, make transparent and to think about the question of being. Thus, in order to ascertain just how Heidegger's efforts to preserve the question of being may be applied to any and all other questions would, therefore, require one to follow Heidegger 'all the way till the end' and see for oneself (as a good phenomenologist is always required to do). This proves to be a task well beyond the author's ability and the scope of this text. Instead, I will now turn to Patočka, a student of both Husserl and Heidegger who represents not only an interesting synthesis and development of their phenomenological work, but furthermore continues to develop phenomenology as a questioning kind of philosophy.

4

Patočka's questioning phenomenology

§23. Chapter introduction

In this chapter[1] I further develop how we can view Patočka's phenomenology as a continuation of Husserl and Heidegger's *questioning philosophy*, in §24, I continue tracing the idea that phenomenology, as sourced in Husserl and Heidegger, utilizes a special kind of questioning. In §25, I then introduce the provisional idea of heresy by comparing it with a religious and philosophical definition. In §26, this background is used in order to arrive at the specific philosophical way in which Patočka develops heresy as a method for his interpretation of phenomenology. Once the philosophical clarification of heresy has been established, in §27 I explore the claim, put forward by some Patočka scholars (such as Paul Ricoeur and Miroslav Petříček), that Patočka's encounter with Husserl's idea of the lifeworld urged Patočka to diverge from Husserl. In a response to these developments, in §28, I consider how the application of heresy defines what phenomenology means for Patočka. Patočka's heretical phenomenology is then presented in §29, as a synthesis of using Heidegger to further Husserl's work. In §30, I consider how Patočka is led to a philosophy of history as an application of preserving the question 'what is history?' as a result of his own particular interpretation of phenomenology, and in §31, I explore how Patočka's phenomenology can further be clarified as a kind of shaken but undaunted philosophy. Finally, in §32, I conclude that in light of these findings, Patočka's method of question preservation can be interpreted as a heretical way for him to take up and develop Husserl's motto and Heidegger's use of questioning.

Patočka's phenomenology can be understood as a kind of *questioning philosophy* that specifically follows the path carved out by Heidegger and keeps the thought and work of Husserl in a state of preserved hindsight.[2] Given that philosophy in general may be understood as questioning, or at least requiring some form of questioning, what makes Patočka's phenomenology unique is that it develops Husserl and Heidegger's idea of question preservation into a theme in its own right. In particular, Patočka shows us how we may preserve questions alongside our efforts to answer them. For Patočka, a preserved question is one that remains secured from being fully eclipsed or resolved by excellent answers. A questioning philosophy is both a collection of preserved questions and a method of doing philosophy that seeks to keep questions in thought, even after or *especially after* powerful answers have already been found or have been developed in response to them. Following Heidegger's lead of adopting Husserl's phenomenological *questions* more than Husserl's *answers*, Patočka augments and radicalizes Heidegger's strategy by what he calls 'heresy': the philosophical process of distinguishing traditional questions from their answers in such a way as to preserve the original *wonder* sourced in questioning.

The philosophical preservation of wonder elicited by a question is woven into the very practice of phenomenology for Patočka; namely in raising its primary questions for oneself. For example, in considering the question 'what is the phenomenon?', in his lecture entitled 'What Is the Phenomenon?' in his work *Plato and Europe* (henceforth *PE*), Patočka states '[b]ut where then is the phenomenon? We do not want to answer this question right away. As far as possible, we want to let it ripen in the form of a problem' (*PE* 18). This exhibits the importance of letting a question confound or problematize. Rather than just connecting question with answer, Patočka shows us how we may use a question for the sake of exploration, to let it return us to a particular moment of experience and, as such, to return us to our experience of the things themselves. He also states, at the end of his fifth *Heretical Essay*, that '[m]odern civilization suffers not only from its own flaws and myopia but also from the failure to resolve the entire problem of history. Yet the problem of history may not be resolved, it must be preserved as a problem' (*HE* 118). The problem of history too, has to be persevered as a question independently and alongside its already traditionally valued answers (e.g. truth, scientific progress, democracy, etc.). The very question 'what is history?' turns out to be valuable for further thinking even after we have answered it rather well in that the wonder elicited *via* such questions is distinguishable from its power of excellent answers.

For Patočka, heretical philosophy is a way to take up, apply and to modify Husserl's motto, and call us 'back to the [questions] themselves'. The result is a philosophy that unifies phenomenology through its *central questions* in such a way as to remain open and to allow for the varying and incompatible answers that emerge from them. Husserl was the perpetual beginner *par excellence*, given that he never left his answers in place but instead continued to return to his original questions again and again, Patočka's heretical phenomenology follows Heidegger's and is revealed to be more in line with Husserl's motto even as it diverges and criticizes his various methods. In this way, Patočka's phenomenology throws a thinker back onto the tradition of Husserl and Heidegger while simultaneously keeping that powerful tradition from eclipsing phenomenology's original questions.

In order to understand how Patočka takes up and further develops phenomenology in view of both Husserl and Heidegger, it is beneficial to first explore how he viewed himself as a student of phenomenology. Patočka's position in response to the development of Husserl and Heidegger is implied by the term 'heretic' which is made in reference to one of his most important works translated into English thus far, entitled: *Heretical Essays in the Philosophy of History* (henceforth *HE*). Traditionally, the study of heresy in Patočka's work is considered historically; however, I aim to examine how heresy can be used as a *leitmotif* to situate Patočka's phenomenology as a *questioning philosophy* that keeps the work and thought of Husserl in hindsight. I, therefore, begin with the question of what 'heretical' means and to whom or what Patočka is a heretic. I argue that heresy connotes a unique kind of questioning that distinguishes an *original question* from the proposed *answer* traditionally or authoritatively presented for it. Interestingly, however, Patočka's heresy does not simply reject or jettison the traditional answer, but rather preserves it as well and further clarifies it by leading a thinker back to its original source (the question that one is trying to answer). Furthermore, the question is also preserved as a source for further thinking and, in this way, heresy is revealed to be an interesting interpretation and synthesis of Husserl and Heidegger's distinct ways to implement phenomenological investigation. Using Patočka's idea of heresy as a lens, I intend to show how the activity of questioning is central to what phenomenology means for Patočka.

§24. The centrality of questioning in Husserl & Heidegger's phenomenology

Husserl's phenomenology was always in a state of continual development and was always presented in the form of an *introduction*. When considering how many of Husserl's students continued to develop phenomenology in new ways beyond him, it is important to keep in mind that Husserl's own penchant for revision is just as important as his various concepts, descriptions, and definitions. Husserlian phenomenology is, thus, divided into two aspects: 1) they comprise a questioning practice that caused Husserl to return to and redevelop his ideas anew again and again and 2) a collection of answers that specifies various stages of Husserl's own development. It is important to bear phenomenology's questioning practice in mind in considering where Patočka follows Husserl and where the two part ways.

Heidegger's phenomenology takes up Husserl's central questions while at the same time distancing himself from Husserl's particular answers and methods. In this way, Heidegger suggests that phenomenology can be best understood as a collection of questions, rather than as a collection of answers. For Heidegger, the questioning philosophy that begins within Husserl's phenomenology is, therefore, preserved and continued when it is distinguished from Husserl's particular answers. Patočka continues this process by developing Heidegger's questioning critique as heresy further: the student's response to the teacher that maintains and preserves the teacher's questions all the while criticizing, preserving and developing new answers for those questions. However, these 'new' developments and answers are never intended to replace or jettison Husserl's ones; on the contrary, they are best illuminated when they are viewed alongside and in tandem with an understanding of Husserl. The primary benefit of Heidegger and Patočka's work can, therefore, be found in the fact that it leads the new student of phenomenology back into the origins of phenomenology by way of Husserl. In this way phenomenology is always moving forward with its answers, but it also maintains hindsight for the original questions that are its impetus and origin. From Husserl's desire that new students of phenomenology read the *LI* in preparation for *Ideas I* (*LI* vol. I, 4), to Heidegger's perpetual return to the question of being, and to Patočka's heresy and philosophy of history, it can be observed that woven into the very development of phenomenology itself there is a renewed appreciation and value for the *question* and for *the activity of questioning itself.*

Thus, Patočka's idea of heresy may in fact be a way to review the very heart and development of phenomenology as *an activity of questioning* in contrast with the more traditional approach of identifying and defining individual philosophies *via* their content (their system, definitions, concepts and principles). However, this other way of viewing individual philosophies for their *central activities* in opposition to their *content* need not be placed in a strict dichotomy. Rather, we can view this distinction as two individual parts of a larger whole: to focus upon an individual philosophy's content (its system, definitions, concepts, principles, etc.) is to view it in a mode of answers, whereas to focus upon an individual philosophy's activities (its concerns, problems, values, projects, etc.) is to view it in a mode of questions. Leaving the issue of whether or not this distinction can be applied to all individual philosophies aside, we can at least say that this answering-questioning distinction not only *applies* to phenomenology but furthermore, as a way of doing philosophy in general, develops from it. If this claim is correct, then we can reconsider what is generally valuable throughout all kinds of phenomenologies. In so doing, we can add to the already valuable power of phenomenological content, an equally but different power of *phenomenological questioning*; importantly not as another distinction, structure or definition to memorize, but something dynamic, vibrant: a practice. This is important because as a mode of thinking, phenomenology's special activity of questioning cannot merely be memorized as its content can be. Rather, the beginner phenomenologist must, in addition to and alongside their efforts of memorizing phenomenological content, also make efforts to practice phenomenological questioning, seeing and thinking. In the language of Patočka's phenomenological philosophy, in addition to 'knowing everything one needs to know' about phenomenology, the beginner must also practice the heresy: questioning everything in the history of phenomenology. In this sense, Patočka's idea of heresy provides a way to re-read and re-review the development of phenomenology from Husserl to Heidegger's thought in terms of a perspective of questioning.

Importantly, as pointed out previously, this appreciation and value for the activity of questioning are not always outlined or explained in the written work of Husserl, Heidegger or Patočka but is certainly emulated by their thought and practice: Husserl's penchant for revision, Heidegger's re-return to the question of being and Patočka's concern for the preservation of history as a question 'what is history?' This penchant for questioning all three philosophers demonstrate is still observable within their texts. The only way to really grasp this activity is to keep it in view while reading through the corpus of phenomenology (Husserl-Heidegger-Patočka).[3] For Patočka, it emerges through his idea of heresy.

§25. Provisional, religious and philosophical definitions of heresy

Although Patočka does not specifically define what he means by heresy anywhere in his work, a definition is visible in how he uses, conceptualizes and practices phenomenology throughout his work nevertheless. For Patočka, heresy at least includes three important and distinct aspects: (1) heresy is a clear and willing choice[4] that therefore requires responsibility (thereby ruling out 'accidental' or 'unaware' heresy); (2) heresy is a mode of thinking that preserves what it criticizes (through its criticism, it recollects and preserves what it 'finds fault with'); and (3) heresy also edifies what it critiques (as opposed to wholly negative criticism that aims to 'get rid of' or to reject what it finds fault with). In a holistic sense, heresy is not *merely* a negative or positive project nor is it *just* constructive or deconstructive for Patočka; instead, it synthesizes all of these aspects together. What word connotes a kind of criticism that ultimately preserves and edifies that which it critiques? It brings to mind the method of Socratic questioning as a line of criticism or inquiry that preserves the active *pursuit* of an idea by removing obstacles in its path (e.g. as observable in various Socratic dialogues: the weakening of definitions, concepts or *answers* that bar the original upsurge of further thinking provided by the original *question* or problem). Socratic questioning can be compared with other kinds of questioning that seek to resolve problems 'once and for all'. Patočka's 'heretical phenomenology' is, in fact, a Socratic way for him to take up and to further develop the mantle of Husserl and Heidegger by preserving the original and central questions of phenomenology alongside their already valued answers. In order to further clarify what heresy means for Patočka, we can contrast his view with the more general and religious definitions of heresy.

In religious terms, the simple definition of a heretic is one who remains within a religion but who holds a view contrary to the orthodoxy, dogma, established beliefs and/or customs of that religion. The English word comes from the Greek *hairesis* that originally meant to 'make a choice' or 'to decide'. This aspect of choice is in line with Patočka's definition regarding the issue of responsibility. In the context of religion, a heretic is an individual who wilfully holds a view contrary to an established system of beliefs. Failing to uphold the orthodox view is not necessarily a problem for a particular religion and does not always count as heresy; what usually constitutes heresy is when an individual chooses to remain *within* a religion or furthermore strives to respond to, modify or change their religion *via* the contrary idea. There are, of course, certain religions that consider the non-religious and all other religions to be heretical to their own, but I am focusing upon the definition of heresy that occurs within a religion or institution.

In a more philosophical sense, heresy occurs when an individual holds a view that is contrary to an institution with which they are affiliated. When it comes to Husserlian phenomenology, we can provisionally draw a distinction among his critical students between those who 'chose to break entirely with Husserl's ideas' and those who 'chose to remain within his phenomenology'. Patočka's heresy would place him in this second group.

Continuing with this more philosophical definition of heresy, we can see Patočka seeking to remain within the 'institution' of phenomenology whilst striving to criticize, change and to develop it. It is important to note that these 'developments' are best understood in light of, and in correlation *with*, the very ideas of that which they are critical (Husserl and Heidegger's ideas). In other words, I do not think Patočka (or Heidegger for that matter) would have instructed their students to forgo or to skip studying Husserl's teachings in favour of their own 'improved' or 'updated' versions of phenomenology. On the contrary, what makes Patočka's criticism of Husserl and Heidegger insightful and *heretical* is that it forces the thinker to return to, and therefore to preserve, the very ideas (those of Husserl and Heidegger) being criticized. The criticism of Husserl's ideas in both Heidegger and Patočka's work is, therefore, not presented as *total progress*, as a Neo-Husserl that replaces the old, but as *heretical*. Thus, Patočka's phenomenology must be viewed in contrast with that with which it struggles (i.e. Husserl's phenomenology).

§26. Patočka's heretical approach to phenomenology

In his short essay entitled 'Jan Patočka: Phenomenological Philosophy Today' scholar Miroslav Petříček attempts to answer the question 'what does "heresy" mean for Patočka, and what is "heretical" in his phenomenology?' (Petříček 3). One of Patočka's central ideas is 'care of the soul' and according to Petříček, Patočka developed it from an encounter with Husserl's concept of *Lebenswelt* (lifeworld). According to Petříček, after Patočka was introduced to Husserl's idea of the lifeworld:

> he was not long in expressing certain reservations with regard to Husserl's conception of phenomenology and phenomenological method. According to Patočka, phenomenology cannot be identified with Husserl's teachings. Moreover, what Husserl conceives of as phenomenology, i.e., the procedure of working back from ossified theses to the living wellsprings of experience, has always been part and parcel of philosophy.
>
> (Petříček 4)

Although he expressed reservations, it is important to note that Patočka certainly did not wholly reject Husserl's various definitions of phenomenology and substitute his own in their place; instead, he sought to *participate* in the questioning pursuit of phenomenology emulated by Husserl and in doing so to return to phenomenology's central problems. In his lecture entitled 'Phenomenology within the Limits of Experience' after discussing Husserl's phenomenology, Patočka states that 'this is how Husserl sees the phenomenon of the world, *at least for a time*, as for instance in *Ideas I*' (BCLW 123, my emphasis). This small phrase 'at least for a time' testifies to the interesting fact that Husserl rarely left his phenomenological conceptions and definitions at rest, but instead always opted to renew and to revise them into further developments by returning to his original questions again and again, despite already having constructed excellent answers for them. This penchant for revision, indeed the very activity of returning to phenomena or to the problems surrounding their access, meaning and signification may all be considered to be part of the essence of Husserl's phenomenology (distinct from Husserl's many definitions, concepts and descriptions). In other words, the questions that Husserl continually returned to again and again are distinct from his various and developmental answers. Indeed, it is this Husserlian mantle of *preserving a problem* by keeping it in question that constitutes heresy for Patočka. Similar to Heidegger, Patočka is heretical to Husserl's answers, but not necessarily his questions, with respect to the tradition of phenomenology.

Many of Husserl's students were inspired, but not always convinced, by Husserl's philosophy. Often cited in this regard is Paul Ricoeur's famous line that the history of phenomenology after Husserl is a history of Husserlian heresies[5] and this is confirmed by Petříček who postulates something similar: 'it is well known that many, perhaps nearly all of Husserl's followers went on (later) to open up their own paths, which quite frequently led in different directions. Such as, for example, the case of Martin Heidegger' (Petříček 4).[6] Although the fact that his students parted ways with him can initially appear to be a kind of criticism for Husserl, after one familiarizes themselves with Husserl's own penchant for revision (the preservation of phenomenology's central questions), the fact that most of Husserl's students went their own way could be evidence that they were more convinced by Husserl's *practice* rather than by his results. In other words, they were convinced by Husserl's motto (*die Sachen selbst*) of returning to experience itself more than by any of his particular methods (psychologism, descriptive phenomenology, transcendental phenomenology, genetic phenomenology, etc.). Petříček states that he 'nonetheless [believes] Patočka's path to be, to a certain extent, peculiar in its characteristic effort to remain as faithful as possible to Husserl' even though Patočka clearly criticizes many of Husserl's claims and 'this is what makes Patočka open only to those Heideggerian suggestions which he can still construe as compatible with an enlarged version of Husserl's phenomenology or "phenomenological philosophy"' (Petříček 4). In this way, then, one can view the development of Heidegger and Patočka's thought as philosophy that, although it is critical of Husserl, nonetheless remained concerned with his original problems and concerns. According to Petříček, this confirms 'why the [lecture] course Patočka taught in his last year at Charles University was not called "Introduction to Phenomenology," but rather – the difference is revealing – "Introduction to Phenomenological Philosophy"' (Petříček 4). Patočka was appointed professor in 1968, but was only allowed to lecture from 1968 to 1972 and otherwise taught in private, giving 'illegal' lectures from his home.[7] Here we can perhaps further clarify the situation of phenomenology by understanding 'phenomenological philosophy' as that collection of *questions* which are central to any phenomenological project whatsoever and which likewise view the various *answers* to these questions as what makes up any and all individual phenomenologies (Husserl's, Heidegger's and of course Patočka's). To further distinguish between phenomenology and phenomenological philosophy, it is helpful to first take a closer look at Patočka's *PE*.

In chapter two of *PE*, entitled 'What Is the Phenomenon? – Phenomenology and Phenomenological Philosophy – Phenomenon and Truth', Patočka considers the difference between phenomenology and the phenomenological. Patočka defines the phenomenon as 'the *showing of existence*: things not only are but also they are manifest [...] In order that something manifest itself, it is necessary that it manifests, appears *to someone*' (*PE* 16–17). Interestingly, after setting up the question of the phenomenon and wondering how exactly appearance works, Patočka says that:

> we do not want to answer this question right away. As far as possible, we want to let it ripen in the form of a problem [...]. We work with the concept of appearing; yet at the same time this concept itself is not clear to us. On the one hand, it is the most common, the most regular; on the other hand, to get to the phenomenon as such, to get to the appearing is not, as you see, so obvious: it is a difficult thing.
>
> (*PE* 18)

Alongside answering the question 'what is a phenomenon?', Patočka also seeks to maintain consideration for this question and in so doing distinguishes the activity of *questioning* as a kind of opening for further thinking different from that of *answering* as a kind of closing that is seeking resolution. Patočka states that 'phenomenology, the science of the phenomenon as such, shows us not things, but rather *the way of givenness* of things, how to get to things, how to draw near to them, how they show themselves' (PE 31). A phenomenologist, through reflection, is able to think about the way in which things appear within and through experience. 'Phenomenological philosophy differs from phenomenology' continues Patočka 'in that it not only wants to analyze phenomena as such, but also wants to derive results from this [activity ... but] phenomenological philosophy *is a not [an] understanding*, or a kind of slipping away from the proper problem of the phenomenon as such. The phenomenon must remain the phenomenon' (PE 32–3, my emphasis). By maintaining and preserving the question 'what is a phenomenon?', Patočka preserves the original path leading back to the wonder initially occurring in *not being able to understand* the way existence appears in the first place. Interestingly, this first instance of 'not being able to understand' is not something wholly negative nor is it just an obstacle that needs to be overcome or discarded; rather it is a state of wonder and through the preservation of a question, we are able to revive and maintain this state of wonder as a *seeking to understand* that always lies prior to and should not be confused with a complete or secured understanding. Distinguishing the original source of appearance, reached *via* a question, from the resolution of this source *via* an answer, is important because in doing so 'we realize that [the] manifesting in itself, in that which makes it manifesting, is not reducible, cannot be converted into anything *that* manifests itself in manifesting. Manifesting is, in itself, something completely original' (PE 24). Here, in addition to a clear allusion to Heidegger's suggestion that being [*Sein*] should never be conflated to a particular entity or thing [*Seiend*], we can furthermore see that the difference between a question and an answer seems to map on top of Heidegger's ontological distinction for Patočka: through questioning, we can engage with or think about the 'manifesting' and through answers we can do the same for 'the manifest'.

If we only consider phenomenology from the standpoint of *answers*, then we would have to conclude that after Husserl invents phenomenology and that nearly none of his students take up and continue it as originally envisioned; the difference between Husserl's original ideas and his students would, therefore, suggest that his followers only criticized, stole or warped Husserl's ideas for their own gain. In the same situation viewed from the standpoint of *questions*, we can recollect the history of Husserl's students and identify those who remain in a *phenomenological philosophy* but who nevertheless produce, develop and adhere to their own phenomenological path (or individual phenomenology). There need not be a false dichotomy here as we can view phenomenology in both ways and benefit; this is indeed how Petříček views Patočka.

In order to further clarify and to situate Patočka's heresy, Petříček compares him to Eugen Fink, Husserl's last assistant. Petříček states that 'in short, Patočka drifts away from Husserl in a process of broadening which has nothing to do with relinquishing or simply overcoming; rather, he attempts to enlarge both the scope and the content of phenomenology' (Petříček 4). In this way, then, Petříček identifies Patočka's 'undertaking [to be] much closer to Eugen Fink's attempt at elaborating the inmost core of Husserl's thought' (Petříček 4) referring to Fink's '*Die intentionale Analyse und das Problem des spekulativen Denkens*' (1951) and 'Operative Concepts in Husserl's Phenomenology' (1957). According to Petříček 'phenomenology, says Fink, should be fundamentally anti-speculative, that is, free from prejudice; it should get at "*die Sachen selbst,*" reach all the way to the "*Lebenswelt,*" the life-world, and uncover the ultimate ground, where the thing itself appears as what is in its "*Sich-Zeigen,*" its self-showing' (Petříček 4). Phenomenological philosophy, therefore, must avoid making any claims that cannot be correlated to genuine and direct experience, as to do so would constitute metaphysics or speculation. Husserlian phenomenology is designed to avoid or reject those ideas that cannot be verified for oneself through correlation to one's own first-person experience. As we will see later, Patočka describes this aspect of phenomenology as a kind of total or absolute responsibility. However it is termed, the value for how things self-reveal seems directly related to a return to and re-appreciation of how the lifeworld reveals itself. For Patočka, the way that Husserl presents the lifeworld as something to be perpetually re-questioned further reveals the power of phenomenological questioning. This brings one to wonder: what does Husserl mean by the lifeworld exactly?

§27. Patočka's encounter with Husserl's questioning of the lifeworld

The idea of the lifeworld is a broad issue in Husserl's phenomenology and will only be touched upon briefly here in order to situate Patočka's response to it. In *Crisis*, the idea of the lifeworld is the attempt to return to an original experience of the world itself. Husserl states that:

> [w]e wish to proceed, here, by beginning anew, staring purely from natural world-life, and by asking after the *how* of the world's pregivenness. At first we understand the question of the world's pregivenness just as it arises within the natural attitude and is understandable by all: namely, as the pregivenness of

the world of existing things through the constant alteration of relative manners of givenness, the world just as it essentially, always, obviously exists for us.

(*Crisis* 154)

The lifeworld is what everyone already understands and takes for granted in an obvious way. It is the attempt of Husserl to bring a thinker back to a state of naïveté about their own day-to-day existence. Husserl continues, stating that:

[w]e wish, then to consider the surrounding life-world concretely, in its neglected relativity and according to all the manners of relativity belonging essentially to it – the world in which we live intuitively, together with its real entities [*Realitäten*]; but [we wish to consider them] *as* they give themselves to us at first in straightforward experience, and even [consider] the ways in which their validity is sometimes in suspense (between being and illusion, etc.).

(*Crisis* 156)

Not only is it important for us to revive our own genuine, concrete and everyday experience for ourselves, but we are also instructed by Husserl to take note of the relativity that also comes with it. This effort to restore the full and rich original and, therefore, a nearly total naive experience of the world, we also find a great deal of raw experiential 'data', the messy abundance of experience we have yet to reflect upon. Husserl states that:

[o]ur exclusive task shall be to comprehend precisely this style, precisely this whole merely subjective and apparently incomprehensible 'Heraclitean flux'. Thus we are not concerned with whether and what the things, the real entities of the world, actually are [...]; we are also not concerned with what the world, taken as a totality, actually is.

(*Crisis* 156)

It is here that Husserl begins to apply a universal epoché wherein we 'exclude all knowledge, all statements about true being and predicative truths for it [...] but we also exclude all sciences, genuine as well as pseudosciences" (*Crisis* 156). In other words, we pursue our ability to raise and properly ask the question 'what is the world?' (or in a more specific formulation 'what is our original experience of the world around us like?'). Again, this question is raised to revive and elicit an original experience of the world; not merely to answer it with some form of knowledge-answer. Importantly, this experience is also not just another *concept* that Husserl has prefigured or designed and simply wants the reader to begin with; on the contrary, what makes the idea of the lifeworld so interesting and perhaps challenging, is that one 'must see it for themselves' in the form of *experiencing it for themselves* in that they must draw it from their own genuine experience. It is a genuine question that calls for actual thinking and contemplation.

The issue of the lifeworld in Husserl's philosophy has a development of its own. According to Iso Kern, although Husserl was already using the term 'lifeworld' prior to 1920:

> it is not until the 1920s, however, that it enters Husserl's philosophy as a technical term for a fundamental problem. Initially, 'lifeworld' is used interchangeably with the 'natural concept of the world [*natürlicher Weltbegriff*]' and 'world of ['natural' or]' simple experience [*natürlicher oder schlichte Erfahrungswelt*].
>
> (Bernet et al. 217)

Thus, there are two definitions for the lifeworld in Husserl's thinking: the first can be understood as an early definition and the second later definition develops more into a problem of its own. According to Kern, the first, early definition develops:

> during the 1920s, [as] the regress from the sciences to their experiential foundation signified for Husserl the return to 'simple' or 'pure' experience. At the time, this meant for him a return to *preconceptual* (prelinguistic, pre-predicative) experience. The world of simple experience, in which all sciences are ultimately founded.
>
> (Bernet et al. 220)

This original and simple experience was a mute, concept-less experience originating from a world prior to the history of intellectual and conceptual thinking (Bernet et al. 221). This suggests that Husserl was in search of a simple, original experience of the world in which he could ground more complex experience. The second definition, emerging later, developed out of Husserl's concern for the crisis he believed was occurring in the sciences after 'he became sensitive to the fact that these sciences had nothing to say with regard to the most important questions for human life, the questions concerning the sense and meaning of life' (Bernet et al. 223). The lifeworld in this later sense related to 'the problem concerning the relationship between the objective sciences and concrete, historical life, or between reality as constructed by objective science and the reality of the subjective lifeworld, stepped into the center of his interest' (Bernet et al. 223). The later definition of the lifeworld did not represent an origin point prior to or independent of history, but the more holistic locale wherein history, culture and the objective sciences develops from. In this light, according to Kern, 'the foundation of the human sciences, in any case, cannot be a mute, preconceptual experience. It can only be a living participation in the cultural world' (Bernet et al. 222). The second definition, therefore, developed more into a question and a problem as to how exactly the objective sciences relate to the subjective experience of the world. Thus, the question of how an encounter with Husserl's concepts of the lifeworld would affect Patočka's view of phenomenology remains.

The significance of Husserl's lifeworld for Patočka is twofold: on the one hand, the question 'what is the world?' represents the very heart of phenomenology to preserve a question alongside its various answers; and on the other, this question provides a way to explore how a phenomenology of dynamism may be attempted. For our purposes here, it is sufficient to consider the idea of the lifeworld as Husserl taking the question 'what is the world?' and/or 'how do we originally experience the natural world around us?' seriously. It is not the aim of this chapter to resolve the problem of Husserl's lifeworld, but in this first sense, the question of the lifeworld does prove to be a useful way to preserve the phenomenon of the world in a state of flux or problematicity for both Husserl and Patočka. That the lifeworld maintained its problematicity meant that both thinkers felt the need to return to, and to reconsider, just how the 'general experience of the world' occurred. This further illustrates the value and power of phenomenological questions, distinct from its equally valuable and powerful answers: although Husserl and Patočka do not agree in their answers regarding the lifeworld, *as a problem* they are united in exploring, defining and, therefore, of preserving it as a worthwhile source for further thinking.

The issue of the lifeworld can be more specifically construed as: 'what kind of structures make up the natural world?' According to Kern:

> over the years, the insight deepened in [Husserl] that actual clarification of the relationship between nature and spirit could be accomplished only by stepping back *from* the guiding, factual, scientific concepts, as products of methodological technique, *to* the world of primordial experience, in which nature and spirit are given [together in primordial intuition].
>
> (Bernet et al. 219)

Here we can observe Husserl's phenomenology in practice as a return to the thing itself through attempts to allow the lifeworld, as a complex phenomenon, to reveal and *re-reveal* itself from itself. This phrasing might sound suspiciously more like Heidegger than Husserl; however, when reconsidering Husserl's phenomenology in light of his penchant for revision, the second 're-reveal' is found to be located in Husserl's own return to the things themselves even though it sounds more like it belongs in a Heideggerian conceptualization. For Husserl, the second 're-reveal' is significant as it further suggests that the phenomenon of the lifeworld is uniquely dynamic in that it resists being totally stabilized as an phenomenological object, but rather continually self-reveals the more one returns to think, question, or phenomenologically investigate it.[8] If one thinks about the lifeworld from the view of an *answer* (concept, definition, static structure, etc.) then the dynamism of the lifeworld remains unaccounted for. However, if one thinks about the lifeworld in the form of the *question* 'what is the lifeworld?' then the lifeworld's dynamism is also accounted for. In addition to this, when the question is preserved even after various answers have been derived for it, then the lifeworld is shown to be inexhaustible *via* appearance: it continues to always reveal and to re-reveal itself when approached in a questioning manner. The possibility of the lifeworld to further reveal itself is preserved when kept in question.

The encounter with the lifeworld is not so much a moment of contention between Patočka and Husserl, but it is perhaps a moment wherein Patočka sees the value in preserving questions. By keeping and thereby preserving the investigation of the lifeworld in question, the phenomenologist is able to attain a higher level of receptivity for the *possibilities* of appearance. Although it is indicated by an encounter with the lifeworld, this insight is quickly revealed to be applicable to any and all kinds of phenomenological questions. A higher level of receptivity for appearance occurs when a phenomenologist preserves questions. Patočka's heresy is thereby revealed to be woven into the very method and historical development of phenomenology, all the way back to Husserl.

§28. What is phenomenology for Patočka?

Now that Patočka's heresy has been clarified somewhat, we can turn to and examine specifically how he understands Husserl and Heidegger and where his own thought diverges from them. The main text that will be used for this is Patočka's *Body, Community, Language, World* (*BCLW*) translated by Erazim Kohák 'published' in 1968. According to Kohák:

> the book has problems. One of them is that Patočka never actually wrote it. The text we have is not even *scripta*, a lecturer's own notes reproduced for students' convenience. It is, rather, *reportata*, a compilation of students' notes

from lectures Jan Patočka gave at the Philosophy Faculty of Prague's Charles University in the academic year 1968–69.

(*BCLW* 179)

Nonetheless, the work was compiled by Patočka's students who then later met to reconstruct the text and one of the students, namely:

> Jiří Polívka undertook the compilation of the final version and dictated the results to Miroslav Petříček, who produced a typescript for private circulation. This was the text [that would later be known] as *Prager Abschrift* [and] would remain the sole source of Patočka's writings abroad until the fall of the Communist regime in 1989.

(*BCLW* 180)

Although these textual issues can make it difficult for a reader to clearly identify and trace Patočka's thought, it does not make it impossible. The *BCLW* text itself is made up of twelve lectures and, for the purposes of this chapter, I will mostly be focusing upon how Patočka presents, understands and modifies the meaning and method of phenomenology, in light of, and in the interpretation of, both Husserl and Heidegger specifically. However, my purpose is not to give a comprehensive view of Patočka's phenomenology as that would be an entire project on its own. Rather, I intend to focus upon how the activity of questioning is understood and presented by Patočka's phenomenology and how his own development and interpretation compares to those of Husserl and Heidegger.

In his first lecture of *BCLW*, entitled 'Subject Body and Ancient Philosophy', Patočka outlines phenomenology:

> *Phenomenology* is a mode of philosophizing that does not take ready-made theses for its premises but rather keeps all premises at an arm's length. It turns from sclerotic theses to the living well-springs of experience. Its opposite is metaphysics – which constructs philosophy as a special scientific system. Phenomenology examines the experiential content of such theses; in every abstract thought it seeks to uncover what is hidden in it, how we arrive at it, what seen and lived reality underlies it. We are uncovering something that has been here all along, something we had sensed, glimpsed from the corner of our eye but did not fully know, something that 'had not been brought to conception.' *Phenomenon* – that which presents itself; *logos* – meaningful discourse.

(*BCLW* 3)

Here we can see that Patočka's interpretation of phenomenology makes use of and synthesizes the specifics of Husserl and Heidegger's thinking. The idea of 'keeping premises at arm's length' and 'searching for the experiential content for such theses' helps to maintain the distinction between the content of phenomenology (premises and theses) and the real and genuine experiences with which they are correlated and this all seems to be quite in line with Husserl's project. The reason for this aim is to protect phenomenology from any and all unverifiable claims; that is, to keep it from ever becoming a philosophical contrivance that cannot be validated by experience (metaphysics). More importantly, in the line to 'uncover something that has been here all along, something glimpsed but which has yet to be brought to conception' seems more in line with Heidegger's phenomenology, specifically in the sense that something opaque and unthematic can still appear (or announce itself) in some way and as such can be further clarified. This speaks to the central point in which Patočka parts ways with Husserl in the question as to exactly what qualifies as an object of consciousness in the first place and whether or not there can be something more primordial than an object of consciousness?

Patočka agrees with Husserl that in an act of consciousness (which is always a correlation with an object *of consciousness*) the act is primarily focused upon the object at which it is directed. This is one of the reasons why the phenomenological attitude is so difficult to bring about. To the beginner phenomenologist (or for anyone for that matter) acts of consciousness occur and happen without any difficulty, they make up the medium of thinking, perceiving, experiencing, etc. Husserl's discovery is that within the activity of thinking, perceiving, experiencing, etc., something is also given to us apodictically: the very *act of consciousness* itself alongside the object it is directed at.[9] We need the phenomenological reduction in order to bring about a distinction between an 'act of consciousness' and the 'object' towards which that act is directed.

Patočka disagrees with Husserl regarding the roles reflection and objectification are to play in phenomenology. Specifically, he rejects the idea that all aspects of experience can be 'captured', can be objectified as an object through a description of the formal structures of consciousness. According to Patočka, 'we cannot deduce, as Husserl does, that the study of our experience, which makes possible access to beings and to being, is a study in reflection (alone), an objectification, that that on which I reflect already has in itself the character of an object which we need but set before our eyes – and there it is, in the original' (*BCLW* 83). In other words, Patočka thinks that there are aspects of experience that resist Husserl's objectification through reflection. Patočka states that:

> in Husserl, reflection is privileged because it putatively provides us with consciousness in the original, only grasped in reflection. That means that

consciousness is already itself grasped in the mode of object givenness, that consciousness has the being character of an objective object of perception, there before our view.

(BCLW 83–4)

Patočka's criticism of Husserl's project is not one of rejection, but one of limitation; Patočka wonders whether or not the phenomenological reduction, and its aim to provide objects of consciousness, will enable the Husserlian phenomenologist to access *every and all kinds of existence*. In other words, could there be a limitation to objectification that fails to account for or to grasp certain peculiar experiences or phenomena? This certainly seems unproblematic regarding existence, understood as 'what is static' or 'what can be stabilized'; however, Husserl's notion of 'consciousness as a static structure of positing an object is a fact, but not all life (all "conscious" life) can be subsumed under this model according to Patočka. For instance, handling a pencil, a hammer, is also a mode of knowing but it makes no sense without a certain context from which it cannot be separated' (*BCLW* 84). Does the very attempt to distil and to separate the 'handling of a pencil' through Husserl's reduction *miss something or lose something?* According to Patočka:

> Husserl does understand consciousness as a series of acts, but always pertaining or relating to an object. Objectification constitutes the firm structure of consciousness; the fixation onto an object is the primordial basis of knowing. The objective guide for analysis is the primordial model of phenomenological work. Consciousness has fundamentally an objectival structure. If we can show a clarity that is in principle non-objectival, and if [...] all modalities of this objectification, are rooted in [something non-objectival], then we have gone beyond Husserl with the help of a Husserlian motif.

(BCLW 84)

In other words, Patočka is interested in whether or not there is 'something' more primordial, something *not an object* that lies beneath Husserl's 'object of consciousness'. If there is something more primordial, then this would not necessarily undermine Husserl's phenomenology, but may in fact further develop and enrich it, provided that what was more primordial could be connected to what can be objectified. Furthermore, it might complicate the method of phenomenological investigation in an edifying way: there might be an additional method for describing and accounting for dynamic and unstable phenomena discovered in the attempt to expand on the method for describing and accounting for static and stabilized phenomena. If experience, as a whole, entails something more primordial than 'objects of consciousness', then a phenomenologist is responsible to explore it.

Here we return to the issue of phenomenological responsibility. Patočka states that 'Husserl's philosophy is a philosophy of pure *theoria*, of pure observation. An absolute science with an absolute responsibility. That was Husserl's immense courage – that drive to responsibility. It places life under the norm of the demonstrable, of truth' (*BCLW* 84). Although this drive for responsibility is clearly valuable and promising for a project of science, 'carrying that idea out concretely however, leads to the opposite of the original intent, that of a philosophy free of presuppositions and fully responsible. The idea of philosophy as a rigorous science can, under some circumstances, be a misleading one' (*BCLW* 84). Although auspicious in scope, phenomenology as a rigorous science might not actually be feasible and yet, even if this criticism is true, it does not discard everything Husserl suggests. Here we can see Patočka showing his agreement with Heidegger, in considering the limits of Husserl's project. Patočka states that 'not every evident givenness need be objectival, demonstrable, not every consciousness need be accompanied by a self-consciousness, not everything evident need be evidently given' (*BCLW* 85). The question here is: what phenomena can we give as examples that fit Patočka's description of something evident but not evidently given, or a phenomenon given that falls outside of (or is not an example of) Husserl's objectification? Patočka's examples are *practices*: the handling of a pencil or a hammer in a particular context.

In this sense, Patočka's critique of Husserl is very in line with Heidegger's. Patočka states that:

> Heidegger was perhaps the first to pose the question of *the origin of consciousness*, not in the sense of natural causes (that belong to psychology, biology), but in principle, in the sense of the ontological conditions of the possibility of clarity concerning the world. A living being lives ahead of itself in its possibilities, realizing its possibilities which it understands in a specific way – nonobjectively, by carrying them out. Practice does project before it a certain clarity about our experiencing: a spatial reality has to be seen. That is the distancing presupposed by all consciousness. Things then emerge out of possibilities as what objectively corresponds to them. Only in this context can things emerge, not, that is, in mere observing but rather in an involved living which identifies with its possibilities and realizes them. That is the *primacy of practice*.
>
> (*BCLW* 85)

Patočka here appeals to Heidegger's existential analytic as a kind of phenomenology that shows how the primacy of practice not only underlies

Husserl's *consciousness of objects* but further falls outside of any kind of phenomenology limited to *objectification*. Interestingly, then, when Heidegger conducts a study of 'phenomena' he must be doing so towards something non-objective. These two different ways in which Husserl and Heidegger consider how phenomenological investigation ought to be properly carried out can be unified without collapsing their individual differences when we view them from the perspective of a question. Where Husserl seeks to explore and to investigate objects of consciousness, he may or may not limit the very notion of appearance to that which can sufficiently be made into an object of consciousness. For Heidegger, the notion of appearance is well beyond the limitations of what can or cannot be made into an object. Heidegger adds to Husserl's original concept of phenomenon as an 'object of consciousness' to include 'semblance' [*Schein*], 'appearance' [*Erscheinung*] and 'mere appearance' [*bloße Erscheinung*] (BT §7). Heidegger's development of Husserl is to consider the many different ways in which appearance itself appears.

One way to further clarify this development is to see that Heidegger shifts from considering the idea of the phenomenon from the perspective of a strict structure and instead revives Husserl's original question 'what is the phenomenon?' or 'how do phenomena themselves appear to consciousness?' To return to Patočka's concern for how phenomena, such as the lifeworld, the lived body, and the primacy of practice can themselves be investigated by phenomenology, this shift from thinking in a mode characterized by stabilization (answers, concepts, definitions, etc.) into thinking in a mode characterized by dynamism (questions, concerns, perspectives, etc.) allows for what was previously invisible or given unthematically in Husserl's phenomenology to be made visible and be given thematically in Heidegger's phenomenology. In other words, with the addition of Heidegger's work, phenomena can now be viewed for how they reveal themselves from themselves in both objective and non-objective ways. Importantly, these two methods do not necessarily compete with one another; instead, they seem to demark different domains of appearance: stable, static appearance and dynamic and unstable appearance.

According to Heidegger and Patočka, overvaluing phenomena in their structure, stabilization and fixity (i.e. to understand them primarily as something objectified) can lead one to unintentionally cover up or miss phenomena in their dynamism, instability and flux (that is, to understand them as *fluctuating possibilities*) entirely. According to Patočka on Heidegger:

> possibilities are not something objective, they are not there to see so we might look at them, rather, they are our possibilities insofar as we do them, realize

them, identify with them. The possibilities that open up to us are present in a special mode so that we are aware of them but not so that they would be objectified but rather in the sense that we understand what surrounds us in light of them. We understand *practically*: that is, we are able to, we are familiar with, we know how to deal with. That is the original meaning of 'to understand.' That is how we first understand ourselves and things.

(BCLW 96)

The 'knowledge' we have of our practical possibilities, the primacy of practice, is of a kind of 'knowledge' that remains non-objective and non-theoretical. A good illustration of this is how an individual is able to use a door – walking up to it, reaching for the doorknob, turning it, opening the door, walking through and closing the door behind oneself – can all be understood and viewed in a theoretical way, but are first learned in a practical way by doing and through practice. When we explore our bodily capabilities, we do not do so in a theoretical way, but instead do so practically. Here it is clear that Patočka has Heidegger's distinction between readiness-to-hand [*Zuhandenheit*] and present-at-hand [*Vorhandenheit*] (*BT* §§9–11; and §§16–18) in mind. According to Patočka, like Husserl, Heidegger is also concerned with 'consciousness' but he just does not use the term and, therefore, defines it in a very different way from that of Husserl. Patočka states:

> what concerns Heidegger is naturally also consciousness, but not consciousness in the classic sense of the correlate of an object which can itself be objectified, which is itself a being of a certain type whose mode of being does not distinguish it from an object. In Heidegger's conception, consciousness – if we can ask about it at all – is something that first arises in the primordial clarity of a being that must accomplish its being, that is preoccupied with its own being. The point is the essential primacy of *practice*. At the very protofoundation of consciousness, of thought, of the subject, there is acting, not mere seeing.

(BCLW 96)

In this way, we can view Heidegger's existential analytic as a way to phenomenologically explore what is supposedly more primordial than what Husserl calls consciousness. This view raises the interesting question of whether or not this puts Heidegger and Husserl's phenomenology at odds with each other, or if they can be viewed as parts of a larger whole. Patočka states that:

> thus Heidegger does in a sense set Husserl's phenomenology aside, though not dismissing it as worthless, only making it problematic as to its *extent*, how radical

it is. It does not deal with ultimate phenomena to which all thought points as to its foundation. It does, however, remain immensely useful as a conceptual orientation.

(*BCLW* 107)

Despite what conclusions we may draw regarding the Husserl-Heidegger comparison, we can at least observe Patočka's response: instead of viewing them in terms of a strict dichotomy, Patočka sees the value of Husserl's absolute responsibility alongside Heidegger's phenomenology of unthematic and vague appearances [*Erscheinungen*]. There is one set of phenomenological questions with their corresponding answers in Husserl and in Heidegger we can find another. The coupling of these two methods brings about a more robust phenomenology.

This further clarifies what heresy means for Patočka as a means to be critical in such a way as to demand that the phenomenologist go back, re-review and re-think original questions and compare them with traditional answers. As a method, the one-to-one relation with Husserl's phenomenology is very clear: just as phenomenology declares 'to the things themselves!', Patočka's heretical phenomenology demands, *in view of our criticism*, that we 'return to Husserl and Heidegger' and review and re-read their phenomenological work again and again. This criticism brings about and secures a special kind of problematicity in that Husserl and Heidegger's answers are cast in doubt, but their *original questions* are made all the more vibrant because of this doubt. Furthermore, even when an answer or set of answers is taken to be true, this ought to never keep one from returning to their corresponding questions anew in order for the problematicity of those questions to perpetually be reconfirmed by their answers.

As Patočka moved away from Husserl in his own phenomenological development, he began to develop his more-celebrated ideas such as openness, the soul and care of the soul. Petříček highlights that:

> these [celebrated ideas] are well-known, established, and familiar things. What I wish to stress is simply this impressive act of interpretation of Husserlian phenomenology, an act which, on the one hand, goes beyond almost all limits of Husserlian phenomenology and, on the other, extends these limits and the scope of phenomenology as such. *It is an act of fidelity and adherence to phenomenology.*
>
> (Petříček 6, my emphasis)

It is here that the peculiar way in which Patočka interprets Husserl begins to become clear. This is also confirmed by Ricoeur who states that Patočka's phenomenology shows 'a path that stays faithful to as well as diverges from the two standard versions of phenomenology [in Husserl and Heidegger]' (*HE* vii-viii). Patočka's response to Husserl is certainly more complicated than merely agreeing or disagreeing with him. Patočka's response to Husserl is one of *heresy* and it is here that Petříček clarifies specifically what this means:

> heresy is the same 'act' as the original creative interpretation which carries on, taking a thought further. It is – perhaps – a sort of 'over-interpretation,' but never a mis-interpretation, since this mode of heretical thinking implies a reflection on the very limits of the thought to be understood, and it implies such an extension of these limits which can transform even the basic definitions and fundamental concepts while preserving the core of the thought in question.
>
> (Petříček 6)

Even in his criticism of Husserl, which led him to other ideas (some even contrary to Husserl's), Petříček suggests that Patočka always stressed an edifying response to Husserl and it is this peculiar *critical fidelity* that makes Patočka a heretic.

A phenomenologist in the mould of Patočka requires one to be a committed heretic (itself a modification of Husserl's eternal beginner). To return to the provisional definition of heresy, we can now see how Patočka's response to Husserl fulfils the three definitions. Patočka's take on Husserl's phenomenology is heretical in the first sense that he does not simply take over Husserl's ideas on the basis of authority, but instead seeks to test or validate them for himself as a way to fulfil the imperative 'to the things themselves!' In so doing, regarding the idea of the lifeworld according to Petříček, Patočka finds that he is unable to agree with Husserl. Although he is unable to correlate or verify Husserl's *answers*, Patočka nonetheless remains fully concerned with the same *questions*: 'what is the lifeworld?' reveals itself to be a way in which to be more phenomenologically receptive to appearance than restricting oneself to an answer. In this sense, Patočka fulfils the second sense of heresy as a mode of thinking that preserves what it criticizes. At no point does Patočka reject the issue of the lifeworld entirely but, on the contrary, keeps it in question by making renewed attempts to develop Husserl's original concern. In so doing, Patočka fulfils the third sense of heresy in that his ultimate aim is to continue and to contribute to Husserl's work rather than to undermine or replace it. In this sense, Patočka's heretical phenomenology further helps us to distinguish between the activity of questioning in a phenomenological way and the specifics of that activity that lend themselves to a categorization as answers.

§29. Patočka's heretical phenomenology as using Heidegger to further Husserl

In his introduction to Patočka's *HE*, Ricoeur conceptualizes heresy in a slightly different way. Therein, Ricoeur states that:

> in tracing the theme of the three dimensions of European humanity [...] the Husserlian and Heideggerean origin of these essays becomes evident; also, one can recognize wherein lies Patočka's heresy, a point of rupture not only with vulgar Marxism – that is too obvious – but, more decisively and dramatically, with views of Husserl and Heidegger about history.

(*HE* ix)

Ricoeur uses heresy here in its more common sense of 'going against a pre-established authority or institution'; interestingly, includes Heidegger as part of what Patočka is heretical towards. According to Ricoeur, Patočka's 'heresy lies precisely in the new definition of the natural world as the world of prehistory, which in turn is a consequence of the characterization of history as problematic' (*HE* ix). Recall that for Husserl, the simple and early definition of the lifeworld was something prescientific that was in danger of being lost if one reduces all of experience to the scientifically accessible empirical world. Ricoeur states that:

> the natural world is not [... just] that which science calls nature, that is, the aggregate of objects accessible to empirical science; nor is it that which positivist materialism takes to be an absolute outside which, in one way or another, is mirrored in the interiority of thought. In this rapid exposition that begins the first essay Patočka is still following his teacher Husserl, though only for the moment. For Husserl, the natural world is prescientific, not prehistorical; it is the world of life, lost by objectification, a world which we would be able to recover, or at least aim at, by means of a regressive, questioning method, like the one practiced by [Husserl].

(*HE* x)

Patočka takes up Husserl's concern for the question 'what is the world?' and develops it beyond an issue of science versus pre-science. However, Patočka's aim seems to remain in line with Husserl's thinking where Husserl thought something essential and valuable was being lost when a thinker only equates existence with what appears empirically, Patočka likewise wanted to argue that something else is lost when a thinker equates existence with phenomenological objectification. Both Patočka and Husserl are arguing for an expansion of existence (what gets taken seriously for further investigation captured by the question 'what is the world?'). According to Ricoeur, Patočka later considers:

> as a consequence [of Husserl's method], the philosopher who turns towards the constitutive phenomena of the world of life reduces himself or herself to the vision of a disinterested subject. With this critique of Husserlian idealism Patočka is clearly in agreement with Heidegger.
>
> (*HE* x)

Again, it should be stressed that this criticism does not jettison all of Husserl's work, but maintains and further develops it in a heretical way: with this observation, Patočka also sets up a new avenue that allows for what is dark and invisible in Husserl's phenomenology to be made into a phenomenon of a different kind. Recall that for Heidegger, the phenomenologist's task is to find unthematic and obscure 'appearances' [*Erscheinung*] and to bring them into focus as phenomena and, in so doing, to allow them to reveal themselves from themselves. In this sense, Patočka is in fact following through with Heidegger's definition but is remaining focused upon a specifically Husserlian problem: the lifeworld.

Patočka's heretical phenomenology is the attempt to bring to light certain aspects of Husserl's phenomenology Patočka felt were dark, invisible or mysterious. Ricoeur states that 'the meaning of phenomenology itself is thereby fundamentally altered [for Patočka]: the phenomenon to which we are open in being-in-the-world cannot be deprived of its mysterious character; what shows itself is only that which emerges out of the *concealment of Being*' (*HE* x). Here it is important to wonder what meaning is intended by 'mysterious character' as Ricoeur could at least mean one of (or all of the) three things: (1) mystery in the sense of something that has yet to be resolved, but which can be (e.g. murder mysteries); (2) mysterious knowledge of the secret kind which can only be obtained from rigorous or arcane means (e.g. esoteric mysteries); and (3) mystery in the sense of something that can be encountered or 'known' to some extent, but which remains intrinsically un-resolvable (e.g. religious mysteries). It should be borne in mind that this idea of mystery is likewise referenced by Heidegger at the end of 'My Way' in which he states that 'if phenomenology is thus experienced and retained [as a possibility], it can disappear as a designation in favor of the matter of thinking whose manifestness remains a *mystery*' ('My Way' 82, my emphasis). The different definitions of mystery likewise change the manner of questioning used.

In each case, the function of a question takes on a different shape: In the first case of a murder mystery, the activity of questioning is used primarily to find the factual or evidential truth, the real murderer and no one else. This kind of detective questioning is used to sift through the subterfuge of cunning and criminal masterminds, to locate and secure what is in fact true, despite the heaps of obfuscation and misdirection. In the second case of the esoteric knowledge, the activity of acquisition-oriented questioning proves to be a feat that aims to overcome a great complexity; for example, in deciphering opaque texts in search of concealed meaning. Here the 'mystery' is found in the *difficulty* of coming to know something secret or complex, one where only the persevering investigator succeeds and the disingenuous do not. In the third case of the religious mystery, the activity of ritual questioning is a kind of repeatable rite that is not done necessarily because it brings one closer to knowledge, but rather usually as a direct act of faith or participation in a religion. The genuine meditation over a religious mystery is to partake in a religion in which mysteries are celebrated (both for what they mean for the believer and in that they are irresolvable, not just un-resolvable). Each of these different manners or modes of questioning greatly distinguishes the kinds of thinking involved in their individual pursuits.

In the case of Patočka, following through on Heidegger's description of the central task of the phenomenologist, we can understand mystery in the sense of taking what remains obscure, invisible or unthematic in Husserl's phenomenology and attempting to provide a way to bring it into focus as a phenomenon, to allow it to reveal itself from itself. Again, the issue comes back to locating something static versus dynamic as Ricoeur concludes when he contends that:

> the hope to recover, underneath the strata of objective knowledge and world views, something that is invariant proves itself to be a deception; rather, one must avow that all historical worlds where the emergence and eclipse of the being of beings gathers itself are 'natural'.
>
> (*HE* x–xi)

Perhaps what made the phenomenon of the prehistorical world invisible for Husserl was his adherence to the search for what is invariant. However, it is Husserl *more than his students* who returned to the questions of phenomenology; it is, thus, more likely the case that it was *because* Husserl was unable to say something invariant about such 'appearances' [*Erscheinungen*] that he refrained from doing so, rather than the suggestion that he was simply unaware of them. If so, then Patočka's criticism is not really a criticism at all but a developmental difference, where the limits of Husserl's phenomenology were expanded or applied to an area of existence; instead, Patočka sought to further investigate what had hitherto been left fallow by Husserl.

Patočka not only moves beyond Husserl's phenomenology, according to Ricoeur, he also does the same with Heidegger's. Ricoeur states that:

> it is here that Patočka's thought takes its departure from that of Heidegger: the concealment of being, in the later Heidegger, meant the alteration between a revealing and a concealing that determined that the world of beings is to be taken now Nature, now Subject, now Spirit. For Patočka, it means the loss of all security, a loss which completely exposes man and his freedom. This is what he calls the problematic condition character of the age of history. This new interpretation of Heidegger is reinforced by the interpretation of Husserl: the natural world is not the prescientific world, but the prehistorical world; that is, the nonproblematic world.
>
> (*HE* xi)

Patočka develops Heidegger's concern for the concealment and unconcealment of being into a phenomenology of problematicity. This phenomenology is characterized by a renewed concern for how life or the world either brings about an engagement and recognition of this problematicity, therefore becoming unsheltered life, or aids us in an escape from sheltered life.

§30. Patočka's philosophy of history as an example of his phenomenology

For Patočka, the issue of Husserl's lifeworld is further bifurcated into the historical and prehistorical worlds. Patočka's approach to phenomenological investigation seeks to explore the importance of participating in history by raising and answering the question 'what is history?' Recall that the context of unsheltered life is not one that lacks traditional meaning, but rather one wherein such meaning has been weakening or shaken; everything that was traditionally accepted is once again thrown back into question. Engaging in history for Patočka, therefore, means preserving the question 'what is history?' alongside its many answers. In this way then we can ascertain in Patočka a continuation of Husserl and Heidegger's work on the activity of phenomenological questioning that seeks to preserve questions as a way to further reveal phenomena.

The shift from the sheltered life of prehistory into the unsheltered life of history proper is marked by problematicity as a total loss of absolute meaning. Patočka states that 'the loss of certitude of the condition of prehistory leads today to the shaking of all accepted meaning' (*HE* xiii). This problematicity is what calls individuals into responsibility, given that they are no longer able to simply stand in a relation to some authority, community or overarching shelter. According to Patočka, unsheltered life requires a confrontation with the possibility of losing all meaning: 'Only by coming to terms with this threat, confronting it undaunted, can free life as such unfold; its freedom is in its innermost foundation the freedom of the undaunted' (*HE* 38–9). In this way Patočka's heretical phenomenology is one of problematicity. 'Beyond this critical point' continues Ricoeur 'life must be understood not from the point of view of the day, that is, of accepted life, but from the point of view of the night, that is, of *Polemos*' (*HE* xiii). Interestingly, this metaphor of day and night applied to the understanding of life suggests that both approaches make up a larger whole.

Shaken, historical meaning is something like a dynamic possibility. In Patočka's terminology, it is comparable to the Greek concept of *polemos*: '*polemos* [is] the flash of being out of the night of the world [which] lets everything particular be and manifest itself as what it is' (*HE* 43). The philosophical questions that illuminate the world and cause us to wonder at it have their genesis in a pursuit of meaning in the crucible of *polemos*, but 'polemos is not the destructive passion of a wild brigand but is, rather, the creator of unity [...] the unity of the shaken but undaunted' (*HE* 43). Here we see Patočka follow through on Heidegger's interpretation of polemos[10] as confrontation or strife: 'Confrontation does not divide unity, must less destroy it. It builds unity; it is the gathering (*logos*) [...] Struggle first projects and develops the un-heard, the hitherto un-said and un-thought' (*Introduction to Metaphysics* 65). The activity of questioning is a place of confrontation where the contents of thought are put into strife. This activity, therefore, becomes the crucible wherein ideas and thought are subjected to testing, construction and deconstruction. According to de Warren, '*polemos* is the violence of ontological questioning that fractures the apparently seamless bond between meaning and being. As a result, the illusion of total meaning and/or an unquestioned relation towards the possibility of meaning is placed in the perspective of problematic existence' (de Warren 2014 221). Although here de Warren notes the connection of polemos to ontological questioning, I think polemos may apply to any activity of genuine questioning whatsoever. The power of polemos is certainly related to the power of a question to re-view ideas, concepts and phenomena in order to further make attempts of destabilization or re-stabilization. The phrase 'shaken but undaunted' here refers to those who continue searching for absolute meaning even though they also understand the possibility that such answers may never be obtained. Although here stated in a theoretical way, Patočka's view emanated out of, and was directly affected by, a real political situation.

In a real political sense, this 'shaken' questioning formed the basis of the 1977 Czech civic initiative Charter 77. According to the political scientist Petr Pithart, who worked with Patočka and others on Charter 77, in his essay 'Questioning as a Prerequisite for a Meaningful Protest' Pithart writes:

> the phrase 'solidarity of the shaken' has doubtless also been used as a prop and an incantation, adding luster to the everyday reality of the persecuted dissidents. That, however, never entirely hid its original meaning: only shakenness as a result of exposure to the forces that move the world, only an acute awareness of danger, makes us feel an urgent need for meaning. If we do not agree that everything is allowed, if we refuse to yield to aggression and nihilism, then that means there is something worth sacrificing for. Sacrificing does not mean dying, but rather suffering for that *something*, and suffering together, i.e., living in the 'solidarity of the shaken'.
>
> (Pithart 159)

These individuals still search for excellent answers to old and important questions even though these answers remain elusive or perhaps even hopeless. Maintaining the perseverance to ask questions in such a situation is, therefore, very difficult. According to Pithart:

> asking questions without even hinting at an answer takes a lot of courage. Perhaps the only time we can succeed in doing so is once we have admitted that the darkness surrounding us is absolute and that there are no signs of hope. In other circumstances, or if we lack courage, we generally ask our questions in a way that implies or even leads directly to an answer. But these are only rhetorical questions.
>
> (Pithart 159)

The feeling of being shaken is, therefore, not just a feeling of resistance but the recognition of a very dire, even hopeless, situation wherein one remains simultaneously fully cognizant of one's bleak situation and yet persists to ask more questions and remains undaunted by it. According to Pithart, in that dark historical time 'Patočka asked authentic questions, with the aim, not to set hands on a sought-after certitude, but ever and ever again to unsettle and to awake. His questions were urgent, frank, and challenging' (Pithart 157). Instead of just providing answers, Patočka 'did not preach truths, but rather encouraged us to the experience of being shaken' (Pithart 160). Through this political leadership, accomplished through writing and teaching philosophy, Patočka encouraged thinking in questions as a political action. In this way Patočka represents a very interesting synthesis of Husserl's and Heidegger's views as a value and preservation of the pursuit or *questioning towards* truth alongside the many different ways one may define and conceptualize truth.

The historical world is a place in which this problematicity is preserved. This problematicity also includes its own structure as a question. The very ground of history is, therefore, also a question of history and, in this way, is not just something static but is also something dynamic. This is difficult to understand as traditional models of thinking tend to remain within static constructs. Instead of *merely* thinking in a mode that looks only for answers, concepts or static constructs, we can broaden our thinking to include a mode that, alongside and balanced with our concern for answers also looks for questions, conceptualizations and dynamic processes. Within this broader scope it becomes clear how a question can persist alongside its excellent answers. According to Patočka, this is the difference between prehistory (a world restricted to answers) and history:

> history is nothing other than the shaken certitude of pre-given meaning. […] Yet the problem of history may not be resolved, it must be preserved as a problem. Today the danger is that knowing so many particulars we are losing the ability to see the questions and that which is their foundation.
>
> (*HE* 118)

In history proper, a thinker sees answers alongside questions and they participate in the guardianship of history proper when they maintain the preservation of questions even in view of incredibly powerful answers. Patočka has learnt this value for a question independent of its possible answers from Heidegger, who exemplifies this process of dedication and guardianship for the question of being. Patočka has not so much built upon and developed Heidegger's concern for the *question of being* as he has followed in Heidegger's more general method of philosophical questioning as such; this is a method that harkens all the way back to the original master, Husserl.

§31. Patočka's phenomenology as shaken but undaunted philosophy

According to Patočka, not only is Husserl's phenomenology a science, it also enriches and expands upon the very notion of science. Taken in its most general sense, science is a kind of knowledge based upon repeatable experimentation.

Stemming from a concern for a subjective versus objective dichotomy, where the former entails descriptions and definitions of personal opinions, emotions, feelings and concerns more ephemeral phenomena and the latter entail descriptions and definitions of cold, factual and systematic phenomena, scientific knowledge aims for what is objective. Objective scientific knowledge is, therefore, knowledge that is 'true for everyone' and therein lies its merit; however, this merit is always discussed in contrast to *what is subjective*. For the most part, the main concern for science is to locate, gather and collect knowledge based on repeatable experimentation and, as such, can tend to be oversimplified as a *means*, apart from our so-called 'subjective' daily lives. In this sense, science can also be viewed as something foreign and *inhuman*, even though people recognize that scientific truth is more valuable or significant then their own subjective thoughts. Although our daily lives are incredibly impacted by scientific achievements across the board, our primary concerns, enjoyments, projects and plans tend to be considered non-scientific. We want to be happy, successful, to fall in love, and take care of our loved ones; although we believe that science can and will help us in these pursuits, we do not believe these projects to be scientific in and of themselves. Thus, if science is important in the 'subjective domain' it is only as a *means or tool* for other subjective projects. According to Patočka:

> Edmund Husserl's phenomenology represents a concurrent reflection about the meaning of things and about the meaning of human life. What makes Husserl's approach distinctive is that (1) it seeks to be a rigorous science and (2) it singles out such rigor not only as one instance but as the central, most important, and profound access to meaning; as such, science can claim a fundamental, crucial significance for human existence. Science ought to and can provide human lives with a 'spiritual meaning,' the content and aim of life we need in order to be truly at home, at one with ourselves, with our life, and with our world. Nor will it provide that meaning by serving as a *means* to something other, something further, but as itself in what it does, by scientific activity as such.
> (*An Introduction to Husserl's Phenomenology* 1, henceforth *IHP*)

Whereas the notion of rigour might bridge the divide of the 'objective versus subjective dichotomy' in the general or oversimplified sense of science, for Husserl, science *par excellence* is one that speaks primarily to those issues concerning human meaning. This oversimplification of science and its effects on society is the main topic of Husserl's last work *Crisis*. Therein, Husserl argues that the very idea of scientific progress is in a state of crisis indicated by a *loss of problematicity*, when people no longer really understand or know what it is that they are doing when they participate in science. Husserl states that the crisis of science:

> concerns not [just] the scientific character of the sciences but rather what [scientists], or what science in general, had meant and could mean for human existence. The exclusiveness with which the total world-view of modern man, in the second half of the nineteenth century, let itself be determined by the positive sciences and be blinded by the 'prosperity' they produced, meant an indifferent turning-away from the questions which are decisive for a genuine humanity. Merely fact-minded sciences make merely fact-minded people. [...] In our vital need – so we are told – this science has nothing to say to us. It excludes in principle precisely the questions which man [...] finds the most burning: questions of the meaning or meaninglessness of [...] human existence.
>
> (*Crisis* 5–6)

For Husserl, science is in crisis and has little or nothing to say about the very humans who undertake it. Crisis is further intensified when those who participate in it can do so without any genuine or real understanding of what it is that they are really doing. The very dividing line of the subjective versus objective dichotomy or the oversimplification of science as a means or tool is part of the crisis. Thus, not only is phenomenology a science but it furthermore expands the scope and value of science by reintegrating the so-called 'subjective domain' back into science.

The origin of Husserl's insight into science comes from a re-investigation into history. The historical origins of science come from the Greek's discovery of the intelligible world. According to Patočka:

> it was the ancient Greeks who first discovered science in the sense of a consistent sequence of reasoning, in the form of mathematical theory [...] the Greeks, though, were not only the first to discover the format of systematic deductive inquiry. They were also the first who did not take the world for granted.
>
> (*IHP* 2)

What does Patočka mean by the phrase 'they did not taking the world for granted'? Recall that the prehistorical world is characterized by sheltered life for Patočka, wherein society and religion protect the individual from facing their own finitude by overwhelming them with situational meaning where every question is already answered. This shelter takes shape in social, political and cultural organizations of meaning which provide a place for every individual and in so doing provide them with an absolute meaning for their life. Thus, where Patočka states that the Greeks were the first 'who did not take the world for granted' we can understand this through the structure of a question: Provided already with the answer as to what the world was already (various religious, mythical, societal, political, etc., formations), the Greeks nonetheless returned to the world and questioned it anew and these questions revitalized the world's possibility to reveal and re-reveal itself anew.[11]

The Greeks discovered something quite interesting and powerful from their renewed questioning and consideration that something could be known regarding the world. Patočka states that 'the Greeks are the first who ask explicitly about the whole which embraces all, ourselves included, and therewith confront the simple wonder of all wonders: that all of this *is* and that the being of that totality is not something obvious like the particulars of life' (IHP 2–3). Furthermore, for Husserl, the Greeks discovered or developed a method that enabled them to access this whole: *ideality*. Husserl states that:

> science has its origin in Greek philosophy with the discovery of the idea and of the exact science which determines by means of ideas. It leads to the development of pure mathematics as pure science of ideas, science of possible objects in general as objects determined by ideas.
>
> (*Idealization and the Sciences of Reality* 301; appendix II from the *Crisis*)

By accessing or inquiring into the world using ideas, by considering an ideal notion first and then examining the way the world 'works itself out' in comparison to it, the Greeks had discovered science but first formed as philosophy characterized by wisdom and wonder before it was filled with facts and systems.

Thus, the path of science is one that runs alongside the path of wonder rather than against it. Indeed philosophy and science both begin with *wonder*; in Greek *thauma*. On this matter, Patočka states:

> our relation to this wonder can be compared only to those relations in which we pass from an accustomed stance into a different mode of life, to the transition from a dream, to the discovery that all had been otherwise, to suspicious suddenly aroused by something we had long passed unconcerned: it is a strangeness, a wonder, an awe, it is *thauma, thaumazein*, from which, according to Plato, wisdom is born. It is worth noting that Aristotle cites as an instance of such an awe-evoking situation the mathematical example that the hypotenuse is incommensurate with the side of a square.
>
> (*IHP* 3)

The proto-scientist as philosopher was originally viewed as a kind of traveling magician, a thaumaturge, who could perform miracles. To examine the term in a more philosophical way, a thaumaturge was someone who could evoke wonder in those willing to listen. Here the notion of 'magic' is not a parlour trick or something of a supernatural kind, but one found in the ability to re-reveal reality in some new way, to enable one to see something ordinary or familiar in an extraordinary or unfamiliar way: the thaumaturge is a 're-revealer'. Patočka states that 'the mysteriousness of the ordinary and the familiar [change for us] so that we could almost say that the more commonplace something is, the more mysterious it is, the more ever before us, constantly manifesting itself, the more dark and impenetrable' (*IHP* 3–4). Here we can see the roots of phenomenology uncovered alongside the roots of philosophy. The very recognition of wonder and mystery is the beginning of the activity of questioning. To wonder about ourselves, our place in the world around us, its meaning and so on is to question. In some cases, these questions are answered rather quickly, but in other areas we find objects, ideas and meanings that seem to spur questioning onward. The more we find that something resists our ability to explain, the more interesting, that is mysterious it becomes. We return to the 'mysterious character' of the world that phenomenology is interested in and see that it does not lie in the fantastical or cosmic, but rather in the mundane, the ordinary, the familiar, *the things themselves*.[12]

§32. Chapter conclusion: The method of Patočka's heretical phenomenology

It is in this sense that the method of phenomenology takes on an interesting clarity as a means by which we view and re-review the appearance of things and the world around us. Phenomenology as a method is, therefore, clearly distinct from the descriptions, discoveries and the phenomena it investigates. Patočka states:

> phenomenology will not consider as its highest goal the transformation into principles, reasons, causes, its ideal will not be an explanation subordinated to the principle of sufficient reason, but rather a comprehension of the thing, that is, of all that has to do with meaning, in the structured richness of its nature and substance. Furthermore, phenomenology will not be a philosophy of the older, argumentative type, focusing on the analysis of internal contradictions and the intricacies of systems and seeking to formulate abstract solutions, it will

seek, rather, to resolve philosophical problems on experiential grounds, *seeing the things themselves*, moving from abstract schemata to the fullness and depth of the sphere of life.

(*IHP* 16)

Is this definition of phenomenology compatible with Husserl's various definitions or developments? If Patočka's definition is considered to be incompatible with any of Husserl's definitions (as specifically described in any one of Husserl's texts) it certainly remains compatible or at least accurately reflects the echo of Husserl's *practice of phenomenology* by returning to the matters themselves again and again.

Now that the development of phenomenology from Husserl, to Heidegger, to Patočka has been traced, the hidden activity of a *questioning philosophy* should likewise be somewhat apparent. Phenomenology as a *questioning philosophy* comprises the central issues, problems and indeed the very questions that drive the individual traditions of any specific thinker whatsoever. Likewise, woven into this tradition of Husserl, Heidegger and Patočka, we can observe how a special use of questions or the activity of questioning remains consistent throughout.

Although Patočka's notion of heresy is usually explored in a historical sense, I have striven to show how heresy leads the beginner phenomenologist back to, and keeps the work and thought of, Husserl and Heidegger in hindsight when used as a *leitmotif* to clarify his phenomenological method. In this sense, phenomenology does not promote dogmatic adherents but participants; instead, the very activity, which includes heresy, is understood as a questioning back that neither takes anything for granted nor on authority. As a participant in phenomenology, one is required to *question everything* so that everything they accept they can also see for themselves. In so doing, the phenomenologist fulfils the vocation of an 'eternal beginner' and likewise avoids any metaphysical theses that cannot be correlated to direct experience.

This task of the heretical method is specifically accomplished when one collects and preserves phenomenology's central questions alongside their various answers. Generally, this is visible in phenomenology as such, in that Husserl's motto (to the things themselves) precedes his methods (psychologism, descriptive phenomenology, transcendental phenomenology, etc.), but in more specific examples too. For instance, it is also visible in the question 'what is the phenomenon?' to which Husserl's incompatible answers contest with Heidegger's. The heretical phenomenologist is tasked with keeping this question in mind even as they explore and come to understand the differences between the answers provided by Husserl and Heidegger. In keeping phenomenology's central questions preserved, one way to view the historical development of phenomenology comes into view alongside the already valued way to view it in terms of its difference (as a collection of answers). Furthermore, Patočka's phenomenology can be viewed in a way that moves beyond, as well as being a development of, Husserl and Heidegger's phenomenology. However, this development is not just a progression of *total progress*, but rather involves a kind of questioning philosophy that maintains and preserves its own questions; the path leading back to the original source is likewise kept in view and is thus *heretical*.

This heretical method is also visible within Patočka's philosophy of history. The *prehistorical* connotes a sheltered life in which absolute meaning provides an answer to every question. In contrast to this, the *historical* connotes an unsheltered life in which questions remain in order to shake and to daunt a thinker to venture to places in which truth does not fully resolve or make peace with thinking, but instead spurns thinking into problematicity, into potentially terrifying and/or unaccountable places. No one knows where a question will lead until they genuinely ask it and even after that, they are always able to ask it anew and in so doing can begin another thoughtful adventure into the unknown. Whereas prehistorical institutions of knowledge require a dogmatic adherence, historical ones require heretical participants: those who participate by raising and maintaining questions alongside deriving and developing excellent answers; however, these answers are never taken over from authority, but are instead retrieved through the individual effort to see for oneself. A heretical thinker is, therefore, one who maintains their thinking in a state of undaunted and unsheltered questioning, that continues to return to the questions themselves in search for truth and values the *questioning pursuit of truth* as much as the truth they may or may not always find in answers.

In a fascinating sense, this heretical method is not really something that Patočka invents, but it is something peculiar to phenomenology. Heretical thinking is revealed to be a follow-through on Husserl's philosophical activity, his motto and the practice of returning to question experience in order to revise his hitherto collected and derived answers. The individualism and preservation of a question in heretical thinking are revealed to be a follow-through on Heidegger's value for resoluteness and the activity of questioning as a means to allow for phenomena to reveal themselves from themselves *via* wonder.

To return to the provisional definition of Patočka's heresy, we can confirm its three aspects in greater detail. (1) Heresy is a clear and willing choice to preserve questions alongside their answers; (2) heresy is a mode of thinking that secures what it criticizes by throwing the thinker back upon the origins of that of which it is being critical; and (3) in its securing and preserving of what it criticizes, heresy aims to edify what it criticizes by keeping it in hindsight (as opposed to the mode of progress that aims to jettison what it finds faulty). Adding to the model of answers, that knowledge must compete for the highest position of truth, the model of questions reveals a way to maintain an additional kind of receptivity to appearance in both experience and in thought *via the activity of questioning*.

5

The logos of questioning

§33. Chapter introduction

Thus far, this text has attempted to trace the power of questioning to elicit originary experiences of the things themselves as they emerge through the historical development of phenomenology (Husserl-Heidegger-Patočka). This power of questioning has emerged in a trajectory that appeared in the following order: firstly, in the practice of Husserl's motto to perpetually return to question the things themselves; secondly, in how this activity is particularity made into a theme in Heidegger's reinterpretation of phenomenology as a possibility; and thirdly, in how this activity is further reinterpreted into Patočka's idea of heresy (maintaining a question even after it has been answered rather well). The application and value of questioning remain a central driving force in all of these examples and as something clearly *exhibited* throughout each philosopher's work and thought, but mostly as an implicit practice that is not always explicitly clarified.

Recall that in Heidegger's interpretation of phenomenology, a mere appearance [*bloße Erscheinung*] can be developed into an appearance [*Erscheinung*] and eventually into a phenomenon proper, as an underlying fluctuation that stabilizes itself into various appearances. Bearing this in mind, we may now apply Heidegger's approach to the thesis of this text: now that the activity of questioning has been brought forth in a review of its historical development of phenomenology in accordance with Husserl's motto, Heidegger's possibility and Patočka's heresy, we have brought into view the vague appearance of the activity of questioning. However, although we have successfully identified the activity of questioning in this way, it has emerged as something imbedded in the *practice* of phenomenology. As such, this chapter aims to further draw out and to clarify the activity of questioning on its own by distinguishing it from the practice of phenomenology. This will ultimately be done in order for us to see just how essential questioning is to phenomenology. In this sense, I am aiming to follow Heidegger's lead in trying to show the logos of questioning, that is, what this activity itself brings into view on its own through a self-showing.

In order to perform a phenomenological analysis of the activity of questioning, in §34, I further explain that what remains most valuable about philosophy is found in its call to genuine questioning, in addition to the already-valued, powerful and excellent answers that result from such questioning. With the activity of questioning freed up for direct analysis, in §35, I then conduct a topographical description of regular questioning and argue that it appears to a thinker through enclosed systems, like problem-solving, and correlates with an experience of curiosity. In §36, I argue that philosophical questioning appears to a thinker as a means to move beyond enclosed systems and is something that correlates with an experience of wonder (*thaumasein*). In §37, the underlying essence of regular and philosophical questioning will be accounted for *via* their experience of stability and instability respectively. In §38, the flux of questioning's ability to stabilize and to destabilize will be further developed. I then conclude, in §39, by considering how the activity of questioning may be further clarified as a mode of thinking characterized by possibility.

If there is one thing that Husserl and Heidegger have shown it is that what is *phenomenologically closest* to a thinker is usually also *theoretically furthest*. The challenge of clarifying the activity questioning is that it seems to disappear within the ease of its use. It is due to the fact that the activity of questioning comes so easily to thinking that keeps it, as an activity in its own right, from becoming an object of investigation. Now that an overview of what phenomenology means for Husserl, Heidegger and Patočka has brought the phenomenon of questioning, into view we are in a position to consider it directly.

§34. Philosophy as a call to genuine questioning

In his work *Basic Questions of Philosophy: Selected 'Problems' of 'Logic'* (henceforth *BQP*), Heidegger uses the introduction to philosophy as a way to show the value of questioning in distinction to that of answering. According to Heidegger, philosophy begins with a call to genuine questioning. He says that 'it is only [through] the very asking of the basic questions that first determines what philosophy is' (*BQP* 3). Rather than beginning with definitions, concepts or rules for what philosophy is, Heidegger suggests that a beginner participate in philosophy by raising basic questions. However, a call to questioning is not enough, it must also be *genuine*. Heidegger states that genuine questioning only occurs when 'we invest everything – everything without exception – in this questioning and do not merely act as if we were questioning while still believing we possess our reputed truth' (BQP 3). Such an appeal is far from a predefined starting place but, instead, sounds more like an attitude of genuineness that can be employed in any act of questioning. However, as is already visible, this 'genuine questioning that invests everything' appears to be quite fragile and flimsy in that it can never guarantee a result. It also seems to be rather 'weak' when judged by the rubric of stability in that it does not lend itself to a strict system, method or stable structure. Whatever genuine questioning is, it is not something that can be blundered into; instead, it is 'organic' in that it must be coddled, nurtured and drawn out of oneself by oneself. Once it emerges within someone, the process of 'getting good at questioning' seems to entail more *finesse* than it does a technical mastery.

A genuine attitude for questioning equates an attitude of open receptivity for what may or may not appear through such questioning, as well as a commitment to follow-through concerning 'wherever' such questioning may or may not lead. In other words, genuine questioning is always a risk that does not know in advance whether or not it will yield anything at all (let alone, anything of value). This reveals that a kind of patience is required for genuine questioning, one that is more of an exploration of mere possibilities that occur prior to, and is therefore distinct from, the kind of solidification of stable truths or results. In order to even begin genuine questioning one must also resist the temptation to begin with an overtly stable point of departure, since thinking through possibilities comes prior to thinking through actualities. Heidegger confirms this by stating that 'the task of this brief preliminary interpretation of the essence of philosophy will simply be to attune our questioning attitude to the right basic disposition or, to put it more prudently, to allow this basic disposition a first resonance' (BQP 3). The 'basic disposition' is clearly not so much a specific approach that we need to first understand in order to employ, but rather is the other way around: we need to start fumbling through the real experience of philosophical questioning until this basic disposition begins to resonate for us. In other words, it sounds like this basic disposition is already possessed by a thinker and, like Meno's slave, instead of being told *what* to do specifically, the beginner questioner must instead make attempts at drawing it out of oneself by *doing*. As a kind of thinking requiring finesse, similar to learning a dance technique, 'right questioning' requires participation, repetition and practice in order to master and, as such, it will always take a lot of time and effort of doing it 'wrong' in order to eventually get it 'right'. This is not to say that there are no techniques in questioning; to participate in the project of phenomenology is something that certainly, as we have already explored, requires many techniques, distinctions, clarifications and so on.

Whereas Heidegger makes efforts to bring about an initial resonance in questioning, Husserl attempts to lead the thinker back to the original moments of instability that always lie prior to any stabilization. Husserl's *LI* represents the attempts to return a thinker to the sources of logic.[1] In later lectures given in 1925, which have been published as *Phenomenological Psychology*, Husserl confirms this by describing what he was originally attempting to accomplish in *LI*. He states:

> In 1900–01 my *Logical Investigations* appeared as the result of ten year long efforts for a clarification (*Klärung*) of the pure idea of logic by a return to the bestowing of sense (*Sinngebung*) or the performance of cognition (*Erkenntnisleistung*) which occurs in the nexus of lived experience of logical thinking [... that] involved a turning of intuition back towards the logical lived experience which takes place in us whenever we think but which we do not see just then, which we do not have in our noticing view whenever we carry out thought activity in a naturally original manner [...]. [These efforts are] to make intelligible how the forming of all those mentally produced formations take place in the performance of this internal logical lived experiencing, formations which appear in assertively judicative thinking as multiply formed concepts, judgments, inferences, etc., and which find their generic expression, their universally objective mental stamp in the fundamental concepts and axioms of logic.
>
> (*Phenomenological Psychology* 14; Hua IX 20–1)

Here we see Husserl making a clear distinction between the concepts, judgements and inferences from the internal logical of *lived experience* from which they emerge and to which they correlate. Although Husserl clearly takes a systematic approach in his investigations and descriptions, his resulting work ought never to be taken on by the reader to be just another system of logic; rather, the *LI* aims to enable the reader to return to the original experience and therefore to the source of logic itself in order to see how what has traditionally been said about logic correlates to this source. Once secure, the very source of these stable answers may be destabilized in order to facilitate further thought. In this way, the *LI* can be used to revive the question of logic, which in turn can be used to revive the source of logical experience itself (what every stable description of logic will correlate with), but this is only one example; phenomenology as a whole represents the efforts to accomplish this very same feat to revive, by way of the activity of questioning, the original source experiences for every and all traditional answers. When we recognize just how powerful this makes phenomenology, its full scope, breadth and applicability to virtually any question, object or experience, then we too should pale in response to it as Sartre did.

From the perspective of the activity of questioning, the phenomenology of Husserl and Heidegger appears much closer together. Heidegger outlines what he calls 'the relation between question and answer in the domain of philosophy' (*BQP* 21). Heidegger states that

> these lectures are proclaiming no eternal truths. I say this to obviate misunderstandings which could easily impede our collaboration. I am not capable of such a proclamation, nor is it my task. Rather, what is at issue here is questioning, the exercise of right questioning, to be achieved in the actual performance of it.
>
> (*BQP* 21)

Two important things seem immediately relevant in the procedure of investigating precisely what 'right questioning' entails: the first is that such an investigation of questioning will require the 'actual performance' of questioning, rather than a mere conceptual analysis of questioning *per se*; the second is that Heidegger's presentation will not provide an 'answer' to this inquiry so much as he tried to lead and to prompt his students into a genuine practice of what it is trying to clarify and explore (questioning); in other words, he is attempting to lead by example. Those who wish to follow do not need to agree with Heidegger's description, but *participate* in such questioning.

This first aspect of the 'actual performance' of questioning is important because it is clearly an allusion to the fact that Husserl's motto preceded his many methods. Philosophical questioning, therefore, is a return to the *questions themselves* and, as such, is clearly not a simple taking over and memorization of traditional answers (which of course only come about *via* the original questions that prompt a thinker to think them). This suggests that it is more important to come alongside questioning for Heidegger, as a practice of participation, and to make attempts of one's own rather than to memorize a so-called 'clear grasp' of what questioning entails conceptually. In this way, Heidegger's approach to questioning is and remains very phenomenological: instead of just 'telling' his students what questioning is or examining a concept for it, he prompts them to practise questioning, to see and experience it for themselves. It is more important for the student to take up the problem in its difficulty for themselves, as it shows itself, than it is for them to give mental assent to the apparent 'solution' (whether it be genuine or not).

The second aspect of Heidegger's presentation, that he will not simply provide solutions to the problems he raises, is important because it shows that what is important is the very exploration and experience of the *problematicity* that the activity of questioning elicits. When the problematicity that a question elicits is threatened by an excellent answer, the proper response is to preserve the question. The preservation of a question to be raised again and again is the affirmation that experience itself is always more than what an answer, concept, view or perspective can capture or correlate. The 'extra' of experience is what cannot ever be fully exhausted through description, no matter how excellent the answer or concept is. In this way, genuinely grasping the *problematicity* of a problem is revealed to be altogether different than merely possessing a question and giving mental assent to its answer. The reduction of philosophy to the possession of answers is thereby avoided when the preservation of the problematicity of thinking is distinguished from the mere one-to-one relation of a problem and its solution.

The gravity of an answer has the tendency to reduce the original possibilities a question may or may not elicit. This is certainly the case when a problem is only posed rhetorically as a direct path to a pre-established answer already worked out in advance. The starting point of philosophy, according to Heidegger, is to genuinely and directly take up any of its many basic questions. The problematicity of an issue is, therefore, brought into view for a thinker when they genuinely take up a questioning position towards it; it occurs when they begin to try and see it from many perspectives, views and start to follow-through on the plethora of available ways to think and to explore the issue. Arriving at a very good answer will, therefore, in no way cover up or eclipse the original path of problematicity that leads to it. In the grand scheme of thinking, excellent answers are revealed to be a rather small part of the whole experience of questioning and answering.

The caution Heidegger displays towards the gravity of answers is a clear development of how his own philosophy is indebted to Husserl's. Heidegger states that his investigation will seem 'to be little enough for one who is pressing on to the possession of answers' (*BQP* 21). There will be answers to consider, but they must be treated with caution, lest they become idols and eclipse the original questions that source them. It is important that a beginner philosopher be confounded and even confused by a question prior to exploring the answers found in the tradition; otherwise, the real philosophical thinking that a genuine question provides may be bypassed entirely for the acquisition of a simple set of questions and their neatly corresponding answers. Here we can see a very clear distinction between experiencing the *exploratory thinking* involved in genuine philosophical questioning and the *mere memorization* of a question and its traditional answers. Again, Heidegger shows a serious *phenomenological* concern for the genuine experience of questioning alongside the traditional collection and verification of answers. It is more important that one really experience the genuine wonder of a question prior to the potential satisfaction of resolution that answers provide.

In philosophy, the activity and structure of a question and an answer are revealed to never be guaranteed and, as such, always include a risk. Heidegger states that

> in philosophy the relation of question and answer is quite peculiar. To speak metaphorically, it is like climbing a mountain. We will get nowhere by positioning ourselves on the plane of ordinary opinion and merely talking about the mountain, in order to gain in that way a 'lived experience' of it. No, the climbing and the approach to the peak succeed only if we begin to mount. The peak might indeed be lost from view as we climb, and yet we keep coming closer to it.
>
> (BQP 21)

Here we see Heidegger reference Husserl in, perhaps, both a critical and reverential way. I take Heidegger's criticism of 'ordinary opinion' and 'merely talking *about*' to be a rejection of a merely conceptual point of departure, wherein one would first theoretically decide what a question and answer mean prior to actually participating in the activity. This might sound like a criticism of Husserl, who spent much of his work on conceptual development and clarification; however, Husserl's penchant for revision is evidence of his perpetual re-questioning of whatever concept he was working on (in fact, Husserl seems to have done this more than Heidegger!).[2] Heidegger's comment can also be interpreted to be reverential to Husserl in that the whole point and project of phenomenology are to seek out and recollect the living experiences that correlate with phenomenology's many *concepts, definitions, systems,* etc. This is precisely what Heidegger is advocating: students of philosophy ought not to simply conceptualize questioning but, *alongside* these attempts, should also make great efforts in practising questioning.

Following Husserl's motto, what remains important for Heidegger in philosophy is the return to the activity of questioning itself in order to genuinely experience it, that is, to practise questioning for oneself. These experiences of how phenomena appear and re-appear when repeatedly questioned are used to correlate to the concepts, descriptions and structures ascribed thereto. Any new students or other phenomenologists who desire to understand the newly minted concepts, descriptions and structures may, as good phenomenologists, return to experience *via* questioning and see for themselves.

It is also interesting that in Heidegger's climbing metaphor the peak is lost from view once one is genuinely climbing. I take this to be a direct criticism of overvaluing conceptual clarity over the 'rough and tumble' messy work of genuine thinking. A thinker who does not take a chance to commit herself to her original pursuit, but instead avoids danger by jumping into an already 'worked out' answer, is simply one who never really engages with genuine thinking. Thinking that begins and persists to remain within the auspicious value of answers thereby irrevocably and unnecessarily limits its own possibility for discovery because it has delimited what may or may not appear in advance of actually searching. For Heidegger, the value of philosophical work comes from the experience of doing it rather than its results. He states that

> climbing includes slipping and sliding back and, in philosophy, even falling. Only one who is truly climbing can fall down. What if those who fall down experience the peak, the mountain, and its *height* most profoundly, more profoundly and more uniquely than the ones who apparently reach the top, which for them soon loses its height and becomes a plane and something habitual?
>
> (BQP 21)

Here we can see that what seems to be intended by the metaphor is that the genuine work and *journey of questioning towards* an answer are to be valued just as much, or perhaps valued more than, the answer to which it may or may not lead. According to Heidegger, a philosopher is someone who should not be judged based on her ability to hold, understand and memorize every correct answer, but rather ought to be judged on the basis of her *questioning pursuit*. The criteria for philosophy would, therefore, be the *experience of thinking* as opposed to the possession of proper content (truth or knowledge). However, for those quick to agree with Heidegger, he furthermore stipulates that

> it is not possible to judge and measure either philosophy, or art, or in general, any creative dealing with beings, with the aid of the facile bureaucracy of sound common sense and a presumably healthy 'instinct' (already distorted and misled long ago), no more than with the empty sagacity of a so-called intellectual. Here the whole and every single thing within [the mountain] can be experienced only in the actual performance of the painful work of climbing.
>
> (BQP 22)

The phrase 'painful work of climbing' brings to mind the many places in which Husserl describes the difficulty of learning and doing phenomenology (*Ideas I*

172–3; 193; 301; *Inaugural Lecture* 132; etc.). In a similar way that Patočka preserves the question of history by likewise keeping it open for further thought (*HE* 25; 118), Heidegger warns us against taking up a new idol in place of the one that we just cast aside. Heidegger states that in the attempt to genuinely take up a question 'anyone here who is only snatching up isolated propositions is not climbing along with me' (*BQP* 22). However, at this point one wonders if perhaps Heidegger falls a little too far on the side of questioning over and against answering.

The effort to show the power of questioning in contradistinction to our already traditional value for answering can potentially recreate the same problem on the other side of the issue: the overvaluing of questioning merely replaces the overvaluing of answers. There are certainly historical moments in philosophy wherein an overvaluing of questioning can begin to undermine philosophy; we must be careful not to merely replace one problem with another.[3]

Despite Heidegger's overt value for questioning over answers, when it comes to the question of just what philosophy is and what it is not, he emphatically and perhaps ironically changes his position from a state of his characteristic openness and instead gives a near manifesto as to what philosophy is *not* stating that

> philosophy is completely different from 'world-view' and is fundamentally distinct from all 'science'. Philosophy cannot by itself replace either world-view or science; nor can it ever be appreciated by them. […] If we attempt to calculate whether philosophy has any immediate use and what that use might be, we will find that philosophy accomplishes nothing. […] Philosophy is overestimated if one expects its thinking to have an immediately useful effect. […] Yet genuine philosophical knowledge is never the mere addition of the most general representations, limping behind a being already known anyway. Philosophy is rather the reverse, a knowledge that leaps ahead, opening up new domains of questioning and aspects of questioning about the essence of things, an essence that constantly conceals itself anew. That is precisely the reason this knowledge can never be made useful.
>
> (*BQP* 4–5)

On the one hand, Heidegger purports to keep the very idea and value of philosophy in question while also giving a detailed description of what it is not. It seems that what is valuable about philosophy amounts to something slippery and easily concealed. It is very easy to assume that philosophy is just a means to develop a picture or view of the world, that it is some kind of prototype or handmaiden to the sciences, that if we just take a good hard look at it, then we will be able to narrow it down to some kind of calculus, and that in so doing would make it into something powerful or useful. Even if philosophy fails in all of these categories, it will then *at least* be a collection of concepts, systems and representations of what is already familiar or, in reverse, be a means by which we can conceptualize, systemize and represent what is unfamiliar, thereby making it into something familiar. Unfortunately, the work of the philosopher today has been reduced to concept invention, clarification and play. In contrast to defining philosophy in these answer-focused ways, Heidegger considers philosophy to be something pre-conceptual, pre-theoretical and pre-scientific.

For Heidegger, that value and power of philosophy is found prior to the acquisition, security and stabilization of an answer. Philosophy is a means for thinking, to leap ahead of knowledge, to open up new domains of questioning; this energizes thought to destabilize what has hitherto been taken to be impervious, unchangeable, etc. Heidegger states that if 'philosophical reflection has an effect [… it is] always only mediately, by making available new aspects for all comportment and new principles for all decisions. But philosophy has this power only when it risks what is most proper to it, namely to posit in a thoughtful way for the existence of man' (*BQP* 5). As a genuine risk of thinking, philosophy cannot guarantee anything in advance of its real implementation. If we say that philosophy is the pursuit of wisdom alongside its already-valued object of wisdom, then we add to this already-valued object the sometimes-overlooked difficult pursuit thereof.

The basic questions of philosophy are, therefore, unique in that their *very asking* after the wonder they elicit can become self-reflexive. The dynamism utilized and applied through the activity of questioning may, therefore, reflexively work back upon the question itself. What follows is an investigation of how questioning appears in an everyday context and develops into a more familiar and powerful form in philosophy.

§35. Regular questioning correlates with an experience of curiosity

What happens when we question? Most of our experience with the activity of questioning takes the shape of inquiring for information into the common structures of *who, what, where, when* and *how*? This kind of regular questioning is one done against a backdrop structure and context that has already been stabilized, systematic and fully worked out in advance. In such questioning, the things we inquire about or seek are already fully stabilized in that they are *already* there, *already* worked out and/or are simply waiting to be indicated. For example, when registering for university, these five questions may be formulated in the following ways: 'who is the registrar?'; 'what documents do I need to bring in order to register?'; 'where is the student registration building located?'; 'when can students schedule appointments with the registrar?'; and 'how do I get to the registrar's building?' Interestingly, in each of these cases the question is posed against the backdrop that assumes an answer is already available and, as such, questioning is just a means of gathering or identifying already-stabilized information. In this sense, the context in which such regular questioning begins and ends is narrow, focused and fully stabilized.

What makes this common way of questioning 'regular' is that it occurs within a medium that is structured, fixed and systematic. The fixity means the inquiry of the question can only amount to a kind of *problem solving*, in which nothing novel is being created and nothing is discarded. The thinking employed in regular questioning is fully secure and self-contained in a system. There is a free motion of thinking within the limits of this stabilized structure however, as the potentiality of regular questioning is fixed in advance, its employment will likewise be limited to some kind of calculation, as a re-arrangement of already-fixed bits of information. In other words, regular questioning amounts to playing a thought-game within an enclosed context.

Regular questioning correlates with our genuine experience of curiosity, given that it appears in a stable and systematic way, enabling one to secure information or to problem-solve. Here, curiosity is defined through the recognition of an overarching system wherein a question amounts to a function. For example, consider a jigsaw puzzle that we know remains within the limits of the following parameters: the number of puzzle pieces is fixed, there will be four corner pieces, the pieces that form the outside will have a flat edge on their exterior side, the picture on the box will match the finished puzzle, and that every piece has a proper place indicated by the fact that it will fit perfectly with its surrounding pieces. In this sense, solving a jigsaw puzzle (depending upon its difficulty) will only require the basic computational trial and error of asking 'how does one piece go with another piece?' When we ask this question, we do so through an already-enclosed system that takes the singular piece to be one that fits within a larger and already-worked-out system (the larger puzzle). In the context of trying to solve a jigsaw puzzle, questioning only amounts to a function within an enclosed system. However, something interesting occurs when one discovers that a particular piece does not belong in the puzzle.

When a question is posed within an already-worked-out system or structure, raising it seems to be likewise limited to that structure. In this context of stability, raising a question is reducible to a one-to-one relation, that is, to calculation. What it means to *question* is therefore restricted to a fixed system of input and output in this framework and in light of that system's function. Like an abacus, calculator or computer, it is the stability of the structure and the systematicity that enables computation to occur in the first place. When a system, inputs or the functions between them become unstable, then the entire process fails to work properly. Interestingly, when this failure to compute occurs in computers or calculators, the result is a notification of 'does not compute' or 'error' whereas in thinking the result is confusion and perplexity.

When we think in a mode of regular questioning, the various possibilities that we entertain and utilize are quarantined from becoming *unstable*. The designs, rules and structures that we utilize in regular questioning remain separate from the possibility of thinking that we employ to flow through them or to 'play' with them. At no point in such regular questioning do these rules or structures destabilize themselves; rather, they are kept fixed so that the original intent of the regular question can be successfully accomplished. In the case of the above example, the original intent is to find and to secure (prefigured) information: the name of the registrar, the documents required, the address of the building, the times at which we can show up, the specific directions that will lead us exactly to the registrar's building, etc. In other words, the kind of questioning that 'threatens' to destabilize the very structure of these things is kept at bay. For example, the question 'where is the student registration building located?' importantly *does not include* the philosophical questioning of just what constitutes a 'building' in the first place. On the contrary, regular questioning requires all of its structures to remain fixed in order for it to be used to problem-solve. What happens, then, when one of these structures loses its fixity?

§36. Philosophical questioning correlates with an experience of wonder (*thaumasein*)

In addition to our regular inquiries for information, we can also question in a more philosophical way wherein we wonder about more meaningful issues (with greater depth, importance or significance). Whereas regular questioning appeared to deal primarily in a stable medium that keeps instability at bay (e.g. puzzle solving), philosophical questioning embraces and elicits instability. This can be observed in at least two ways: philosophical questions remain valuable for further thought even after excellent answers have been uncovered for them and, in so doing, these answers to philosophical questions can spur thinking onward, rather than resolving thinking completely.

Perhaps one of the most basic questions that move us into wonderment is the question 'who am I?' This question has been chosen for a specific phenomenon of philosophical questioning as it is an unavoidable experience to wonder about oneself, to wrestle with one's identity, and to imagine and postulate who one might become in identity, vocation and character. In addition to being unavoidable, this question is also unique in that even after one finds an incredibly excellent answer for it (or potentially the *best* answer for it) the question itself remains inexhaustible; that is to say, it remains a worthwhile question to ask and answer anew, no matter how well it has been hitherto *addressed* and *resolved*. Apart from some potentially pathological states of mind, the question 'who am I?' seems for the most part to remain inexhaustible in an *edifying* way.

Even at an early age, we encounter the question 'who am I?' in a regular way and answer it accordingly with our name, our age, our gender, our address, our position in our family, our relation to our friends and in other static ways. Although some of these factors change over time (e.g. our age or address), we nonetheless use them to ground and orientate ourselves in the world. As we grow up, we begin to discover interesting things about our classmates such as 'they have parents just like we do', 'they do not have siblings in the same way as we do' and 'they have different ideas they hold just as strongly as we ourselves do'. These discoveries usually lead one back to the question 'who am I?', but now in a different sense. The already-worked-out answers (our name, age, etc.) available for this question remain valuable and to hand, but now the question shifts to a more philosophical mode: 'do I have value?', 'how important am I?', 'what am I capable of?' and 'what ought I to do with my life?' In this sense our question 'who am I?' takes on a deeper and more significant search for meaning that our already-possessed static answers fail to resolve.

As a child grows up and receives educational training, they may answer the question 'who am I?' with an identity of 'I am capable' (of reading, of being creative, of thinking critically, etc.). Interestingly, this answer does not resolve the question so much as it spurs it on: now that the questioner identifies itself as *being capable of* ..., the original question 'who am I?' is further opened to new and additional potentialities that are now made possible *via* this answer. For example, after recognizing that they are creative, a child might wonder at the prospect of becoming an artist or at the prospect of finding themselves athletic, may wonder about the prospect of playing sports professionally. Importantly, instead of resolving the question of who they are in a static way, these answers instead propel the child into greater and greater action in response to the dynamism and wonder of who they may become. This exemplifies how philosophical questions may remain worthy of asking *because* of an answer posed for it, rather than being resolved once and for all.

As a child grows into a young adult and continues to receive education, their thinking may again and again return to the question 'who am I?' and in so doing may continue to elicit wonder. In addition to the more proto-philosophical questions such as 'who am I?' and 'what am I capable of?' a student may eventually encounter the more celebrated and traditionally established questions of philosophy: 'what is the meaning of life?', 'how shall I live?', 'what does it mean to exist?', 'what can I know?', etc. The wonder elicited by these classic questions prompts one's thinking to explore not only the potentiality of thinking itself, but also the great wealth of powerful answers that have already been derived for them by the tradition of philosophy. However, this wonder is not impervious. When a student of philosophy comes to understand one of the tradition's excellent answers, the wonder elicited by questions can and may be entirely resolved and, therefore, be lost in a pejorative sense. For example, after coming to understand how Aristotle answers the question 'what is being?' or how Descartes answers the question 'what is consciousness?', a student can find that the original wonder initially elicited by these questions is entirely lost in its resolution by such excellent answers. It can happen that after one fully grasps the power of an excellent answer, the original question that sourced it is reduced to a rhetorical construction: when raised, the question merely points to the already-worked-out answer.

No matter how excellent and powerful Aristotle's answers may be, we find in Heidegger a renewed way to raise the question of being and likewise for Descartes great accomplishments we have Husserl's renewal of the question of consciousness. Importantly, the wonder of philosophical questions that persists after already coming to understand these powerful answers is not placed in opposition to those answers. After coming to an understanding of Husserl and Heidegger's contributions, students do not then discard their understanding of Aristotle, or worse still, suggest that new students merely skip straight to Husserl and Heidegger. Quite the contrary, much of the more advanced philosophy is best taught only after students have already explored the old masters. In this sense, due to the wonder of philosophical questions, the progress is one defined by a holistic accumulation over time, rather than a series of updates that reject their predecessors. Just as Patočka, in his efforts to raise the question of phenomenology, always keeps the work and thought of Husserl and Heidegger in hindsight, so too can we view every question alongside its powerful answers but held at bay. We complete the circle when we recognize the value in applying the same questioning to even Husserl, Heidegger and Patočka and recognize this as a way to participate in philosophy as such.

It is observable in these phenomenological descriptions of curiosity in regular questioning and of wonder in philosophical questioning that the activity of questioning itself emerges on a horizon of stability and instability. The essence of regular questioning seems to be an experience of stability, both as a means by which we can collect and utilize information and as a means by which we can stabilize meaning. The essence of philosophical questioning seems to involve an experience of instability, as a means by which we can both explore meaning in a dynamic way and destabilize meaning. These issues of stability and instability therefore require a closer examination.

§37. The stability and instability of questioning

The very structure of a question revolves around a narrowing or broadening of the 'level' of possibility it is permitted to elicit in its asking. On its own, a question elicits possibility and, depending upon what a thinker aims for a question to do, this power of possibility is modifiable. In a regular question, the destabilization activated by a question is structurally limited to the domain in which it is directed. In other words, we only have a regular question when its larger context can be fully stabilized, thereby making it into a function. In contrast to this structure and limitation in a philosophical question, everything may be destabilized for the sake of further thinking. The initial difference between a regular and philosophical question is signified by its modification to allow or disallow the level of possibility it brings forth and engages (or in other words, the possibility it opens or closes itself off to). A regular question has its possibility *limited* in order to keep what it searches for confined to its relevant field of inquest. When a question's elicited possibility is left unchecked, then any intended goal of finding something becomes untenable. The process of any investigation is, therefore, a practice of trying to modify and balance the optimal amount of elicited possibility a question provides with its originally intended goal and this involves an exchange of instability and stability. In this sense the more philosophical a question becomes, the less useful it becomes.

A philosophical question is an unwieldy and potent thing. It is this *potential to destabilize* that the activity of questioning in a philosophical sense proves to be incredibly powerful, even to the point of undermining the search for answers. Sometimes an answer is missed due to a question's scope being too limited; at other times it is missed when it is too broad. A philosophical question is rather peculiar in that the destabilization activated thereby may be applied to everything and anything, even the *very question employed*. The adventure of thinking in questions, of what is opened up for thinking by a *genuine question* is reminiscent of Bilbo's excellent line in J.R.R. Tolkien's *Lord of the Rings*: 'It's a dangerous business, Frodo, going out your door [...] You step onto the Road, and if you don't keep your feet, there's no knowing where you might be swept off to' (Tolkien 83). At the heart of every question is a *quest*. Some quests know specifically what they are after and find just that, whereas others can change dramatically in the middle or unintentionally uncover things that were never being sought for. This means that the journey an inquiry elicits is one of exploration.

In a more austere example, we can think of Kant's introduction, section III of the *CPR* entitled 'Philosophy *needs* a science that *determines* the *possibility*, the principles, and the *domain* of all cognitions *a priori*' (*CPR* Introduction <B>, A3B7, my emphasis). Why does philosophical thinking require such determinations? What is Kant protecting philosophical thinking from, exactly? The answer seems to be the power of a question to destabilize. The power of a genuine question to destabilize seems opposed to a project of truth; if not kept in check, questioning can become endless, lead into error and may even destabilize the very enterprise of thinking employed by a question. The power to destabilize can undermine the entire project of philosophy (depending upon how one defines that project). For Kant, the problem of metaphysics is one domain in which philosophical questioning and answering have spun out of control. Kant's celebrated and often-quoted passage speaks of the 'drug-like' and 'self-destructive' effect that the power destabilization employed in free thinking and questioning possesses and remarks that

> the charm in expanding one's cognitions is so great that one can be stopped in one's progress only by bumping into a clear contradiction. This, however, one can avoid if one makes his inventions carefully [...]. The light dove, in free flight cutting through the air the resistance of which it feels, could get the idea that it could do even better in airless space. Likewise, Plato abandoned the world of the senses because it set such narrow limits for the understanding, and dared to go beyond it on the wings of ideas, in the empty space of pure understanding.
>
> (*CPR* A5/B9)

Whether a question's power to destabilize is viewed to be wholly pejorative or beneficial, it is at least worthy of further consideration. However, certainly the contention *that* genuine questioning may 'destabilize too much' reveals something interesting about how the activity of questioning itself appears as *a possibility* for a thinker. Thus, even prior to figuring out specifically what questioning is or what it entails, it seems to at least initially appear as something deceptively charming and/or volatile, capable of destabilizing anything and everything. It is clear why such a power to destabilize would appear as threatening and undesirable in the historical pursuit of truth and knowledge.

Historically, philosophy begins as a collection of the most powerful destabilizing questions and later develops into different collections and sub-collections of questions. Every domain of philosophy that claims to begin with a set of propositions, however they are arrived at (self-evident, logical theorems, politically important, personal resonance, etc.), will likewise be uncovered to be correlated to a set of valued questions that *always precede them*. Whether or not these valued questions have been identified or not by the disciplines founded upon them, the ground from which one values their starting questions seems to depend upon the thinker's choice or willingness to *think* them. It seems that there is a tendency in thinking to quickly forget the questioning-path that originally leads to a celebrated answer after that answer has been uncovered.

We can see the extent to which a question applies or limits its power to destabilize also determines its potential use. The more a question is intended towards a use, the more its destabilizing power must be limited, focused or fixed. However, the more limitation that is placed upon a question's power to destabilize, the less possibility it elicits. Likewise, on the other side of the spectrum, the more one allows a question to evoke the possibility to destabilize anything and everything, the less *useful* the question becomes. There is a direct correlation between a question's potential use and the set limit of its destabilizing power. A torrent of thought usually feels multifaceted, wherein one's thinking moves effortlessly from thought to thought among the stream of consciousness in many directions at the same time, making connections like a flash of lighting through a cloud. Although the experience of philosophical questioning tends to produce very little content, *the very experience of the possibility that philosophical questioning accesses, utilizes and moves through* leaves the thinker with something that is difficult to describe. It is this general, common and everyday experience of curiosity that seeks stability and the overpowering experience of wonder to destabilize any and all ideas, which the remainder of this chapter now seeks to explore, examine and describe.

Within the activity of questioning, we find that the experience of instability proves to be very difficult to describe. As Kant has already outlined in his *CPR* (A3B7),[4] this instability can give rise to a level of potentiality in thinking that, although creative and joyful, may also lead into error and furthermore may render various philosophical projects untenable (i.e. a grounded and consistent metaphysics) if it has not been tempered properly. Kant's critique is paramount for the kind of philosophy he seeks to establish, but it also sets the standard historically and conceptually for valuing stability over and against instability. Indeed, Kant's metaphysics is a system designed to protect itself against the flux of questioning by limiting it in advance. The very idea of Kant's critique of reason is to first work out the proper amount of limited fluctuation allowed for reason, prior to raising and working out metaphysical questions. As metaphysics, it is a project of safe stabilization. In other words, Kant first stabilizes reason before allowing it to be used in a project of philosophical system building. This theme is clearly taken up by Husserl's aim to secure a means to do phenomenology in an absolute and scientific way (very much a follow-through and development of a historical concern for science of which Kant's work is a milestone).[5] These efforts to work towards a value for stability are contrasted by Heidegger's aim to show that the wonder (*thaumasein*) elicited by a question will always be prior to and distinct from the answers derived in response to it; Patočka aims to show the primacy of practice and something that is experiential but is resistant to total objectification. It seems that on the one side we have advocates for stability (Kant and Husserl), whereas on the other side we have advocates for instability (Heidegger and Patočka) and yet, in our use of questioning and answering, we find experiences of both instability and stability emerge alongside each other. Thus, instead of working to build a system or to destroy one that is already traditionally valued, phenomenology can enable us to gain a better view of stable and unstable ways of thinking.

§38. The flux of wonder and curiosity

If philosophy and science begin in response to the wonder[6] of the world around us, then it is likely that this wonder can be questioned in both a regular and a philosophical way. The disposition that genuine philosophical thinking brings upon a thinker turns out to be a powerful way to view and re-view the world around us. Heidegger states that a disposition can confine man in his corporeality as in a prison. Yet it can also carry him through corporeality as one of the paths leading out of it. In each case the world is brought to man in a different way; in each case his self is differently opened up and resolved with regard to being.

(*BQP* 134)

The disposition one holds within the activity of questioning may bring the world into wonder or may drain wonder away from it. Heidegger makes a critical comparison between wonder and curiosity and states:

> It has long been known that the Greeks recognized *thaumasein* as the 'beginning' of philosophy. But it is just as certain that we have taken this *thaumasein* to be obvious and ordinary, something that can be accomplished without difficulty and can even be clarified without further reflection. For the most part, the usual presentations of the origin of philosophy out of *thaumasein* result in the opinion that philosophy arises from curiosity.

(*BQP* 135)

The real decisive element that makes the distinction between wonder and curiosity can be traced to the idea of destabilization: curiosity is more in line with regular questioning in that it seeks to find a resolution to a framed problem, whereas philosophical questioning pursues a destabilization that may, if left unchecked, undermine the very frame it begins with and occurs in response to worldly encounters that have yet to be framed for the most part.

That philosophy begins in wonder is a sign that it begins in flux or begins with something that is itself always capable of returning to a state of flux (i.e. experience). Wonder is a response to something unfolding that strikes us in a peculiar way. The problematicity recognized through wonder reveals an element of destabilization that is potentially metastatic in that it may or may not spread to further ideas. Curiosity is a response to something already viewed in a problem-solution framework wherein either a potential solution still needs to be uncovered or the problem needs to be reformulated so that a different solution can emerge. Curiosity is the recognition that something is missing within a larger system or framework and, in this sense, reveals an *already-limited* power of destabilization. Curiosity is what drives regular questioning, wherein the possibility curiosity permits remains limited in order to resolve what has originally caused it. This is distinct from the wonder (*thaumasein*) elicited by philosophical questioning wherein the possibility it enables remains potentially unlimited and unstructured. Heidegger states that when philosophy is only understood in terms of the regular questions of curiosity, then 'we fail to realize how decisively the reference to *thaumasein* as the origin of philosophy indicates precisely the inexplicability of philosophy, inexplicability in the sense that here in general to explain and the will to explain are mistakes' (*BQP* 136). Although this might sound like an unfair critical remark about curiosity, Heidegger's point is that where curiosity seeks to explain, wonder does not. In response to what causes a question, curiosity presupposes an explanation or resolution whereas wonder (*thaumasein*) leaves a thinker 'awe-stricken'. To put it another way, curiosity seems to draw our attention 'inward', into focus, upon a missing or hitherto uncovered piece of a larger system (i.e. our response to the last few jigsaw puzzle pieces or the recognition that we have run out of pieces but still have a few holes left on the puzzle board). Distinct from this, wonder seems to draw our attention 'outward', expanding and moving in every direction at once, which seems to threaten the stability of any larger 'whole' or context, but it also leads a thinker into contemplation. Importantly, a state of wonder is one of receptivity and allowance wherein the thinker marvels at that which appears and a state of curiosity composes the will to explain, to account for and to situate what is in view.

The difference between curiosity and wonder can be understood as what remains restricted to a system: curiosity perpetually tries to apply a system to a phenomenon in the hopes of framing it. This system is intentionally designed to only permit knowledge and is continually tested, updated and re-modified with each passing curiosity in pursuit of the goal that an ultimate super-systematic explanation will be reachable in response to all passing phenomena. Within such an enterprise, even though this goal is never attained, it nonetheless determines the path of what counts as a worthy question or not nonetheless.[7] In the case of a specific science, this goal would determine whether or not any given question would count as a 'scientific question' in the first place. This is very different from a thinker who wonders, given that this *thaumasein* is not *just* the recognition that a new idea or phenomenon has yet to find a place in the ongoing systematic explanation of all things; on the contrary, *thaumasein* occurs when one experiences either something that has yet to be conceptualized (something novel) or occurs when one recognizes the failure of a concept to fully correlate to the experience to which it relates (something in development or something excessive still remains untamed, unaccounted for).

In phenomenological terms, we would aptly say that a thinker experiences *thaumasein* in response to the genuine experience of the dynamism of phenomena and, in response to these experiences, then becomes curious as to how one may or may not be able to describe, conceptualize and define exactly what occurs in experience (i.e. to make efforts to stabilize what has emerged in flux). The former occurs when we question experience, whereas the latter occurs when we seek after true answers that qualify as knowledge. Heidegger states that 'thus the known, the understandable, and the explicable here form a background not further attended to, from which the marvelous emerges and is drawn away' (BQP 137). Whereas curiosity seeks resolution, wonder seems to only be possible outside of or beyond what is curious; it is only when a genuine failure to explain something that curiosity develops into wonder.

So long as one is not reduced to the other, wonder and curiosity ought not to be viewed in opposition; they each have a different role to play in questioning. Wonder is a genuine experience of amazement in the face of what first appears as inexplicable. This experience leads to the curiosity to explain, describe and systematize what was originally encountered through wonder and thereby leads us back into wonder in our failures to fully systematize our experiences. Heidegger claims that

> amazement is a certain inability to explain and ignorance of the reason. This inability to explain, however, is not by any means equivalent to a determination and a declaration that the explanation and the reason are not available. On the contrary, the not being able to explain is first and essentially a kind of being caught up in the inexplicable, being struck by it; and upon closer inspection the amazement does precisely not want to have the marvelous explained but instead wants to be teased and fascinated by the inexplicable as what is other, surprising, and uncommon in opposition to what is commonly known, boring, and empty. Nevertheless, amazement is always a determinate and singular event, a particular occurrence, a unique circumstance, and is always set off against a dominating determinate background of what is precisely familiar and ordinary.
>
> (BQP 137)

Therefore, what is amazing and wondrous will always be viewed against the backdrop of what is explainable. What is important about wonder for Heidegger is the ease to forget it after one has made attempts to resolve it; even after a great deal of historical and traditional explanation has been attempted and found convincing, the distinction between wonder and curiosity can become blurry and difficult to discern. Heidegger's point is that the original encounter with the wondrous is never fully resolved, it can only be forgotten or worse, the forgetting is taken as a kind of permanent resolution wherein the forgetting is valued as an accomplishment rather than as a loss (such as is visible in the question of being). The reason for this is that the wondrous is part of genuine experience, whereas the resolution of curiosity will always remain an object of knowledge. It is always good to develop our knowledge further, but when our progress in obtaining knowledge begins to eclipse our ability to directly engage with experience or when we limit our ability to experience based on our already-obtained knowledge, then we have let the original intent of knowledge acquisition obfuscate the experiences that originally correlate with them. In this particular case, the overvaluing of curiosity in the light of answer acquisition can lead us to completely overlook the original questions that started the whole project of philosophy. The proper response to such a situation is a great thinker to remind us to return to experience itself and this is precisely what Husserl, Heidegger and Patočka urge their students to do.

§39. Chapter conclusion: Thinking in a mode of possibility

To question is to think in a modality characterized by possibility. The activity of questioning is revealed to be a powerful way to relate to experience in two important ways: (1) one way that affords various stable phenomena as well as various ways to stabilize phenomena and (2) one way that affords various unstable phenomena as well as various ways to destabilize phenomena. What I have shown is that alongside our ability to fashion powerful answers to any question, as a means to elicit further possibilities, questions need to be preserved even after excellent answers have been developed for them.

The activity of questioning is how a thinker attains thinking in a mode characterized by possibilities. This kind of possibility is not yet a concept, but is instead the original or genuine experience of thinking that all concepts, descriptions or definitions of possibility correlate with. The emergence of possibility, found through the activity of questioning, also seems to keep revealing itself anew in different and dynamic appearances. Each time one returns to the possibility elicited by a question, it appears in a new and different way. As such, the possibility elicited resists a merely static definition or structural description. Whatever this possibility is, it at least does not seem to be something that is static or when found to be somewhat stable, it does not remain so for very long.

The historical development of phenomenology Husserl-Heidegger-Patočka gives us some help in this situation. By examining these thinkers we have discovered that phenomenology is always composed of something static alongside something dynamic: the static is the previously stabilized list of contents (e.g. phenomenological books, descriptions, distinctions, concepts and systems) and the dynamic is the always preserved questions that lead a thinker, a seasoned veteran or a neophyte, back to the things themselves (e.g. what is phenomenology?, what is the phenomenon?, what is perception? and what is experience?). The central practice of phenomenology shows us that if we want to investigate an aspect of experience, we must always ground that investigation in a return to experience itself that, as a question, remains preserved for further thought even after excellent concepts, descriptions and definitions have been found. We have already discussed how answers stand alongside their questions when it comes to these central topics of phenomenology. For the most part, scholarship seems to value answers that exhaust their original questions. Thus, there is no need to further support the value of answers, but what is now required is to support a value for the questions that lead to such answers.

Although it is certainly rare for a question to become so exhausted that it is no longer worth asking anew, Husserl shows us that this in fact occurs in his time regarding the great questions as 'what is a number?', 'what is logic?' and 'what is science?' Husserl's greatness is found in his ability to renew these general questions *just as much as his phenomenological answers*. Heidegger shows us that it also occurs with the questions 'what is being?', 'what is truth?' and even Husserl's own work *via* the question 'what is phenomenology?' Patočka shows us that it occurs with the questions 'what is history?' Thus, the occurrence of a question becoming so well answered that a thinker finds it difficult to ask it anew is something that might not happen on the individual level alone, but also at the social, political and historical levels. In this way, then, the historical development of phenomenology Husserl-Heidegger-Patočka has not only enabled philosophy itself to revitalize its central questions: 'what is experience?', 'what is perception?' and 'what is consciousness?' it also may serve the larger domain of philosophy by showing the value of keeping questions or the activity of questioning itself preserved for further thought.

Upon closer examination, the activity of questioning is revealed to be a means to stabilize and destabilize our perception, ideas and ways to relate to and think about experience. This power has been explored by starting with our everyday experience of curiosity and then developed into the more traditional experience of wonder within philosophy. The power of thinking to stabilize itself into concepts, definitions, systems and descriptions may be understood as *thinking in a modality of actuality* (stability). The success of this mode is found in philosophy's collection of ideas, texts, concepts, thinkers, etc. As a valuable enterprise, this mode of thinking requires no further support; in fact, if anything the gravity of its success needs to be countered or tempered. As has already been shown through the development of phenomenology, overtly powerful answers tend to get in the way of their original questions more frequently that the opposite occurs. This auspicious value of static and stable answers has further threatened to eclipse an inquiry of their source altogether; had it not been for phenomenology, itself a rediscovery of the power to question, this inquiry may have fallen away into complete oblivion.

Conclusion

Academics primarily work, think and write with questions, but through the busywork of academia, it is easy to overlook the phenomenon of questioning itself. Philosophers are famous for remaining preoccupied with life's 'big' questions, those issues and problems that resist being fully resolvable, and in so doing always seem to be worthy of asking and answering again and again, no matter how much time is spent researching, writing and thinking upon them. At many moments in the history of philosophy, this 'inability to answer' a question can be considered to be pejorative or can be taken as a symptom that the entire philosophical enterprise needs to be re-implemented in a new and 'better' way.[1] However, it might in fact be a boon that certain questions resist being completely answered or remain worth asking, even after excellent and powerful answers have been found for them.

'What is being?' 'What is the meaning of life?' 'What does it mean to be good?' Questions are more than just paths of inquiry; they are also indicative of a culture, a generation and even a historical era. For a cultural example, one can consider the Canadian value for multiculturalism as an answer to the question 'what is the best Canadian way to organize a society?' What is interesting is that for many Canadians, the project of multiculturalism (as a question we are seeking to answer) is more important than whether or not we can successfully implement such an idea (i.e. to definitively answer this question).[2] For a generational example, one can consider the attribution of Bob Dylan to be the 'voice of a generation' specifically in reference to his song and album of the same name *The Times They Are a-Changin'* which not only captured the spirit of his day, but its repetitive refrain was also taken up as an anthem to answer the question 'what shall we do in response to our current political situation?'[3] Contrast this with a more recent folk singer, namely that of Elliott Smith's bleaker yet celebrated song *Ballad of Big Nothing*, a beautiful and energetic rhythm played alongside the lyrics of 'Do what you want to, whenever you want to though it doesn't mean a thing/Big nothing'. Smith perhaps epitomizes the current generational struggle with the same question as Dylan ('what shall we do in response to our current political situation?') but postulates the answer of nihilism; this is a view he perhaps confirmed by committing suicide. For a historical example, one can observe how the Pre-Socratics were generally preoccupied with answering the question 'what is the ultimate basis of all things?' postulating various answers such as water for Thales, *aperion* for Anaximander, air for Anaximenes, harmony for Pythagoras of Samos, fire for Heraclitus, the one for Parmenides and so on.[4] In each of these cases, behind the different answers, one can find a similar questioning pursuit to find the ultimate basis of all things. Thus, the origins of Western philosophy may be valued for its questioning *as well as* a repository of already-valued of answers.

Questions can define, segregate and unite people. According to Husserl, the question 'what is truth?' lies at the spiritual heart of the project of Europe originating with the Greeks and Western philosophy itself. He states that '[w]e pose the question: How is the spiritual shape of Europe to be characterized?' (*Vienna Lecture* 273). Husserl answers this question by claiming that the spirit of Europe is a philosophical project for truth and science performed in the service of all humankind.[5] However, even though the question of truth has the power to potentially unite all people who wish to participate in its spiritual project, the very same question also has the power to segregate. To the same extent that we cherish and value a thinker like Husserl, one who desires to unify thinkers under philosophy's biggest questions, such efforts also threaten to segregate. Husserl also reveals himself to be a thinker who is somewhat subject to the ethnocentric political issues of his day (for good or ill). Husserl continues, stating:

> Thus we refer to Europe not as it is understood geographically, as on a map, as if thereby the group of people who live together in this territory would define European humanity. In the spiritual sense the English Dominions, the United States, etc., clearly belong to Europe, whereas the Eskimos or Indians presented as curiosities at fairs, or the Gypsies, who constantly wander about Europe, do not.
>
> (*Vienna Lecture* 273)

Even though it is clear that the idea of Europe can unify, it can also be a source of ethnocentrism; a few pages later, after comparing European culture to Indian culture, Husserl also remarks that

> [w]e feel this precisely in our own Europe. There is something unique here that is recognized in us by all other human groups, too, something that, quite apart from all considerations of utility becomes a motive for them to Europeanize themselves even in their unbroken will to spiritual self-preservation; whereas

we, if we understand ourselves properly, would never Indianize ourselves, for example. I mean that we feel (and in spite of all obscurity this feeling is probably legitimate) that an entelechy is inborn in our European civilization.

(*Vienna Lecture* 275)

'Entelechy' is a realization of potential that Husserl suggests defines the spiritual meaning of European civilization and it is this sense of potential that other people groups are able to recognize and through which they desire something similar for themselves. Although Husserl does not specifically say it here, he implies that such realization for potential is not present in other non-European civilizations. This is ethnocentric to be sure, but in Husserl's defence it is important to clarify that by the phrase desire to 'Europeanize themselves' he means to participate in the teleological project of truth. As such, successful participation would importantly not necessarily mean the cultural appropriation of European languages, political structures, social values, etc. Although to what extent there is overlap between a spiritual and a socio-political definition of Europe would need to be addressed in order to avoid an ethnocentric application of Husserl's project. This criticism notwithstanding, it remains clear that a quest for scientific truth in philosophy can both bring individuals together as an ideal question to try and answer, and be a means to divide individuals. Interestingly enough, prior to developing or considering *answers* to the question 'what is philosophy?', as a *pursuit of the truth* it remains open to any and all participants and interpretations as to how such a pursuit *would get underway* and or appear *in practice*. When we shift the focus away from how a particular historical or cultural group attempts to *answer* this question towards the unity of the question itself, the activity of questioning is shown to be a way to reveal the unity of divisive views without collapsing their incompatibility.

Many of the celebrated philosophers can be connected to a central question, perhaps one that they kept asking again and again or perhaps one that they answered so well that after their contribution no one ever believed another thinker could genuinely ask that question again. Philosophy, which is commonly defined as the 'love of wisdom', might in a more encompassing and holistic sense be defined and understood as the love of questions. In the work he wrote with Félix Guattari entitled *What is Philosophy?*, Gilles Deleuze[6] interprets 'philo-sophy' as a kind of *friendship for wisdom* stating that 'the Greeks might seem to have confirmed the death of the sage and to have replaced him with philosophers – the friends of wisdom, those who seek wisdom but do not formally possess it' (Deleuze 2011 3). In the same way as we love our friends but do not really possess them, a philosopher might best be understood as a friend to questions or a friend to the activity of questioning. Restricting the value of philosophy to the possession of excellent or true answers could be expanded to also include the difficult pursuit of trying to acquire such answers *via* questioning. Instead of idolizing and seeking merely to possess and accumulate 'true answers', the philosopher can be a friend to questioning and the kind of thinking elicited *via* the activity of thought. To do so would not necessarily undermine the value and prestige of excellent or true answers, but it would broaden this value to the pursuit and journey to such answers alongside their acquisition.

With questions such as 'what is the meaning of Europe?' and 'how should we organize healthcare?' we can see that questions are important not only in universities, but also in other social and political institutions. Yet questions can be found even closer to home. Questions such as 'who am I?', 'how shall I live?' and 'what am I capable of?' show us that questions not only permeate our intellectual, social and political lives, but also our personal and spiritual life. We read philosophers to see the kinds of approaches they take to certain questions, or to closely analyse the answers that they give. We read philosophers to try and think like them, to take on their views, concepts and to adapt their approaches to problems and their answers. It seems that the activity of questioning may be found on all levels of existence: from the most mundane concerns to the highest theoretical issues of meaning and science. If so, then surely at each level, the value of *merely questioning* ought to be as important as, albeit implemented differently, than the value of answering. One conclusion that may be drawn in response to the entire history of philosophy is that the power of an answer is the supreme goal of inquiry.

Answers are what science and philosophy seek. We want to know the answer to what being is. We want to know how to be good, so that we can live well. We want to know how to save the European Union so that we can craft a more politically secured future. With each philosophical and later scientific discovery of true, compelling or excellent answers, humanity is elevated. However, have we, in our value for answers, not reduced the value of a question to that of the power of an answer? Are questions without answers and un-answerable questions therefore worthless for philosophy?

University education already places sufficient value and prestige upon excellent answers. Although this is not a problem in and of itself, this predilection for answers may obfuscate and undermine a project of research as Husserl, Heidegger and Patočka have shown in their work. This is perhaps most clearly displayed in the traditional understanding of logic, object and experience that Husserl aims to overcome with his presentation of phenomenology in his *Inaugural Lecture*. Likewise, the traditional understanding of being that Heidegger aims to destroy in *BT* or the traditional way to ask the question 'what is history?' Patočka works so hard to revive and to preserve as a worthwhile problem to perpetually reflect upon. Indeed, this re-discovery and re-valuing of a question's power to illuminate and re-vitalize experience lie at the heart of phenomenology. This questioning attitude lies prior to any and all methods and, in this way, may be pre-theoretical and pre-conceptual. If so, then a philosophy that restricts itself to theoretical conceptualization will always prove incapable of addressing its own source.

In the face of the false dichotomy that between questioning and answering one must be valued more than the other, phenomenology reminds us that such a thought may in fact be the force of an already-assumed answer. Behind every answer lies a question, that when revived frees one from the undesirable assumption that one activity must be valued over the other. In fact, this elementary ability to re-question any and all ideas, experiences, premises, histories, cultures, systems and truths could reveal that questioning may in fact be the original abyss out of which thinking itself emerges. However, as much as I have left the door open to argue that questioning reigns supreme over and against that of answering, I think that it is more productive to simply engage with and to further clarify the power of the activity of questioning and leave these issues open for further thought. That being said, based on my research in phenomenology there certainly seems to be more 'space' for the abundance of phenomena on the side of questioning than there is on the side of answering.

Perhaps instead of trying to argue which activity (of questioning versus answering) is more significant, valuable or important than the other, we can shift the perspective and observe that the history of philosophy already understands and values answers rather well. Thus, instead of arguing that questions must supersede their answers, we can simply try and show how and why philosophical inquiry is complemented with a clear grasp of the power of questioning. Evidence for how a balance of the activity of questioning alongside that of answering is already visible in the historical development of phenomenology.

Throughout the previous chapters, I have traced the development of questioning through phenomenology from Husserl, to Heidegger, and Patočka. I first raised the activity of questioning as an experience worth clarifying. In order to situate a clear investigation I have traced the more specific appearance of questioning within the traditional development of phenomenology, given that this activity already permeates our thinking and appears in many different ways.

Beginning with Husserl's motto 'to the matters themselves', now reinterpreted as a questioning means to *re-experience* the things themselves, I have highlighted the important distinction between the *content of phenomenology* (the collection of descriptions, concepts, structures, etc.) and the *practice of phenomenology* (using questions as a means to return the phenomena themselves in order to re-experience them anew). Following this legacy, Heidegger has been shown to follow Husserl's questions more than his answers and, in so doing, develops phenomenology into a philosophy that preserves questions as much as it aims to answer them. Continuing this *questioning philosophy*, Patočka explicitly develops what remains more implicit in the work and thought of both Husserl and Heidegger, namely, phenomenology as understood as a collection of preserved questions that elicit original experiences for further consideration.

I then highlighted Husserl's perpetual return to phenomena (what accounts for his penchant for revision) and the very flux of phenomena to perpetually reveal and re-reveal themselves. Husserl's *practice* of returning to the things themselves makes re-experiencing phenomena a priority and its possibility is secured by keeping them in question. The dynamism of phenomena to reveal and re-reveal themselves is incompatible with the stability of concepts, descriptions, systems or structures but may nonetheless still be brought into view for investigation *via* the activity of questioning. However, although Husserl's *practices* implicitly exemplify this practice (in that his motto precedes his methods and is indicated by his penchant for revision) Husserl never explicitly develops the activity of questioning. As a philosopher always aiming for the truth, Husserl perhaps becomes too caught up with the results of his phenomenological answers and in so doing overlooked the original power of his questioning; this is certainly what Heidegger would have us believe. Heidegger claims that the *practice* of continually returning to question an experience again and again tends to get eclipsed by the excellent answers derived by this practice. However, as is visible from Husserl's claim in his last and unfinished work, in which he states that 'I seek not to instruct but only to lead, to point out and describe what I see. I claim no other right than that of speaking according to my best lights, principally before myself but in the same manner also before others' (*Crisis* 18), it is reasonable to believe that Husserl remained aware of the importance of raising phenomenological questioning for oneself and to keep experience in question as a means to further explore, describe and clarify the things themselves.

The volumes of phenomenological texts written by Husserl, therefore, only make up part of what must be learned in order to become a phenomenologist; the other part involves taking up Husserl's practice of genuinely engaging in the activity of questioning in order to re-experience the phenomena themselves. This other part of phenomenology is excellently summarized in Reinach's charge that 'to talk about phenomenology is the most idle thing in the world, so long as that is lacking which alone can give talk concrete fullness and intuitiveness, namely, the phenomenological *way of seeing* and the phenomenological *attitude*' (Reinach 180). The practice of *returning to experience* with phenomenological questions in order to *re-elicit* the original emergence of phenomena is, therefore, used as a practice to verify phenomenological *descriptions*. This is why merely memorizing the many descriptions, concepts and systems accounted for in the content of phenomenology is to only grasp a part of what phenomenology fully entails.

Heidegger claims that Husserl himself falls prey to the tendency to overlook an original question in favour of an excellent or powerful answer. This, Heidegger suggests, is visible through development of phenomenology from *LI* to *Ideas I*. Regardless of whether we find Heidegger's criticism of Husserl convincing or not, we can acknowledge Heidegger's point regarding the relationship between a *questioning mode* of thinking, which lets phenomena persist in their fluctuation versus that of an *answering mode* of thinking which attempts to stabilize this fluctuation. Heidegger's concern for unstable, opaque and dynamic phenomena that resist total stabilization prompts him to develop phenomenology in a different way than that of Husserl. In particular, Heidegger's phenomenology develops into the preservation of the question of being.

In response to the complicated comparison of Husserl and Heidegger, I have shown that what first appears to be a divide between Husserl and Heidegger is really a division regarding the definitions of experience, science and philosophy. I gave a defence of Husserl against Heidegger's critique and I furthermore established a way to view Heidegger's work as a continuation of Husserl's original questions, even though it develops separately from Husserl's answers. Both thinkers take seriously the same phenomenological questions, but they derive different and incompatible answers. Regarding the specific example of 'what is a phenomenon?', Husserl highlights the varying moments of a (1) unity, (2) profile, (3) act of consciousness and (4) mode of consciousness, whereas Heidegger highlights moments of revelation: (5) a phenomenon is when x reveals itself from itself, (6) a semblance [*Schein*] is when x reveals itself as pseudo-x, (7) an appearance [*Erscheinung*] is when y announces itself in the place of x where x shows itself as it is and (8) a mere appearance [*bloße Erscheinung*] when y announces itself in the place of x but x does not show itself. The important role of the question 'what is a phenomenon?' is shown to be how all of the different answers relate to one another. By genuinely taking up this question, we are able to elicit all of these aspects for ourselves and to see how each answer can be verified by our own experience of how phenomena genuinely emerge. Furthermore, as participants in phenomenology, in addition to employing the question 'what is a phenomenon?' to verify Husserl and Heidegger's answers, we also keep this question preserved as a means to allow *for new answers* to come to the fore – to remain open for hitherto unconcealed ways in which the phenomenon itself may further reveal itself. We, therefore, can see how the activity of questioning is used for both the verification of previous phenomenological claims, and a means for further research. In this sense, Husserl and Heidegger's phenomenology does not just concern questions and the activity of questioning but, in addition to this, calls one to genuinely practise this activity.

Viewing Husserl and Heidegger's respective developments of phenomenology through the activity of questioning further reveals how a phenomenology of opaque, fluctuating and dynamic phenomena is possible. Whereas Husserl's work can be characterized as aiming to establish a phenomenology of stability, understood as a collection of apodictic evidence that grounds the essential structures of conscious life, Heidegger's work can be characterized as one that aims to establish one of instability, understood as a collection of problems highlighting how things appear, appear partially, appear in incomplete ways and sometimes only hint at their appearance and, in doing so, do not appear all. For Heidegger, phenomenology is a process of locating fleeting and mere appearances and making efforts to develop them into phenomena that self-reveal; this is accomplished through the recollection of questions that have been covered up by excellent traditional answers. Heidegger's efforts are primarily aimed at the question of being, but his strategy and the way he develops the use of questioning may be applied to *any and all* phenomenological questions.

Patočka makes further advances regarding Heidegger's strategy of question retrieval and preservation and, in so doing, provides the most explicit development of Husserl's phenomenological practice. Patočka's idea of heresy is clarified as a way to further develop phenomenology pursued as *questioning* rather than as a set of *answers*. Heresy involves taking up a question alongside its already-developed answers, to know and to understand these answers in such a way as to hold them apart from, and thus to preserve, the original question asked. Once retrieved, the original question enables a thinker a way to return to the flux of phenomena, from which one can both verify traditional answers and develop new ones. In this sense, Patočka fuses Husserl's original notion of flux (the experience of the phenomena themselves) with Heidegger's notion of a question (as displayed in his treatment of the question of being). This emphasis on the activity of questioning in general is something that both Husserl and Heidegger clearly display in their research and writing, even though it usually remains more implicit in their practices. In this sense, what is connoted by 'heresy' may not be Patočka's invention so much as a further clarification and development of Husserl's original impetus to keep the problem of the things themselves in view. In this sense then, *questions themselves* are treated as phenomena by Patočka in the peculiar sense that one can experience *them* (by genuinely raising and thinking about them). In so doing, one can allow questions to further reveal and re-reveal appearances.

In light of the work Husserl, Heidegger and Patočka have done in interpreting and in the development of the activity of questioning in phenomenology, we draw out of phenomenology a way of thinking in questions in general. The activity of questioning represents a powerful way to interact with possibility in thinking and experiencing as a means to stabilize and destabilize our experience, ideas and claims. As a clue to explore the phenomenon of possibility itself, it would be interesting and beneficial to use the activity of questioning as a means to phenomenologically investigate possibility as it emerges alongside the role of questioning in phenomenology.

Despite the fact that all three thinkers hold different and, in some cases, incompatible answers, they can all nonetheless be unified under the same phenomenological questions. Instead of trying to determine the 'correct' configuration of phenomenology between Husserl, Heidegger and Patočka, we can expand our view of them into a wider context of questioning and answering: each take up the questions 'what is phenomenology?', 'what is the phenomenon?' and 'what is experience?' in their own way. Although some of their answers are similar, overlap or counter each other, they all emanate from the same questions. Furthermore, this unity of a question does not collapse the individual differences between Husserl, Heidegger and Patočka but in fact removes or at least weakens the need for a 'correct configuration' in the first place. Instead of a system of philosophy, phenomenology provides questions and answers: the former represents a practice that the beginner must undertake and master in order to fully experience for themselves, and thereby fully understand, the latter.

This unity of phenomenology's questions is hinted at by Spiegelberg's suggestion that phenomenology may be holistically understood as a dynamic movement, rather than as a set of strict ideas. As something 'dynamically in motion', participation in its central activity (*of questioning*) is revealed to be just as valuable as having a clear grasp of the results of that activity (*answers*). The central activity of phenomenology is the effort to allow things to self-reveal by repeatedly returning to them again and again. It makes sense, therefore, to apply this to the very movement of phenomenology itself and Spiegelberg suggests that 'the Phenomenological Movement changed so much, and to the very end, that it cannot be presented adequately except by showing how it developed. [...] Phenomenology itself is given through various appearances. In fact, there is room for something like a phenomenology of phenomenology' (Spiegelberg 1960 xxvii).[7] In his foreword to his text *Sixth Cartesian Meditation: The Idea of a Transcendental Theory of Method* Fink confirms that '[i]ndeed in Husserl's phenomenology the idea of a phenomenology of phenomenology, a reflection on phenomenologizing, is an essential moment of the systematic conception' (Fink 1995 1). The activity of questioning is clearly at the centre of the activity of 'phenomenologizing', albeit in a modified sense. Fink has in mind here an activity of phenomenological practice that coincides with a *'transcendental theory of method*, which therefore is the phenomenological science of phenomenologizing, the phenomenology of phenomenology' (Fink 1995 12). In other words, not the most general and basic kind of questioning but a particularly transcendental depiction of phenomenological questioning. As such, this would require another interesting methodological clarification (Husserl-Fink). However, as this text has argued, we must view Husserl's motto prior his methods (perhaps any method whatsoever), based on the more general idea that the activity of questioning is something always prior to that of answering. As an additional method, Fink's transcendental theory of method is certainly valuable; however, it is one that remains on the side of answering. As a movement, phenomenology encompasses many individual methods.

To avoid collapsing phenomenology from a movement into one of its many methods, one must preserve the question 'what is phenomenology?' even alongside their equally important efforts to clarify for themselves any or all of the hitherto developed methods that constitute an answer to this question. In this sense, to participate within a particular method of phenomenology can, therefore, be distinguished from participation within the larger *movement* of phenomenology. Defining the sense of 'movement' he has in mind, Spiegelberg states that '[p]henomenology is a moving, in contrast to a stationary, philosophy with a dynamic momentum, whose development is determined by its intrinsic principles as well as by the "things"' (Spiegelberg 1960 2). This dynamic momentum can be further clarified as a collection of genuine questions as the means to access the 'things': in their very asking, their possible answers remain open, in flux, as opposed to rhetorical questions that are only raised to lead a thinker to a pre-established answer. Although there are many already-established and uncovered answers to various phenomenological questions, given that it deals with a direct appeal to genuine experience itself, there remains within every and all phenomenological questions something *inexhaustible* that must be *seen for oneself*.

Each of the main phenomenologists considered (Husserl-Heidegger-Patočka) has interpreted and developed this return to the things themselves in their own way and in so doing has revealed a way to view all of them (and perhaps of all of phenomenology) in a peculiar unity of a question: they each take up and seriously consider the same (or similar) central questions of phenomenology, even though they develop and pursue different and incompatible answers. This turns out to be the reason why phenomenology *resists* a strict definition; why it is part of participating in phenomenology to always take on a process of *clarification*; why it is usually considered as a movement (Spiegelberg), conception of method (Heidegger), something to be kept in question (Patočka) or as something that one must return to again and again as an eternal beginner (Husserl). To be a phenomenologist, therefore, requires more than merely giving mental assent to particular concepts, definitions and systems but furthermore demands that one take up its central *practice*: raising phenomenology's questions for oneself. The very thing that keeps phenomenology difficult and elusive is, therefore, revealed to be its greatest strength: as a philosophy, phenomenology requires one to participate in its central activities as well as to master its content.

The activity of questioning that phenomenology utilizes reveals a rediscovery (or re-emphasis) of something that is not strictly phenomenological. This follows on from Heidegger's suggestion in 'My Way' that what Husserl discovers in phenomenology is related to early Greek thinking or to the very mode philosophical thinking itself ('My Way' 78). Husserl also suggests that the difficulty of phenomenology is akin to the difficulty of making one's way into philosophy itself (*Ideas I* 193). In this sense, phenomenology is not so much an invention or re-discovery of a lost way of thinking, but is an adaptation of an ability to question that every person already possesses. If true, then, this fact further safeguards phenomenology from being reduced to a discipline, mere method, system or metaphysics (again here defined as a contrivance). This is perhaps why phenomenology turns out to be rather difficult to understand and practise, given that it is composed of both content as well as a peculiar practice.

Phenomenology sources its discoveries in experience, but notably in the *inexhaustibility* of experience to perpetually reveal and re-reveal, to be an unending source for thought and further reflection. Is the inexhaustibility of experience something that can be *known* as a fact or a *stabilized* claim? Strictly speaking, and based on my analysis, I do not think so. As an answer claim, 'that experience is inexhaustible' would in a sense threaten the ability of philosophy, and therefore of phenomenology, to make true claims about the world. However, as the historical development of phenomenology has shown in a limited sense, at each stage whenever an answer or a set of answers are considered 'final' or 'complete', this ultimately leads to a pejorative restraint of science and philosophy even as it also coincides with great accomplishments and advancements. Furthermore, to suggest that we may totally exhaust what we can know about experience would bring us back to the very problem we are seeking to avoid or overcome. In light of this, it seems we run into an either/or answer problem; however, perhaps this dead end is not arrived at due to what we are investigating, but in fact stems from the way in which we are approaching it. Perhaps this problem stems from an approach to philosophy that is *answer oriented* and is therefore avoidable if we approach it in a more question oriented way.

In light of my analysis, viewing the question-answer relation in an either/or construct is itself unnecessary. Although neither are exactly the same, nor are they equally balanced, both questioning and answering are needed for what they individually provide for thinking. As such, we can exchange our claim 'that experience is inexhaustible' for the question 'is experience inexhaustible?' and in so doing can maintain our ability to gather true claims whilst simultaneously remaining open for those claims to be re-revealed anew, displaced altogether and/or replaced by newer or more interesting ones. This is done out of respect for the dynamism of experience, an aspect that seems to appear and conceal itself in so doing. What emerges in flux is the very process of something stabilizing and the process of something destabilizing. A phenomenologist keeps such fluctuation in view with their questions even as such experiences themselves resist being fully captured by any of our answers. In this sense, there is much more to the question 'is experience inexhaustible?' than there is in the answer claim 'experience is inexhaustible'.

The inexhaustibility of experience is not something that can be claimed or argued for so much as it represents a problem that phenomenology attempts to engage with. The history of philosophy is, in a sense, a response to the question 'what is experience?' Exhaustively systematizing experience remains possible only when we restrict experience to a particular limitation, but interestingly, that limitation will always be a limitation of experience itself. Observe that two answers are under consideration here: (1) 'experience is exhaustible once the proper system is developed for it' and (2) 'experience is *not* exhaustible no matter how one attempts to systematize it'. The first answer cannot be confirmed until a great achievement has been made (which has yet to be done), but the second answer seems to condemn philosophy to relativism or perhaps even nihilism. However, the question to which both these answers respond remains separate: 'what is experience?' As much as Husserl perhaps wanted phenomenology to be that 'great achievement', and equally the amount of criticism Heidegger levelled against viewing phenomenology as that achievement, we see the boon of preserving this question. From the perspective of the question, both answers remain *possible* in that they emerge for us as something worthy of further thought. As phenomenology raises and reflects upon the question 'what is experience?' it too remains open to what may emerge. Phenomenology is valuable in that it not only begins with, and always returns to, experience itself, but furthermore and in so doing preserves the question 'what is experience?' beyond the rhetorical path leading to a particular answer.

To what did Husserl return again and again in order to modify and improve his ideas, descriptions, definitions and systems? How did Heidegger find a means to bring into view the ontological difference, to locate and make transparent a deeper analysis of consciousness *via* his existential analytic? Why did Patočka struggle to develop a heretical way to develop phenomenology from within? Each thinker *did not* contrive their concepts or ideas; instead, they found them correlated to their own genuine experiences. Husserl returned to *experience* again and again, in order to test and to verify his ideas, descriptions, definitions and systems and each time he did, he found ways to further develop, clarify and improve his ideas. Heidegger saw in his own *experience* of everydayness the ontological difference and a peculiar way of human existence that seemed entirely pre-theoretical. Through being a student of both thinkers, Patočka *experienced* phenomenology itself as a means of returning to a problem again and again, to let it ripen and reveal phenomena for further thinking.

Interestingly enough, *experience* is not only the common source and place in which phenomenology begins; it is also the site to which a student of phenomenology must perpetually return. The discoveries of phenomenology are not just newly minted concepts to be discussed, agreed or disagreed with. The beginner phenomenologist must not just merely memorize and give mental assent to the ideas, concepts, descriptions and systems of phenomenology, but rather as a *participant* they must make attempts to verify and genuinely see for themselves the *experiences* that correlate to such ideas, concepts, descriptions and systems. In this sense, the return to one's own experience to verify any concept is always something additional to the very process of 'acquiring' or 'minting' a concept in the first place. This two-fold process of *beginning with* and always *returning to* experience is accomplished *via* the 'vehicle' of questioning. That experience can reveal and re-reveal itself shows us that a question is importantly always *more than* its answer, *more than* what it reveals and *more than* the thinking that it elicits. As an activity that can elicit the emergence of phenomena in many different ways, questioning shows us that it has a powerful and dynamic ability to relate to experience. However, as a kind of possibility or dynamism, this quality of a question to be *more than* can never be fully stabilized and, as such, it can never be modified to guarantee a particular result in advance. Questioning is revealed to be something that may lead to an answer or it may simply lead to a constellation of thoughts that never solidifies, comes together or coalesces into anything at all.

There have been many attributions, claims and descriptions of the 'beginner phenomenologist' throughout this text; however, this has all been a trick of sorts played on the reader. This is because in phenomenology there are no authorities and no masters. Husserl is sometimes referred to as 'the master' in response to his self-description c. 1902: 'Thus I am, after many years, still the beginner and the student. But I want to become the master! *Carpe diem*' (*The Idea of Phenomenology* 1). In honour of all of his pioneering achievements in founding and developing phenomenology, as well as emulating its central practice, Husserl is considered to be the original master. However, at the end of his career and in his last and unfinished work the *Crisis*, he beautifully states that we phenomenologists

> are absolute beginners, here, and have nothing in the way of a logic designed to provide norms; we can do nothing but reflect, engross ourselves in the still not unfolded sense of our task, and thus secure, with the utmost care, freedom from prejudice, keeping our undertaking free of alien interferences [...] and this, as in the case of every new undertaking, must supply us with our method.
>
> (*Crisis* 134)

Thus, a phenomenologist not only *starts out* as a beginner, and *persists* as a beginner, but furthermore it turns out that they *remain* a beginner through and through until the very end. In other words, it is not that phenomenology requires some kind of blank slate beginner admission, but rather the *willingness to participate in the practice of being a perpetual beginner*. In his work *What Is Called Thinking?*, Heidegger states that '[t]he teacher is ahead of his apprentices in this alone, that he has still far more to learn than they [...]. The teacher must be capable of being more teachable than the apprentices' (*What Is Called*

Thinking? 15). In other words, a teacher is not only a perpetual beginner, but must also be *more of a beginner* than her students so that they can emulate how to learn. This attitude and practice go hand in hand with the activity of questioning, as the very means by which one re-asserts their status as an eternal beginner.

The power of a question teaches a thinker to mature beyond the desire to rig the philosophical 'game' of concept-play and concept-clarity in advance (at least as it applied to phenomenology). The problems and, therefore, genuine questions of philosophy and phenomenology teach us to return to the things themselves. The rough and tumble of genuine thinking is messy, difficult and concludes without results most of the time. Although we seek to possess and to understand those precious answers, the few great thinkers who have managed to carve out and clarify them for us, the mere amount of time we spend as students *pursuing them* over and against *ascertaining them* shows us that our value for questioning needs to be kept safe and separate from our desire to possess answers.

All phenomenological investigations have one important and essential thing in common: a point of departure from, a continual return to and a necessary correlation with experience *via* the activity of questioning. As I have shown, the central role of this questioning activity is visible throughout the historical development of phenomenology and acts as a means by which to elicit wonder. The wonder that we encounter through experience prompts us to question and when we genuinely pursue our questions this can lead us back into a state of wonder. This state of wonder can and may lead to a resolution, but may be distinguished from that of an answer when taken on its own and understood as a separate experience. The *ability* or *experience* of questioning itself is now distinguishable from any or all concepts of questioning because the *fluctuation* of experience will always occur prior to its stabilization into answers.

For the many incredible accomplishments of Husserl, Heidegger and Patočka, we can learn by seeing what they saw and by questioning as they questioned. We might not be able to answer all of our questions, but that will not stop us from becoming more proficient in our ability to question and, in so doing, bring the wondrous ever closer to our gaze and let it become all the more wondrous. In that regard, Fink is certainly correct to assert that phenomenology concerns the wondrous and we can add to this claim that it not only concerns, but also begins with, always takes place within and perpetually returns us back to the *wondrous*.

Notes

Introduction

1. By practice I mean the return to one's own genuine experience of phenomena understood in its most robust, general, dense and multifaceted sense. This practice is accomplished when we perpetually re-question our own experience in such a way as to keep the things themselves we are investigating in view alongside the descriptions we make of them. In other words, it is an activity that must be perpetually executed and as such it is not just a formal or conceptual aspect of how to understand phenomenology; it is a practice that must be constantly *practised*.
2. Unlike a technique, the practice of Husserl's motto is more of a *finesse*, that is, it is an activity that can only be 'mastered' through perpetual repetition, under the realization that one only 'masters' a finesse when they recognize it must always be performed anew.
3. In Husserlian phenomenology, the idea of knowledge always goes hand in hand with a community. Although Husserl grounds knowledge in intuition, it is always an intuition that must be repeated by that individual and all other individuals in a community in order to verify and validate any claim. In his article 'Desiring to Know through Intuition' Husserl scholar Rudolf Bernet states that '*[e]ven if intuition and, more generally, knowledge are acts of an individual consciousness for Husserl, the possibility of these acts nevertheless depends on conditions which do not fall within the province of this consciousness.* [...] [K]nowlege is necessarily carried out in the first person and yet [...] this person never holds, by herself, all the keys to her knowledge. A third person can thus know – not the knowledge of the first person, but the same object as her' (Bernet 2003 164). Thus, every knowledge claim is only worth as much as the community can make of it by their own attempts to test it and, in so doing, trying to see it for themselves.
4. An excellent example of this is observable in the exchange between Hume and Kant on the issue of causality. In his work entitled, *An Enquiry Concerning Human Understanding* (henceforth *Enquiry*), Hume famously states that '[a]ll reasonings concerning matter of fact seem to be founded on the relation of *cause* and *effect*. [...] I shall venture to affirm, as a general proposition, which admits of no exception, that knowledge of this relation is not, in any instance, attained by reasonings *a priori*; but arises entirely from experience, when we find that any particular objects are constantly conjoined with each other' (*Enquiry* 29–30).

Hume's answer to the question 'what is causality?' is that causality is *not* based on *a priori* reasoning and only amounts to constant conjunction as opposed to a necessary connexion. To put it in other words, Hume claims that the effort to answer the question 'what is causality?' *via a priori* reasoning is impossible, hence unanswerable when asked in that particular way. However, when the question 'what is causality?' is re-thought by Kant in the form of 'how are synthetic judgements *a priori* possible?', he is able to re-engage with Hume's question in a new way and states that 'Hume, who among all philosophers came closest to this problem', concluded that in light of his answer he believed 'himself to have brought out that such an *a priori* proposition is entirely impossible' (*CPR* B19–20). In addition to the often-cited and celebrated line where Kant attributes Hume to have awoken him from his dogmatic slumber (*Prolegomena to any future metaphysics*, henceforth *Prolegomena* 57; 4: 260), Kant also states that Hume 'rightly affirmed: that we in no way have insight through reason into the possibility of causality, i.e., the possibility of relating the existence of one thing to the existence of some other thing that would necessarily be posited through the first one' (*Prolegomena* 103; 4: 310). In light of the findings of his *CPR*, Kant claims a few lines later that he has 'sufficiently shown that [the concepts] and the principles taken from them stand firm *a priori* prior to all experience, and have their undoubted objective correctness, though of course only with respect to experience' (*Prolegomena* 104; 4: 311). Not only does Kant show how Hume's question may be asked in a new way, but now that Kant has answered the question 'what is causality?' so *excellently well* it is once again considered unnecessary to genuinely raise this original question anew; this is the case, at least until another philosopher does to Kant what he did to Hume.

5   The English translator Dallas Willard translates *Sachen* as 'facts', but this English word can be misleading as Husserl use of *Sachen* encompasses more than just facts. As such, I have decided to use the English words 'things' or 'matters' to avoid confusion concerning Husserl's motto.

6   In his article 'Limits of Conceptual Thinking' Bernet states that '[w]hen one objects to a standardized mode of thinking in which knowledge is a matter of recognition, in which recognition becomes the identification of something familiar, and in which all experience is made dependent on its matching our concepts, then an alternative way of thinking must start with sensuous experience and how it gives rise to concepts. *In such a view the meaning of concepts can never be entirely conceptual, because concepts are formed on the basis of an experience, the meaning (or lack of meaning) of which is not yet conceptual.* Such a dependence of concepts on the meaning of preconceptual experience also entails that conceptual thinking cannot any longer be considered a matter of an intellect simply following logical rules and blindly applying or projecting ready-made conceptual forms on

a meaningless matter. Under these premises, phenomenology presents itself as a promising starting point' (Bernet 2014 227, my emphasis).

7   By 'prior' I mean that an experience of a phenomenon must occur before its conceptualization. Thus, this priority has nothing to do with Kant's notion of the *a priori*. In phenomenology, the activities of concept creation, concept use and concept reflection are closely related to the activity of questioning. Bernet states that 'the need for concepts emerges from and in perception – more particularly when the meaning of what one actually perceives becomes problematic, when the continuity of a perception is interrupted by the question: "What is it that I perceive?" This question ordinarily leads not only to a more attentive perception or to a thematization of what one perceives; it also leads to a search for names and categories. The most common origin or genesis of concepts thus lies in their answering needs arising in perception. Once a conceptual answer is given, the further course of experience can then be either perceptual or conceptual. The answer can also be delayed when what one perceives is too strange or when an appropriate concept is not available and must still be created' (Bernet 2014 229). Thus, thinking and questioning do not merely emerge by way of concepts, but all three seem to work with each other. We can experience something strange and then seek to conceptualize it; in doing so, the phenomenon may further reveal itself and this, in turn, causes more thinking and questioning and so the process repeats.

8   As will be developed in greater detail throughout this text, appearances are static and stable whereas phenomena are fluctuating and dynamic. The non-linear reciprocity between the two generates experience and discovery, whereas the attempt to understand and clarify this reciprocity comprises phenomenological research. However, when the *results* of that research become powerfully clear, descriptions have a tendency to eclipse the original phenomena they are intended to clarify and account for. Thus, the importance of remembering that phenomena precede their appearances preserves their potentiality to further self-reveal.

9   For an application of how the preservation of questions can be edifying to other phenomenological projects, see 'The Multicultural Philosopher: How the Preservation of Questions Provides Insight into Social and Political Phenomena' (Hubick 2016) in *Identity, Belonging and Human Rights: A Multi-Disciplinary Perspective*.

10 I am using the J.N. Findlay English translation that is based on the second German edition published in 1913.

11 I use the title *Ideas* to refer to Husserl's philosophical development of transcendental phenomenology (approximately 1913–38), but when quoting him, I signify each specific book (I-III).

12 For an example of how one can apply Husserl and Heidegger's activity of questioning to the theological idea of 'special divine action', see 'Our Openness to

Religious Phenomena: Thinking in Questions as a Way to Understand Possibility' (Hubick 2016) in *ET-Studies* 7:2.
13 Hubick, Joel. (2017) "Heretical Hindsight: Patočka's Phenomenology as Questioning Philosophy". *Journal of the British Society for Phenomenology*. DOI: 10.180/00071773.2017.1387685 (pages 1–19). (Taylor & Francis Ltd, http://www.tandfonline.com).
14 For an application of how the role of questioning can be applied to the issue of plagiarism and philosophical responsibility, see 'A Philosophical Response to Plagiarism' (Hubick 2016) in *Teaching Philosophy* 39:4.

Chapter 1

1 In his critical essay of phenomenology titled 'Husserl and the Problem of Idealism', Theodore W. Adorno states that '[t]he idea that a philosopher must produce a fixed set of irrefutable findings, an idea which Husserl himself certainly would have shared, presupposes that all the tasks he sets for himself can actually be fulfilled, that there can be an answer to every question he raises. This assumption, however, is disputable' (Adorno 5). Even though Husserl certainly seeks to answer his questions as best as possible, and pursued absolute and essential answers, he is in fact the most radical re-questioner in the entire phenomenological movement. Although Husserl wanted to find true descriptions that appropriately account for lived conscious experience, his willingness to re-question experience and all his already-collected findings reveal something quite contrary to Adorno's description of Husserl as 'the most static thinker of his period' (Adorno 5 7).
2 The most famous account of realizing the extent of phenomenology is, of course, Jean-Paul Sartre's encounter with Raymond Aron as recounted by Simone de Beauvoir in her work *The Prime of Life* where even an apricot cocktail can be considered a worthy object of phenomenological inquiry (de Beauvoir 112).
3 In his work *Conversations with Husserl and Fink*, Dorion Cairns states that 'Husserl began by asking me if I had any questions, to which I answered that I had recently been attempting to get a general idea of phenomenology, and that I was feeling it very difficult to know where to begin, as everything which came later seems to have a bearing on what had gone before. This circumstance, [Husserl] replied, was what had kept him so long doubtful about the proper introduction' (Cairns 1976 27).
4 As quoted from Spiegelberg's essay 'From Husserl to Heidegger: Excerpts from a 1928 Freiburg Diary by W. R. Boyce Gibson'. *Journal of the British Society for Phenomenology*. Volume 2 (Spiegelberg 1971 63).
5 Kisiel's review of Heidegger's *Prolegomena zur Geschichte des Zeitbegriffs* (*History of the Concept of Time* henceforth *HCT*) is not to be confused with this translation of Heidegger's lectures into English. See bibliography for more information.

6   In his introduction to Heidegger's *What Is Called Thinking?* translator J. Glenn Gray curiously states that '[d]espite [Heidegger's] great love for the Greeks and his familiarity with Western philosophic thought, I believe it is a fundamental mistake to read Heidegger as a follower of this or that previous thinker. He seems to me to have no basic dependence on any predecessors, not even his previous thought' (Gray xiv). Not only is this claim rather extreme, but a few lines later Gray describes Heidegger as someone who '[t]oday, at age seventy-nine, he starts every morning afresh, without any secure base in past systems of thought and still dissatisfied with what he himself has worked out' (Gray xiv). This claim is rather ironic because such a description would perfectly fit Husserl as well.

7   Sheehan repeats a similar claim in his essay 'What if Heidegger Were a Phenomenologist?' stating that '[t]he first step is to realize that Heidegger's work was phenomenological from beginning to end' (Sheehan 2013 382). In a footnote to this claim, Sheehan quotes William Richardson's work *Heidegger: Through Phenomenology to Thought* stating that '[i]t is singularly important to realize that Heidegger never abandons the phenomenological attitude that seeks only to let the phenomenon manifest itself' (Richardson 537). However, the two claims that Heidegger was a phenomenologist from 'beginning to end' and that he 'never abandoned the phenomenological attitude' are not exactly the same. I certainly agree that Heidegger continues to develop Husserl's phenomenology, but the claim that Heidegger remains a phenomenologist is in danger of simplifying the different meaning of phenomenology between Heidegger and Husserl (certainly, if one does not attempt a comparison of the two). That said, I certainly agree with Richardson's claim that Heidegger remains interested in the phenomenological attitude, but again only so far as it is understood *via* the activity of questioning and even there, I would likewise claim that such an interest undergoes an extensive development from the way it was originally developed and practised by Husserl. Thus, in order to preserve how Heidegger and Husserl's phenomenologies are quite different, even incompatible with one another, requires an extensive comparison of Heidegger with Husserl. In more recent scholarship, Sheehan published *Making Sense of Heidegger: A Paradigm Shift* (2015), a text that further develops his original claims in his essay 'A Paradigm Shift in Heidegger Research' (2001) in which he states that '[s]ince Heidegger's focal topic never was "being" in any of its forms, and since the term "being" in the current secondary literature is plagued by so much confusion and absurdity, we would do well to follow Heidegger's example and abandon the word "being" as a marker for *die Sache selbst*' (Sheehan 2001 187–8). In the book, Sheehan again claims that he 'reads [Heidegger's] work strictly as [Heidegger] himself declared it to be – namely, *phenomenology*, which means that it is about one thing only: sense or meaning ([Sheehan] takes them as the same), both in itself and in terms of its source' (Sheehan 2015 xii). Leaving the issue open for

further thought, I agree with reviewer Lucian Ionel's criticism that 'Sheehan not only emphasizes that Heidegger's ultimate project seeks the source of meaning, but considers that Heidegger gives a "final answer" to the question of how the disclosedness of Being is possible. [… However in] spite of Sheehan's rigorous analysis, whether that is truly Heidegger's last answer is questionable' (Ionel 596). As I will argue, when it comes to Heidegger's presentation of phenomenological questioning, the preservation of questions remains just as important as the attempt to develop excellent answers for them. Even already in Husserl one finds an appreciation of questioning that goes beyond finding a 'final answer' or a complete resolution. In light of Heidegger's efforts to 'reawaken an understanding for the meaning of this question [of being]' (*BT* 1/1), I am unsure about interpreting Heidegger's work as something that aims to provide a final answer of any kind.

8   'Mythic' is a term Prof Martin Moors once used to capture the strange areas of research, tone and conceptual language used by the so-called 'later Heidegger'. As this text's textual analysis is restricted to the so-called 'early Heidegger', I think that it is important to remain neutral on the issue of whether or not Heidegger remains as a phenomenologist to the very end.

9   Just as an interesting side note: in his work entitled *Sixth Cartesian Meditation*, Fink writes that '[i]ndeed, in Husserl's phenomenology the idea of a phenomenology of phenomenology, a reflection on *phenomenologizing*, is an essential moment of the systematic conception' (Fink 1995 1, my emphasis). Fink's account of the activity and practice of *phenomenologizing* sounds very similar to Heidegger's account of a basic experience of *philosophizing*.

10   Kisiel & Sheehan state in a footnote that '[t]he original German text reads: "*und in dieser Wirkung seine wahre Wirklichkeit sich erwirken will*"' (Kisiel & Sheehan 506). This phrasing remains open to the interpretation that Heidegger believed Husserl's true 'effect' was located in his radical question to elicit a radical kind of thinking in those who genuinely followed-through on raising such questions for themselves.

11   Was Heidegger self-aggrandizing his own philosophy and merely using Husserl's work as a means for his own gains or was Heidegger fulfilling Nietzsche's famous line that 'one repays a teacher badly if one always remains a pupil only' (Nietzsche 59)? The answer is likely somewhere in the middle, but as a *question*, this issue is worth thinking about.

12   In 'My Way', Heidegger clearly describes his response to Husserl's *LI*, but a similar pattern can be identified in some of his other works in which he is not so candid. For example, in his work *Kant and the Problem of Metaphysics* (henceforth *KPM*), Heidegger stresses the importance of reading Kant's *CPR* as a work of metaphysics and not epistemology, stating that '[l]aying the ground as the projection of the inner possibility of metaphysics is thus necessarily a matter of letting the supporting power of the already-laid ground become operative' (*KPM* 2). In other

words, Heidegger reads Kant's *CPR* phenomenologically, as a work of discovery, using Kant's question '[h]ow are synthetic judgments *a priori* possible?' (*CPR* B19), not as a way to systematically setup metaphysics as an error-less epistemology, but as a phenomenological way to return to the central issues of metaphysics itself *via* an activity of *questioning*. To avoid simplicity, Heidegger's reading of Kant has been heavily criticized and rightly so, for he himself admits that the 'allegation of violence can indeed be supported by this text' (*KPM* xx); however, the pattern to re-read thinkers in light of the power of questioning remains clear: '[T]he [*KPM*] remains an introduction, attempted by means of a questionable digression, to the further questionability which persists concerning the Question of Being set forth in *Being and Time*' (*KPM* xviii). Again, I am not arguing that Heidegger's interpretation of Kant and or Husserl is necessarily correct, only that Heidegger's practices reveal a pattern of reviewing traditional questions *phenomenologically*, as a means to revive original experiences so that a reader is able to not only understand the answer a text provides, but view it additionally in light of the *original question the text aims to answer*.

13   In his essay 'The Body at the front: Corporeity and Community in Jan Patočka's *Heretical Essays in the Philosophy of History*' scholar Darian Meacham states that 'shaking' is 'a term which Patočka uses to designate the experience of radical loss of received meaning, or the sedimented meaning of tradition. [...] This idea in turn constitutes Patočka's notion of history in a proper sense, as opposed to the prehistoric, which is exactly the sedimentation of meaning that we would normally call historical' (Meacham 356). Shaken meaning is the recognition that an idea appears both, in its traditional pre-given value and something that is questionable (worthy of further consideration).

14   In his article 'The Significance of the Concept of *Thauma* in Patočka's Philosophy of the History of Art' scholar Felix Borecký states that '[p]re-historical people accepted the global meaning without questioning it, and were in agreement with it in the society' (Borecký 49). To accept meaning without questioning it for oneself precludes the possibility of confirming or seeing for oneself *why* the claim is true and this makes taking responsibility for one's own meaning impossible.

15   In his book review of *Edmund Husserl: Psychological and Transcendental Phenomenology and the Confrontation with Heidegger*, entitled 'The Essential Possibility of Phenomenology' (1999), in addition to giving a detailed review of the work, scholar Burt Hopkins makes an indirect interpretation of this famous line of Heidegger's. Hopkins' claim is that Heidegger's critique of Husserl's phenomenology takes 'issue with phenomenology's current actuality (i.e., Husserl's formulation of its point of departure) [in such a way as to] present his own thought as being consistent with the inherent *possibility* of phenomenology' (Hopkins 206). In this sense, then, Hopkins considers Heidegger's idea of phenomenology, understood as possibility, to be an expression of Heidegger's

ambivalence towards Husserl's phenomenology: seeking to take up Husserl's project in a radical but not necessarily non-phenomenological way. A more elaborate version of this paper appears in *Husserl Studies* (2001).

16 For an alternative analysis of what phenomenology understood as a possibility could mean, see Franco Volpi's paper 'Phenomenology as Possibility: The "Phenomenological" Appropriation of the History of Philosophy in the Young Heidegger' (2000). Volpi's analysis focuses primarily upon a historical account of how Heidegger reads and responds to the tradition (specifically Aristotle and Kant) in light of phenomenology. Furthermore, Volpi's paper is structured to be more of a defence against those who suggest that Heidegger's phenomenology need not be indebted to that of Husserl's, rather than a detailed explanation and exploration of what phenomenology understood as a possibility may or may not entail.

17 In his paper '"What Is, Is More than It Is": Adorno and Heidegger on the Priority of Possibility' (2011), Iain Macdonald claims that this famous phrase of Heidegger equates the 'priority of possibility' (Macdonald 46–9). He states that Heidegger and Adorno have in common 'this specific thought: *there is a kind of possibility that is superior to actuality and real possibility, traditionally conceived*' (Macdonald 46). Although I agree with Macdonald's efforts to trace an argument in Heidegger for a positive 'kind of possibility that is to be distinguished both from possibilities that conform to actuality and from those that are merely logical [… and that such] a version of absolute potentiality [is] available *within* our own, human experience of what is' (Macdonald 32), I am reluctant to agree that this makes possibility take priority over actuality (this claim itself understood as a confirmed and stable answer). I would instead consider Macdonald's position to be an excellent way to answer the question 'what is possibility?' and yet, as an *answer*, I would further suggest that Heidegger's concern for possibility entails both a preservation of the very questioning of it and some interesting responses, concepts or answers for it. In this sense, Macdonald's 'priority of possibility' may in fact threaten to, once again and through the provision of an excellent answer, eclipse the original question of possibility. That said, his efforts to relate Heidegger's project to that of Adorno's are very interesting and thought-provoking.

18 Buckley writes that 'while it is certainly true that "destruction" is an essentially "positive" notion, there is implicit in the notion a certain "violence". It is perhaps in this negative side of "destruction" that Heidegger comes closest to Husserl' (Buckley 182). Here Buckley quotes Husserl writing that '[w]e shall attempt to strike through the crust of the externalized "historical facts" of philosophical history, interrogating, exhibiting, and testing their inner meaning and hidden teleology' (*Crisis* 18). The difficult task is therefore to see how Husserl and Heidegger may be viewed together in their value for questioning without collapsing their differences. Indeed, a question proves to be a valuable idea as two completely different answers can still be unified under the same question.

19 In his essay entitled 'An Approach to Husserlian Phenomenology' Dorion Cairns states that '[t]he peculiar character of Husserlian phenomenology lies not in its content but in the way the latter is attained. Whatever its sense, an account is phenomenological in the Husserlian sense if, and only if, it is produced "phenomenologically." Mere acquaintance with the doctrines of Husserlian phenomenologists is therefore not acquaintance with Husserlian phenomenology as such. To be acquainted with an account as phenomenological in the Husserlian sense, one must also know Husserlian phenomenological method' (Cairns 1973 223). This clearly states that what makes one a phenomenologist is not the mere understanding of answers but a genuine grasp and practice of the questioning activity that yields these answers.

20 Another clear summary of what comprises genuine 'phenomenological work' is given by scholar Nicolas De Warren in his essay 'Tamino's Eyes, Pamina's Gaze: Husserl's Phenomenology of Image-Consciousness Refashioned' in which he states that 'Husserl's thinking remains in motion, driven by the framework of his philosophical ambition. In this regard, Husserl's characterization of his enterprise as a project of *research* is fundamental to the theory and praxis of phenomenological philosophy; […]. Most importantly, this ethos of research is manifest in the conceptual work called for by phenomenological thinking. In charting a course through Husserl's writings, we must enter into his thinking as we would enter a laboratory of thought in which conceptual distinctions are minted, examined and tested to experience. We are not dealing with a one-sided affair of cutting experience to pre-fabricated notions, but committed to the give and take of "things themselves" from which conceptual understanding emerges through the synthesis of fulfillment and disappointment that Husserl describes as the trial and tribulation of evidence and trajectory of philosophical discovery' (de Warren 2010 308–9).

Chapter 2

1 As will be discussed, it is difficult to demarcate Husserl's methods, but in general they are as follows: Psychologism, Descriptive Phenomenology, Transcendental Phenomenology and Genetic Phenomenology. As the focus of this analysis is to trace how the activity of questioning plays an essential role in the formulation of all of his methods, less time is spent clarifying the specifics of these methods.

2 The very idea of 'returning to *see* the things themselves' is a somewhat contentious idea in both internal Husserl studies regarding what properly constitutes phenomenological research, as well as a common point of external criticism of Husserl's phenomenology itself. As Spiegelberg states: '[t]he call "*Zu den Sachen*"

has at times been interpreted too naively as meaning nothing but "turning to objective realities in the world outside", rather than to "subjective reflection". But this would be in conflict especially with Husserl's later interpretation of phenomenology' (Spiegelberg 1960 121–2). Some critics claim that Husserl's phenomenology ultimately relies upon some kind of esoteric experience that 'there is – to put it no stronger than this – something dismal and dogmatic about a philosophy whose utility, cogency, and plausibility depend essentially, not on objective arguments, rational analysis, or the critical consideration of evidence available to all, but rather on the individual philosopher's having undergone some esoteric experience the nature of which he is then in principle unable to communicate' (David Bell, *Husserl* 162). Other critics claim that Husserl's methods ultimately end in failure that '[t]he most important lesson of the reduction is the impossibility of a complete reduction' (Maurice Merleau-Ponty *Phenomenology of Perception* xxvii). Although I do not aim to engage with these many criticisms directly, I will address them indirectly by reconsidering Husserl's motto as a kind of *questioning practice*. As will be further clarified, a *question* is not just a concept, nor is it just an experience but rather enables one to relate to their own experience in such a way as to develop a concept in the first place.

3   In his short autobiography entitled *My Own Life* Dorion Cairns provides a rather telling anecdote about Husserl: 'And [Husserl] said to me once: "When I go back to what I have written in an earlier meditation, I always go back to that which is most obscure to me and I wrestle with that problem. I never go on and leave a problem unsolved and that is why I shall never write a philosophy. My work is not that of building but of digging, of digging in that which is most obscure and of uncovering problems that have not been seen or if seen have not been solved." All of his works are, therefore, *introductions* to phenomenology, introductions with the aim of uncovering and, if possible, solving the most profound problems' (Cairns 1973 10).

4   An experience that has been subjected to the phenomenological reduction is still an individual experience and is not yet an essence; however, the reduction does clarify the experience as a phenomenon. In order to further clarify the phenomenon as an essence, its factuality must be purified into a generality and this is accomplished by applying the eidetic reduction at which point it counts as a pure phenomenon and is, therefore, no longer an individual or empirical experience. Phenomena that have been purified are technically no longer individual or empirical experiences; however, in order to clarify an experience in the first place, to identify and apply the reduction thereto requires one to question their own experience. Thus, pure phenomena are still *sourced* in individual experiences prior to their reduction and it is for this reason that every subsequent phenomenologist is able and indeed called to verify every previously made phenomenological claim for themselves by way of their own experiences.

5   In his work *Introduction to Phenomenology*, Husserl scholar Dermot Moran also cites the following texts on exploring the issue of 'tracing Husserl's intellectual development' (Moran footnote 21, 486): Robert Sokolowski, *The Formation of Husserl's Concept of Constitution*; Theodor DeBoer, *The Development of Husserl's Thought*; Walter Biemel, 'The Decisive Phases in the Development of Husserl's Philosophy' in R.O. Elveton, ed., *The Phenomenology of Edmund Husserl. Selected Critical Readings*; and J.N. Mohanty, 'The Development of Husserl's Thought' in B. Smith and D. Woodruff Smith, eds, *The Cambridge Companion to Husserl*.

6   According to Dermot Moran, 'Husserl's assistant, Eugen Fink, has offered a convenient way of approaching Husserl's development, proposing three stages: the first he labels *psychologism* (1887–1901), though more accurately, it represents Husserl's *struggles* with psychologism; the second Fink labels *descriptive phenomenology* (1901–1913); and the third phase, *transcendental phenomenology* (1913–1938)' (Moran 65–6).

7   Bernet et al. state that 'it is possible to identify three principle types of path taken in the work of Husserl [... which may be characterized as] broad strokes within the horizon of Husserl's attempt to come to terms with the history of modern philosophy' (Bernet et al. 65).

8   The authors state that 'we see here the possibility "of an introduction to transcendental phenomenology and phenomenological philosophy by way of the history of ideas" (*Erste Philosophie* II, 3), which could well constitute a fourth type of way (cf. [*First Philosophy*] I; [*The Crisis of the European Sciences and Transcendental Phenomenology: An Introduction to Phenomenological Philosophy*], parts I and II)' (Bernet et al. 256).

9   Bernet et al. posit that 'Husserl's distinction between static and genetic phenomenology belongs to a relatively late phase of the development of his phenomenology' (Bernet et al. 195ff). Static phenomenology aims to describe experience as we find it, whereas genetic phenomenology attempts to account for how the structures we find we already have of experience come about in a dynamic way, built up from the most basic (time consciousness) all the way up to 'higher' ones (consciousness with all its many distinctions, structures, powers and abilities).

10 According to Bernet et al. 'Husserl published relatively little, but he has written a great deal, so that his philosophical *Nachlass* consists of more than 40,000 handwritten pages, mostly written in shorthand (Gabelsberg system)' (Bernet et al. 245).

11 Dan Zahavi numbered Husserl's *Nachlass* in the region of 'some 45,000 pages' (Zahavi 8).

12 Dorion Cairns in his essay 'An Approach to Husserlian Phenomenology' makes a similar claim, but where I use the word 'motto' Cairns uses 'method' by arguing that '[t]he theory of this method is itself phenomenological in the Husserlian

sense – and this indicates that Husserlian phenomenological method, in some form, is prior to Husserlian phenomenological methodology as well as to the rest of Husserlian phenomenological theory [...]. The [methodologies] can be understood only after the method in its rudimentary form, and certain results of rudimentary method, have been grasped' (Cairns 1973 223–4). The term 'motto' is better suited here as it brings to mind a practice *in medias res*, rather than 'method', which can simply mean 'a way to take up a particular practice'.

13 This is summarized rather well in Eugen Fink's work *Sixth Cartesian Meditation* in which he advances the notion that '[t]he phenomenological system itself as the architectonic of transcendental philosophy cannot be drawn up ahead of time, but is only to be *obtained from the 'matters themselves' by passing through concrete phenomenological work*' (Fink 1995 8).

14 Thomas S. Kuhn's book *The Structure of Scientific Revolutions* is a good general account of how this flux affected the way in which individuals were thinking about and developing the idea of science in the twentieth century. Given the novel discoveries of the time, the continual progress of truth building upon truth is not discarded, but it is cast back into question. As science encountered strange new problems, for which it did not have the means to account for, radical restructuring began at nearly all levels of scientific organization. In Ian Hacking's introduction to Kuhn's book, he uses the example of physics stating that 'the generation preceding Kuhn, the one that wrote so extensively on the scientific revolution of the seventeenth century, had grown up in a world of radical revolution in physics. Einstein's special (1905) and then general (1916) theory of relativity were more shattering events than we can well conceive' (Kuhn xiii). Thus, the generation preceding Kuhn (approximately 1890–1920) was not just one filled with new discoveries, as every scientific period could be fairly described as being, but more interestingly, the discoveries being made were changing the very way science itself was to be properly defined, understood and implemented. Not only were new objects being discovered in this period, but also *new ways to* discover, define and demarcate the very idea of objectivity itself were emerging. It was clear to Husserl that in order to move forward, he and his generation had to turn the *power of questioning* employed by science back upon itself and its tradition: one must question the ideas and methods of tradition itself in order to find the original *problems* these ideas and methods aimed to resolve or account for.

15 According to Kuhn, 'the decision to reject one paradigm is always simultaneously the decision to accept another, and the judgement leading to that decision involves the comparison of both paradigms with nature *and* each other' (Kuhn 78). The development of new paradigms results from a clash of questions: 'what is nature?' with 'how does this paradigm resolve our current problems in explaining nature?'

16 The claim that the phenomenon self-reveals is open to a certain line of criticism: in *LI*, Husserl states that '[t]he appearing of the thing (the experience) is not the thing which appears (that seems to stand before us *in propria persona*). As belonging in a conscious connection, the appearing of things is experienced by us, as belonging in the phenomenal world, things appear before us. The appearing of the things does not itself appear to us, we live through it' (*LI* vol. II, 83). Here Husserl is clear that the 'appearing' itself does not appear; however, his next line that 'we live through it' suggests that we may still nonetheless become *aware* of the distinction between the appearing of the thing and the thing itself. Under a singular definition of appearance, this is problematic; however, under the question 'what is appearance?', used as a means to elicit varying ways we experience appearance itself, the varying ways it 'emerges within and through our experience' suggests there is more than one singular definition of appearance. Further, each definition needs to be properly identified in order to distinguish it from other ways it shows itself. As Husserl distinguishes between the appearing thing, the thing itself and the manner in which we live through the experience of appearance, it is fair to say that such distinctions constitute different ways in which appearance self-reveals (restricting the use of the word 'appearance' in the broadest sense). The very work of the phenomenologist is shown in the attempt to try and elicit, describe, and clarify for oneself each of these different ways of appearing.

17 To avoid confusion, I am following Robert Welsh Jordan's decision to keep with the practice of Dorion Cairns' translation of the German *Gegenstand* as 'object' with a small 'o' and *Objeckt* as 'Object' with a capital 'O'. For more information see footnote 1 on page 133 in Husserl's *Inaugural Lecture*.

18 The original German is: '*Zur näheren Charakteristik dieser Wissenschaft und ihrer Methode führen wir zunächst eine einfache Unterscheidung ein, nämlich die zwischen Phänomen und Objekten im prägnaten Wortsinn*' (Husserl 1976 369).

19 In *Crisis*, Husserl writes that '[t]he ground of experience, opened up in its infinity, will then become the fertile soil of a methodical working philosophy, with the self-evidence, furthermore, that all conceivable philosophical and scientific problems of the past are to be posed and decided by starting from this ground' (*Crisis* 100).

20 This quote is an allusion to Kant's idea of transcendental philosophy. In the *Crisis*, Husserl examines the relationship between his own view of transcendental philosophy and how it relates to Kant's. Husserl writes that '[o]f course this most general concept of the "transcendental" cannot be supported by documents; it is not to be gained through the internal exposition and comparison of the individual systems. Rather, it is a concept acquired by pondering the coherent history of the entire philosophical modern period: the concept of its task which is demonstrable only in this way, lying within it as the driving force of its development, striving forward from vague *dynamis* toward its *energeia*' (*Crisis* 98). There is a fascinating

comparison to be made between Husserl and Kant's respective senses of just what transcendental philosophy means and fully entails. In particular, how for Kant it must be limited to a speculative, yet rational, argument based on validity alone, that is 'transcendental philosophy is a philosophy of pure, merely speculative reason' (*CPR* A15/B29), whereas for Husserl it may be genuinely experienced and, therefore, phenomenologically validated.

21 In his efforts to lead by example, Husserl's writing can initially appear to be rather strange: there is a kind of systematic effort to 'do justice' to whatever phenomenon or experience he is describing. However, at other moments it is rather unclear why he speaks about a topic for such length only to jettison it entirely at the start of the next section or chapter. His effort to fully explore various aspects of a particular experience can at times be rather rewarding; whereas, when such effort ends without much payoff, it can be rather confusing or at best frustrating. In the senses of 'doing justice' and being thorough, Husserl may be considered systematic; however, rarely does he suggest or imply that his ultimate goal or purpose is to produce a *system*.

22 Spiegelberg writes that despite the '[r]umors and misunderstandings to the contrary notwithstanding, Husserl's commitment to the ideal of a rigorous science never wavered, however outdated it appeared in an atmosphere of growing hostility to science, especially in Germany. It only assumed different forms and emphasis in the midst of a rapidly changing intellectual climate' (Spiegelberg 1960 77).

23 Buckley also states that 'Herbert Spiegelberg has pointed out that despite the omnipresence of this word, it rarely receives a singular definition by Husserl' (Buckley 21).

24 In an undergraduate course on Kantian Philosophy, Prof. George Di Giovanni once said 'mathematics is a sophisticated way to say nothing at all' (paraphrased). In this sense, systematicity can actually eclipse the very thing it is originally aiming to clarify. Furthermore, this reveals how system and systematicity can become a form of idolatry that is valued independently of what it was originally aiming to signify.

25 In his article entitled 'Husserl's Concept of Philosophy', Karl Schuhmann states that '[t]o philosophy pertains – and this was Husserl's great discovery – that it be not only a science directed to the world, but also a science of its necessary correlate which is *consciousness* of the world. Now, the science of this essential correlation between what appears and its appearance, the science of the "phenomena" (in the objective as well as the subjective meaning of this term), is precisely *phenomenology*. Philosophy, this is to say, becomes complete only if it investigates not only the world of objects, but also the consciousness of them' (Schuhmann 277–8).

Chapter 3

1. In this chapter I will use two English translations of *Being and Time*. The reason for this is that both translations highlight different aspects of certain passages. All references will have both the English and original German pagination respectively; Joan Stambaugh's translation will be referenced as '(JS *BT* ##/##)' whereas John Macquarrie and Edward Robinson's translation will be referenced as '(M&R *BT* ##/SZ ##)'. There have been many different ways to try and translate Heidegger's ontological difference in his use of the German *Sein* and *Seiendes*. For this chapter, I have prioritized Macquarrie & Robinson's use of the English terms 'entity' and 'entities' for '*Seiendes*' and 'being' without a capital letter for '*Sein*'. I do so because I agree with them where they state that '[t]here is much to be said for translating "Seiendes" by the noun "being" or "beings" (for it is often used in a collective sense). We feel, however, that it is smoother and less confusing to write "entity" or "entities"' (M&R *BT* footnote 22). Furthermore, as I am also using Stambaugh's translation, in order to be consistent on this translation, I have sometimes substituted 'entity' and 'entities' in square brackets in place of her use of 'being' and 'beings'. I have added the German in square brackets in places where the distinction is unclear.
2. I use the word 'apparent' because, as I have already argued in earlier sections, there is an interesting way to salvage Husserl's value for systematic descriptions that does not coincide with the production of a mere system. However, although I think Heidegger ultimately gets Husserl wrong on this point, due to Husserl's ambiguity, I still think that the recognition of the danger of a merely system-oriented phenomenology is nonetheless an essential way to get Husserl right. Thus, in order to explore this issue and allow ourselves to view Husserl as Heidegger may have, it is important to suspend our already-developed understanding of Husserl's project and to follow Heidegger's description wherever it may or may not lead.
3. This situation is made more complicated by the fact that Heidegger never actually finished *BT*, even though some of his works, such as *Kant and the Problem of Metaphysics*, may be understood as continuations of his thought they still represent later modifications and developments in Heidegger's thinking. However, even as an unfinished work, *BT* still represents a work of questioning more than it does as a presentation of answers.
4. For a detailed account on the difficulty Husserl had in revising his *LI* that is also free of any interpretive Heideggerian contamination, see Ullrich Melle's chapter 'Husserl's Revision of the Sixth Logical Investigation' in *One Hundred Years of Phenomenology*. This chapter specifically explores that '[t]his conception of a complementary relationship between the *Ideas* and the new edition of the *Logical Investigations* gave rise to a dilemma. It was impossible to raise the *Logical Investigations* completely and as a whole to the level of the *Ideas*' (Melle 111).

5   In 'My Way' Heidegger states that 'Husserl's teaching took place in the form of a step-by-step training in phenomenological "seeing"' ('My Way' 78). Although Husserl's notion of 'seeing' is a common point of contention, here it is clear that for Heidegger it took the form of a *practice* one had to become familiar with rather than a set of propositions one had to either agree or disagree with.
6   For Heidegger, the sixth investigation was important for understanding the meaning of phenomenological 'seeing'. Heidegger states that 'the distinction which is worked out [in the sixth investigation] between sensuous and categorical intuition revealed itself to [him] in its scope for the determination of the "manifold meaning of being"' ('My Way' 78). However as confirmed by Melle, 'in October 1913 the new and revised edition of the *Logical Investigations* was published – without the Sixth Investigation' (Melle 112–13).
7   Recall in §13 that although letter fragments indicate that he wanted to 'make all "systems" impossible once and for all' (Spiegelberg 1973 183) that as is visible '[f]rom statements in some of his letters and fragments now found in his unpublished manuscripts it appears that Husserl [also cherished] the plan of condensing his final insights into something he himself called a system' (Spiegelberg 1973 183).
8   Husserl also believed that this was obvious to everyone else as he adds that 'anyone who knows the old work [*LI*], will see the impossibility of lifting it entirely on to the level of the *Ideas*' (*LI* vol. 1 4).
9   These lists of students have been taken from Moran 77–84.
10 Similar to Adolf Reinach, it is likely that many of Husserl's students were more inspired by Husserl's practices, rather than they were by the results of his practices.
11 In the Editor's Epilogue, Petra Jaeger states that '[t]his lecture course of 1925 is an early draft of *Being and Time*, even though the theme of temporality is not yet actually covered here' (*HCT* 321–2).
12 By historiological, Heidegger means something like the 'objects' of history; as things that are already stabilized, they would properly be understood as appearances of historical phenomena. A phenomenology of history would then rightfully *precede* the stabilization of such appearances, in that it would open up their underlying sources as phenomena (once retrieved, such phenomena would then also be allowed to generate additional appearances).
13 Regarding Husserl specifically, the idea that a 'scientific phenomenology' is a superior kind of phenomenology is also problematic for Heidegger because it unnecessarily limits the value of phenomenology within the rubric of science. Scientific phenomenology can of course be valuable, but when its teleology is considered *the way* to practise both science and phenomenology, then something problematic has occurred according to Heidegger. This is because when properly understood, the practice of phenomenology will always be prior to that of science; thus, to consider 'scientific phenomenology' as superior to both endangers one to lose the priority of phenomenology to that of science.

14 As an interesting side note, the danger of a scientific mode of disclosure that ultimately results in the collapse, or in this case to the over stabilization of phenomena for the sake of a scientific project, may be an early point of development for Heidegger's idea of enframing [*Gestell*]; later presented in his essay 'The Question Concerning Technology' (Heidegger 2008 307–41).

15 In his article entitled 'The Interpretation of Galilean Science: Cassirer Contrasted with Husserl and Heidegger' scholar Lawrence E. Cahoone argues that 'the alleged "anti-scientific" orientation of Husserlian and phenomenology is misleading' (Cahoone 2). What appears to be 'anti-scientific' about Heideggerian phenomenology turns out to be a clarification of its limits. Cahoone states that 'despite their positive interpretation of the ideal *praxis* of natural science, Husserl and Heidegger consider the natural or the exact sciences to be the spokesmen for a *doctrine* they hold in philosophical contempt; namely, "naturalism" or "objectivism". These terms designate the view that the real world is the world exclusively described by the natural, physical sciences, or, the view that the physico-natural order is the primary, most fundamental order for inquiry' (Cahoone 15–16). The problem is more subtle in that it is the consideration of science to be *the only* or *ultimate way* to investigate experience. However, this does not mean that both Husserl and Heidegger have exactly the same views or propose similar solutions.

16 It is important to add that although a phenomenology study opens up an 'original area of research which precedes' a scientific study, the former in no way undermines the latter. In fact, usually such phenomenological research merely enriches already fruitful study by showing how there is *always more* to a phenomenon than what has subsequently appeared (this occurs when the scope of what is *permitted* to appear is not fixed in advance).

17 The particular way that Heidegger defends Husserl's *LI* from being reduced to a theory of logic is strikingly similar to what he goes on to claim of Kant's *CPR* in his work *Kant and the Problem of Metaphysics*.

18 See Richardson's introduction to his work *Heidegger through Phenomenology to Thought* (Richardson 3–24).

19 In his article 'Being, My Way', a review of Rüdiger Safranski's *Martin Heidegger: Between Good and Evil*, Sokoloski states that 'Martin Heidegger was taken by a single issue in his philosophical thinking, the question of Being. Everything he wrote, even his commentaries on other writers, got pulled explicitly into that one overriding question' (Sokolowski 1999).

20 Regarding the first answer, Heidegger states that 'so if it is said that "being" is the most universal concept, this cannot mean that it is the one which is clearest or that it needs no further discussion. It is rather the darkest of all' (M&R *BT* 23/4). Even if it is granted that being is the most universal concept, this does not also mean that it is the most transparent concept. Concerning the second answer, he responds that 'the indefinability of being does not eliminate the question of its

meaning; it demands that we look that question in the face' (M&R *BT* 23/4). Merely stating that being is indefinable should not cause us to turn away from further exploring it, but should instead drive us all the more to further clarify it. Regarding this point, he claims that 'the very fact that we already live in an understanding of being and that the meaning of being is still veiled in darkness proves that it is necessary in principle to raise this question again' (M&R *BT* 23/4). In short, Heidegger's response to these traditional answers is that they do not answer the question so much as keep one from genuinely raising it. What is even more interesting is that he also claims that '[b]y considering these prejudices, however, we have made plain not only that the question of being lacks an *answer*, but that the question itself is obscure and without direction. So if it is to be revived, this means that we must first work out an adequate way of *formulating* it' (M&R *BT* 24/5).

21 Stambaugh translates '*selbst durchsichtig*' as 'lucid in advance' whereas Macquarrie & Robinson translate it as 'transparent to itself'.

22 In his essay 'What, after all, Was Heidegger about?' Heidegger scholar Thomas Sheehan provides an alternative way to understand these three moments and states that '[t]he three movements of any question are what Heidegger calls the *Befragtes*, the *Gefragtes*, and the *Erfagtes*. These terms stand for, respectively, the "object", the "optic", and the heuristic "outcome" of the inquiry' (Sheehan 2014 258). I, however, prefer to leave the original German words un-translated.

23 Another possibility is that the *Erfragtes* of any genuine question may in fact need to remain unclear in such a way as to remain open for what may or may not emerge in response to such a question. As Heidegger says 'what is to be *ascertained* [...] will require its own conceptualization' (JS *BT* 5/6), this might be an intentional way to leave the question open, to whatever emerges on its own so we may describe and conceptualize it without interference from already-stabilized concepts.

24 In attempting to clarify the meaning of the *Erfragte* in Heidegger's *Grundfrage* in Traditional ontological terms, Sheehan defines it as '[Let "X" formally indicate the sought-for outcome]' (Sheehan 2014 260). Later he further applies this to Heidegger's concern for '*Das Sein selbst in dessen Wesen*' in 'ontological terms: [...] *Erfragtes = in dessen Wesen*: We seek the *essence* or *whence* of such being. In more appropriate phenomenological terms: [...] *Erfragtes = in dessen Woher*: We seek what makes meaningfulness possible at all' (Sheehan 2014 262). I think that for Heidegger the *Erfragte* is to remain open and I am not sure whether Sheehan's revision of it into ontological terms is helpful or not. If the *Erfragtes* is the essence of being, this could be problematic depending on how 'essence' is defined.

25 In his article entitled 'Heidegger's Critique of Husserl's and Brentano's Accounts of Intentionality' Moran provides a rather clear case study of this claim regarding the issue of intentionality. In it Moran states that 'Heidegger is going over and rethinking the same ground as Husserl, though his radically different language for articulating Dasein's being-in-the-world helps to overcome problems in what

he thought of as Husserl's still too Cartesian way of articulating the intentional relation. But, as we have seen, there are many features of Husserl's account which are simply repeated by Heidegger and not necessarily in a deeper manner' (Moran 48). However, although Husserl can be viewed as being overly theoretical, I agree with Moran that in Husserl's defence 'as Husserl's manuscripts continue to be published, they often reveal a greater sensitivity to the practical and the engaged than is evident in the programmatic statements of phenomenological method published during his life' (Moran 61). Without yet agreeing or disagreeing with Heidegger's views of Husserl, we can at least see how such views characterized the way Heidegger scoped *BT* in response to Husserl.

26   Sheehan states that for Heidegger '[t]he phenomenological reduction issues in the practitioner's first-person experiential engagement with *phenomena*, that is, with things only insofar as they are manifest and meaningful within understanding. But these phenomena are neither the experienced objects by themselves nor the experiencing subject by itself. Phenomena are always correlations: object-as-experienced-by-a-subject, or equally a subject-as-experiencing-an-object. The relation between a phenomenologically reduced object and human understanding is what constitutes the meaning of the object' (Sheehan 2013 384). In comparing Sheehan on Heidegger's definition of the phenomenon with Bernet on Husserl's definition, at least as it was formulated by the *LI* (already covered above in §10 'What Is the Phenomenon for Husserl') it is observable how Heidegger in *BT* can be interpreted as remaining within Husserl's phenomenology. However, Sheehan unnecessarily limits the meaning of phenomenology to theory. At the end of his essay Sheehan defines phenomenological theory as 'intellectually thematizing the structure and possible activities of [the] human being – as Heidegger himself did in *Being and Time*' then further claims that 'Heidegger's real goal, however, lies beyond theory, in existentiel practice. It has to do with taking up and instantiating one's own personal life what his phenomenological investigations merely talk about' (Sheehan 2013 397). Given the already-established distinction between phenomenology, understood as a collection of *answers* versus how it is understood as a collection of *questions*, even Husserl's phenomenology shows itself as 'something' beyond merely a theory or collection of theories and certainly already interested in what 'lies beyond theory' and is found within genuine experience itself.

27   As a further warning, the reader is encouraged to suspend all the clarifications made of Husserl's use of terms (i.e. phenomena understood as unity, profile, etc.) for the majority of this chapter. Although a comparison between the two is considered later, in the difficulty of trying to ascertain Heidegger's view of phenomenology, the reader is encouraged to appeal to Husserl as little as possible to avoid further complications of an already-complicated endeavour.

28 'But are we nowadays even perplexed at our inability to understand the expression "Being"? Not at all. So first of all we must reawaken an understanding for the meaning of this question. Our aim in the following treaties is to work out the question of the meaning of *Being* and to do so concretely' (M&R *BT* 1/1).

29 This is where the issue can get a bit tricky as both appearance and phenomenon may be understood as something 'self-revealing'. Heidegger states that '[t]he expression "appearance" itself in turn can have a double meaning. First, *appearing* in the sense of announcing itself as something that does not show itself and, second, in the sense of what does the announcing – that which in its self-showing indicated something that does not show itself' (JS *BT* 28/30). In the analogy of disease and symptom, the symptom has this double meaning: first, a symptom announces itself in the place of an underlying disease that does not self-reveal and second, even as something that announces on behalf of something else, the symptom is still a case of self-revealing. Appearances are always working on behalf of an underlying phenomenon, whereas phenomena are always only working for themselves. Furthermore, this might explain how and why initially understood phenomena may turn out, after further investigation, to be the appearance of a deeper phenomenon. Although this threatens to undermine the certainty of any claim (you might have to perpetually re-investigate it to be sure) it elevates the importance of questions: similar to Husserl, Heidegger's take on phenomenological research entails the infinite task of repeating questions, raising them again and again to confirm and re-confirm what we claim of them.

30 Kant states: 'I freely admit that the remembrance of *David Hume* was the very thing that many years ago first interrupted my dogmatic slumber and gave a completely different direction to my researches in the field of speculative philosophy' (*Prolegomena* 57; 4: 260).

31 Kant states that Hume 'rightly affirmed: that we in no way have insight through reason into the possibility of causality, i.e. the possibility of relating the existence of one thing to the existence of some other thing that would necessarily be posited through the first one' (*Prolegomena* 103; 4: 310).

32 The issue of logos is present in many of Heidegger's works (*BT* §7B; *HCT* §9a; *Fundamental Concepts of Metaphysics* §8; *Ontology – The Hermeneutics of Facticity* §2; *Introduction to Phenomenological Research* §2; just to name a few). Thus, like many of Husserl's ideas, it is difficult to say something specific about it without being drawn into a lot of extra-textual explanation and linguistic and terminological clarification of his original German or use of Greek. That being said, like many of Heidegger's ideas, the fundamental insight he is trying to convey is deceptively simple and is something that we all experience on a day-to-day basis. For this reason, in this section I have tried to avoid a technical presentation as much as possible. For an excellent technical examination of how Heidegger's idea of

truth presented in *BT* is indebted to Husserl's *LI* see Bernet's 'Phänomenologische Begriffe der Unwahrheit bei Husserl und Heidegger' English translation forthcoming as 'Phenomenological Concepts of Untruth in Husserl and Heidegger'.

33 In *HCT* Heidegger puts it in a different way: 'In discourse, to the extent that it is genuine, what is said should be drawn from [...] what is talked about, so that discursive communication in its content, in what it says, makes manifest what it is talking about and makes it accessible to the other party' (*HCT* 84).

34 In Bible school, a common joke was to quote the Bible and say 'Judas hung himself [...] Jesus replied "go and do likewise"'. Both lines are taken out of context to create a humorous implication, the first from Matthew 27:5 and the second from Luke 10:37.

35 Two classical riddles that exemplify this are as follows: 'a box without hinges, key or lid, yet golden treasure inside is hid' and 'what always runs but never walks, often murmurs, never talks, has a bed but never sleeps, has a mouth but never eats?' Inauthentically, these riddles may be understood syntactically as sentences that describe something that can be imagined but only in a confusing way. Prior to their being resolved, the very syntactical arrangement of words or the descriptive images they pose is usually done in an artful way that conceals what it aims to elicit (the riddles' resolution). Trying to imagine a box without hinges or something that runs but never walks seems strange until the idea of an egg or a river resolves the confusion. Authentically, the riddles now may be viewed on both levels: (1) for the clever obfuscation it poses through its specifics and (2) how its solution when brought into view resolves its specifics.

36 In *Fundamental Concepts of Metaphysics*, Heidegger writes that '[r]evealing, "taking from concealment", is that happening which occurs in the *logos*. In the *logos* the prevailing of beings becomes revealed, becomes manifest' (*Fundamental Concepts* 27).

37 Another good example that illustrates inauthentic and authentic logos can be observed in reading. Many times, reading and re-reading the same passage can give the feeling of 'knowing what the passage specifically states' (i.e. what each of the individual words and their specific arrangement mean) without fully understanding 'what the passage is trying to manifest' (i.e. what all the words together are ultimately intending to illuminate). Furthermore, after a repetition of reading and thinking, the feeling of approaching an insight is also common; this occurs when we recognize that we are 'on the way' to the insight but do not yet fully 'have it'. This difference is further indicated in whether or not someone can explain an idea in their own words versus if they can only repeat the technical definition of it (the former would be authentic logos whereas the latter inauthentic).

38 Heidegger states that '[i]f we keep within the horizon of the Kantian problematic, we can give an illustration of what is conceived phenomenologically as a "phenomenon", with reservations as to the other differences; [...] For manifestly space and time

must be able to show themselves in this way – they must be able to become phenomena – if Kant is claiming to make a transcendental assertion grounded in the facts when he says that space is the *a priori* 'inside-which' of an ordering' (*BT* 54–5/31). Attached to this last sentence, Heidegger quotes Kant 'Cf. *Critique of Pure Reason*, "Transcendental Aesthetic", Section I, p. 34' I believe referring to the passage where Kant states 'that which allows the manifold of appearance to be intuited as ordered in certain relations I call the **form** of appearance. Since that within which the sensations can alone be ordered and placed in a certain form cannot itself be in turn sensation, the matter of all appearance is only given to us *a posteriori*, but its form must all lie ready for it in the mind *a priori*, and can therefore be considered separately from all sensation' (*CPR* B34/A20).

39 Heidegger states that truth is an activity of 'taking entities out of their hiddenness and letting them be seen in their unhiddenness (their uncoveredness). The ἀλήθεια […] signifies the "things themselves"; it signifies what shows itself – *entities in the "how" of their uncoveredness*' (*BT* 262/219).

40 In *IPR* Heidegger writes that '[t]he expression φαινόμενον is accordingly not a conceptual category, but instead a manner of being, *how something is encountered* and, indeed, encountered in the *first* and, as such, *first legitimate* way. [… It] is a determination of being and is to be grasped in such a way that the character of *showing itself* is expressed […] it is what is always here, what we encounter the moment we open our eyes. It does not need first to be disclosed, but is frequently covered up' (*IPR* 10).

41 Of course, every text is not only about *one question*, but may in fact address multiple questions or multiple ways to take up the same question. This is also why there can be, and are, many edifying interpretations of any one single text. However, it is easier to clarify Heidegger's distinction between truth as correspondence versus truth as *aletheia*, when we assume that there is only one question at work in a text.

42 Recall that in *Conversations with Husserl and Fink*, Dorion Cairns states that '[e]arlier in the conversation, when, in fact, I first spoke of evidence, Husserl spoke, as often before, of the importance of the phenomenon of "*Fortgeltung*" < continuing acceptance, continuing validity >, that what I hold valid today, or this minute, continues in validity the next minute. Or can be returned to as valid' (Cairns 1976 41). In this sense, we can see that Heidegger maintains Husserl's value that truth is a result of a perpetual activity of questioning.

43 Recall that in the *LI* Husserl writes that 'phenomenology […] lays bare the "sources" from which the basic concepts and ideal laws of *pure* logic "flow", and back to which they must once more be traced, so as to give them all the "clearness and distinctness" needed for an understanding and for an epistemological critique, of pure logic' (*LI* vol. I, 166). Furthermore, in describing the *LI* he also states that 'these investigations make no claim to be exhaustive. Their aim is *not to provide a logical*

system, but to do the initial *spadework* for a philosophical logic which will derive clearness *from basic phenomenological sources*. The paths taken by such an analytic investigation will also naturally differ from those suitable to a final, systematic, logically ordered statement of established truth' (*LI* vol. I, 174, my emphasis).

Chapter 4

1. A version of this chapter has been published in a journal article. Reprinted with permission from the publisher. Original article information: Hubick, Joel. (2017) "Heretical Hindsight: Patočka's Phenomenology as Questioning Philosophy". *Journal of the British Society for Phenomenology*. DOI: 10.180/00071773.2017.1387685 (pages 1–19). (Taylor & Francis Ltd, http://www.tandfonline.com).
2. By 'hindsight' I simply mean the process of moving forward whilst at the same time keeping an eye on where one has come from, as opposed to a new development that entirely departs from its origins. Regarding the activity of questioning, hindsight takes shape by aiming to answer a question while at the same time keeping previous answers in mind and ultimately keeping the question itself in view.
3. This claim need not be limited to the phenomenology of Husserl, Heidegger and Patočka but for the limited scope of this chapter I am only intending to show that this is the case for Patočka's phenomenological developments in view of both Husserl and Heidegger. I am also not suggesting that this is the only way to view Patočka's phenomenology; however, this may in fact be an interesting and useful way to situate him in light of Husserl and Heidegger nevertheless.
4. In her article entitled 'Heretical Dimensions of Self Responsibility' scholar Laura Tusa Ilea writes that '[t]he genealogy of responsibility is connected to heresy – in the sense of a practical decision that goes beyond any theoretical back-ground determination' (Ilea 341). This is linked to the original Greek meaning of heresy '*hairesis* as decision, choice, inclination' (Ilea 345).
5. Ricoeur 1987 9.
6. For a more detailed account of the development of phenomenology leading up to Husserl and the many different ways phenomenology is taken up, re-interpreted and re-defined by Husserl's colleagues and students, see Spiegelberg's *The Phenomenological Movement: A Historical Introduction*.
7. This information is taken from the current Charles University in Prague, Faculty of Arts webpage (http://www.ff.cuni.cz/home/about/famous-alumni/#patocka) accessed on 5 June 2016.
8. Recall that for Husserl, in *LI* and in *Ideas I* as viewed from his inaugural lecture at Freiburg in 1917 titled 'Pure Phenomenology, its Method and its Field of Investigation' a phenomenon is an object of consciousness that can be real or ideal, fixed or in flux, actual or illusory, foreign or immanent, etc., but must *appear* to

consciousness in some way. Likewise, for Heidegger as viewed from *Being and Time* §7, the issue of the phenomenon concerns concealment and unconcealment, thereby adding to Husserl's idea of a phenomenon: semblance [*Schein*], appearance [*Erscheinung*] and mere appearance [*bloße Erscheinung*]. Patočka's take on the lifeworld, therefore, seems to keep both Husserl's and Heidegger's definitions in mind. The position that for Husserl the lifeworld cannot be a phenomenon at all can possibly be further clarified as an *unstable* phenomenon.

9   Husserl states that '[c]orresponding everywhere to the manifold data of really obtaining, noetic content is a manifold of data in a correlative "*noematic content*" or, in short, in the "*noema*" – [...]. The data in such noematic content are identifying in an actually pure Intuition [*Intuition*]. Each perception, for example, has its noema, at the lowest level, its perpetual sense, i.e., the *perceived as such*' (*Ideas I* 174–5).

10 For a more detailed discussion about Heidegger and Patočka's use of polemos see Nicolas de Warren's essay 'Homecoming, Jan Patočka's Reflections on the First World War', specifically footnote 25 on page 220.

11 According to the scholar Borecký, it was '[t]hanks to *thauma*, [that] the ancient Greek no longer naively accepted his life as something self-evident, but fundamentally transformed it into an *initiative* revealing philosophy, politics, and history' (Borecký 55).

12 For a further discussion of how thauma relates to the history of art in Patočka, see Felix Borecký's essay 'The Significance of the Concept of *Thauma* in Patočka's Philosophy of the History of Art' in *Acta Universitatis Carolinae Philosophica et Historica* (Borecký 47–56).

Chapter 5

1   In the *LI*, Husserl states that 'phenomenology [...] lays bare the "sources" from which the basic concepts and ideal laws of pure logic "flow", and back to which they must once more be traced, so as to give them all the 'clearness and distinctness' needed for an understanding and for an epistemological critique, of pure logic' (*LI* vol. I, 166).

2   It is perhaps a phenomenological irony that although Husserl frequently speaks of being systematic and that Heidegger criticizes systems, as we view them with historical hindsight, it is Heidegger's philosophy that appears to be more of a system than Husserl's, perhaps owing to Heidegger's historical influence eclipsing that of Husserl's. And yet, what is history if not a collection of answers? When we take up Patočka's heresy and review history as a question, then that 'influence' shifts, and we begin to see just how far reaching Husserl's ideas and practice in fact show themselves. So now, let us learn the lesson and let go of the

question versus answer dichotomy and see all three thinkers for the confluence of phenomenological thinking they exhibit.
3. We must also be careful not to overvalue questioning, as it is not the ultimate ground of our experience either. Husserl suggests that it is the life-world that is the ground of experience as something that 'belongs to what is taken for granted, prior to all scientific thought and all *philosophical questioning*, that the world is – always in advance – and that every correction of an opinion, whether experiential or other opinion, presupposes the already existing world, namely, as a horizon of what in the given case is indubitably valid as existing, [...]. Objective science, too, asks questions only on the ground of this world's existing in advance through prescientific life' (*Crisis* 110, my emphasis).
4. Kant writes that 'precisely in these latter cognitions, which go beyond the world of the senses, where experience can give neither guidance nor correction, lie the investigations of our reason that we hold to be far more preeminent in their importance and sublime in their final aim than everything that the understanding can learn in the field of appearances' (*CPR* A3/B7).
5. Husserl writes that '[s]uch a fully conscious will for rigorous science dominated the Socratic-Platonic revolution of philosophy and also, at the beginning of the modern era, the scientific reactions against Scholasticism, especially the Cartesian revolutions. Its impulse carries over to the great philosophies of the seventeenth and eighteenth centuries; it renews itself with most radical vigor in Kant's critique of reason and still dominates Fichte's philosophizing. Again and again research is directed toward true beginnings, decisive formulation of problems, and correct methods' (*PRS* 76).
6. In *Metaphysics*, Aristotle states that '[f]or it is owing to their wonder that men both now begin and at first began to philosophize' (982b12/p. 1554).
7. Regarding the example of this occurring in science, in her work *The Life of the Mind*, Hannah Arendt writes that '[t]he very concept of an *unlimited progress*, which accompanied the rise of modern science, and has remained its dominant inspiring principle, is the best documentation of the fact that all science still moves within the realm of common sense experience, subject to corrigible error and deception. When the experience of constant correction in scientific research is generalized, it leads into curious "better and better", "truer and truer", that is, into the boundlessness of progress with its inherent admission that *the* good and *the* true are unattainable. If they were ever attained, the thirst for knowledge would be quenched and the search for cognition would come to an end. This, of course, is unlikely to happen [...]' (Arendt 54–5).

Conclusion

1. There are exceptions in the instance that the inability to answer a question is taken as something positive or edifying: Plato's depiction of Socrates and issues of *aporia* reveal a value in presenting yet-to-be-answered questions; for example, the *Meno* problematizes the question 'what is virtue?' (*Meno* 71a) and *Laches* problematizes the question 'what is courage?' (*Laches* 190d-e). In his *Metaphysics*, Aristotle states that '[f]or it is owing to their wonder that men both now begin and at first began to philosophize […] And a man who is puzzled and wonders thinks himself ignorant' (Aristotle 982^b 10–25). The process of bringing about a genuine wonder or puzzlement towards the question under investigation is shown to be valuable in many of these early philosophical texts. The use of *aporia* to begin with initial puzzlement or to bring one's thinking back to a state of puzzling openness is valued even when it is never fully resolved. In this sense, one can observe a value in the *questing* of a question that has yet to, or never will, find its resolution in an excellent and powerful answer.
2. In my article 'The Multicultural Philosopher' I explore a 'dynamic model' of multiculturalism claiming that '[a] dynamic model which contained and maintained possibility alongside its actuality would be something in flux, something with a life of its own and something that continued to change and develop despite the successes or failures of its application. A dynamic model may also cease to be or develop into something unintended; it would not do to try and shape it, rather we would have to allow ourselves to be shaped by it. A dynamic model would not have a solid structure at its centre but would have a question; a question which, although it had generated powerful answers, would be preserved in order to promote further thinking' (Hubick 2016 8). This would be one way to consider the Canadian question of 'what is multiculturalism?' but one could also do the same for the American question 'what is democracy?' or the European question 'what is science?'
3. It is interesting that although this is widely held to be the case, Dylan himself rejected it. In an interview with National Public Radio's host Steve Inskeep, after being asked about being named the 'voice of a generation' Dylan replied that '[t]hat was just a term that could create problems for somebody, especially if someone just wants to keep it simple, write songs and play them. Having these colossal accolades and titles, they get in the way' (Inskeep, Smith. 'Bob Dylan: A Conversation' www.npr.org. https://www.npr.org/2004/10/12/4080202/bob-dylan-a-conversation (accessed 6 December 2017).
4. In the *Texts of Early Greek Philosophy: The Complete Fragments and Selected Testimonies of the Major Presocrates* edited by Daniel W. Graham, one can find references in each philosopher's fragments attesting to the 'ultimate basis of all

things as being': water for Thales (29; Aëtius P I.3.I, S I.10.12); *aperion* or 'the boundless' for Anaximander (49; Diogenes Laertius 2.1-2 (AI)); air for Anaximenes (75; Diogenes Laertius 2.3 (AI)); fire for Heraclitus (151; Aëtius P I.3.II, S I.10.14); and the one for Parmenides (221; Hippolytus *Refutation* I.II.I-2 (A23)).

5 Husserl states that '[t]he genuine spiritual struggles of European humanity as such take the form of struggles between the philosophies, that is, between the skeptical philosophies – or nonphilosophies, which retain the word but not the task – and the actual and still vital philosophies. But the vitality of the latter consists in the fact that they are struggling for their own true and genuine meaning and thus for the meaning of a genuine humanity' (*Crisis* 15). In light of this, philosophers are the guardians of this spiritual project of truth, 'we are what we are as functionaries of modern philosophical humanity; we are heirs and cobearers of the direction of the will which pervades this humanity; we have become this through a primal establishment which is at once a reestablishment [*Nachstiftung*] and a modification of the Greek primal establishment. In the latter lies the *teleological beginning*, the true birth of the European spirit as such' (*Crisis* 71). However, in addition to being guardians of the truth, should we not also aim to be guardians of the *questioning pursuit of truth* as well?

6 The relationship between Deleuze and phenomenology is contentious. According to Deleuze scholar, Corry Shores, 'Deleuze is often considered an anti-phenomenologist' but that does not stop Shores from making 'constructive use of his critiques on traditional phenomenology' (Shores 2012a 7). In his article entitled 'Body and World in Merleau-Ponty and Deleuze', Shores also states that his 'analysis [...] is interested in not so much in what *was* the relationship of Deleuze's ideas to phenomenology, but more in what it *could become* when we treat his criticisms as constructive critiques. Might it be possible to do phenomenology in a Deleuzean way?' (Shores 2012b 182). To answer his own question, Shores quotes Miguel de Beistegui who raises the question '[h]as phenomenology not characterized itself throughout precisely as this ability to become and evolve? And is this not the historical lesson of phenomenology: that it is itself a flow, with unpredictable bends and meanderings, which, whatever their intensity, in the end always reinvent phenomenology [...]. [...] there is no "letter" of phenomenology: no primordial word, no consecrated text, no originary truth that one could betray: only an endless series of heresies, which is, at least in philosophy, the only possible form of fidelity, that is, the fidelity in and through genuine questioning' (Beistegui 68). Self-describing his own philosophical method in his 'Letter to a Harsh Critic', Deleuze explains his philosophical method in that 'I saw myself as taking an author from behind and giving him a child that would be his own offspring, yet monstrous' (Deleuze 1995 6). Such criticism is anything but traditional; however, it can still be enlightening, albeit perhaps a bit sensational. In his journal article 'Deleuze

and Phenomenology' scholar Stephan Günzel states that Deleuze's philosophical method is one of conceptual persona that aims to not only identify something but also show how it is lively and dynamic. Günzel states that '[a] conceptual persona is a proto-literary figure that appears in philosophical texts not only to *illustrate* a concept, but to *dramatize* its function. […] This is to say, philosophy is not about representing (the world), but about bringing into relation the elements of a concept, and a conceptual persona may achieve just that […]. Deleuze argues that these dramatizations of concepts allow philosophy to pose *problems* […]. Philosophy is not about examining the truth of statements of fact or propositions, but about the creation of concepts, by which a problem is posed' (Günzel 34–5). In other words, although Deleuze is perhaps a bit of a 'fringe phenomenologist' or critic, he nonetheless follows in Husserl's footsteps in attempting to bring the reader back into a questioning state towards their own experience of the world. Again, the point is *not just* to bring about a reflection on any particular philosophical idea, but to return to the original genesis state of any and every concept whatsoever: revived and returned to, again and again, through the activity of questioning.

7   In his essay 'Desiring to Know through Intuition' (2003) Bernet states that in the *LI*, 'the *Sixth Investigation*, prior to the introduction of the doctrine of the transcendental reduction, the meditation on a "phenomenology of phenomenology", [is introduced and] will be pursued throughout Husserl's work' (Bernet 2003 154). This supports the idea that alongside the specific work of phenomenology, as defined by any of Husserl's specific methods, there is an additional but broader work of allowing phenomenology itself to appear. Therefore, even in one of the original ways Husserl presents the project of phenomenology, it is presented as an ongoing and unfolding problem.

Works Cited

Adorno, Theodore W. 'Husserl and the Problem of Idealism'. *The Journal of Philosophy*. Volume 37:1 (1940) (pages 5–18).

Arendt, Hannah. *The Life of the Mind*. Harcourt Inc.: New York, 1978.

Aristotle. *Metaphysics*. Taken from *The Complete Works of Aristotle: The Revised Oxford Translation*. Edited by Jonathan Barnes. Volume II. Princeton University Press: Princeton, 1984.

Augustine. *Confessions*. Translated by William Watts. Harvard University Press: Cambridge, MA, 1997.

de Beauvoir, Simone. *The Prime of Life*. World Publishing: Cleveland, 1962.

De Beistegui, Miguel. 'Toward a Phenomenology of Difference?'. *Research in Phenomenology*. Volume 30 (2000) (pages 54–70).

Bell, David. *Husserl*. Routledge: London, 1992.

Bernet, Rudolf. 'Desiring to Know through Intuition'. Translated by Basil Vassilicos. *Husserl Studies*. Volume 19 (2003) (pages 153–66).

Bernet, Rudolf. 'The Limits of Conceptual Thinking'. *Journal of Speculative Philosophy*. Volume 28:3 (2014) (pages 219–41).

Bernet, Rudolf. 'Phenomenological Concepts of Untruth in Husserl and Heidegger' English translation forthcoming of 'Phänomenologische Begriffe der Unwahrheit bei Husserl und Heidegger'. *Heidegger und Husserl*. Edited by R. Bernet, A. Denker and H. Zaborowski. Freiburg: Alber, 2012 (pages 108–30).

Bernet, Rudolf. 'The Phenomenological Reduction: From Natural Life to Philosophical Thought'. *Metodo: International Studies in Phenomenology and Philosophy*. Volume 2:4 (2016) (pages 311–33).

Bernet, Rudolf, Iso Kern and Eduard Marbach. *An Introduction to Husserlian Phenomenology*. Northwestern University Press: Evanston, 1999.

Borecký, Felix. 'The Significance of the Concept of Thauma in Patočka's Philosophy of the History of Art'. *Acta Universitatis Carolinae Philosophica et Historica*. Volume 1 (2014) (pages 47–56).

Buckley, R. Philip. *Husserl, Heidegger and the Crisis of Philosophical Responsibility*. Kluwer Academic Publishers: Dordrecht, 1992.

Cahoone, Lawrence E. 'The Interpretation of Galilean Science: Cassirer Contrasted with Husserl and Heidegger'. *Studies in History and Philosophy of Science*. Volume 17 (1986) (pages 1–21).

Cairns, Dorion. *Conversations with Husserl and Fink*. Edited by Richard M. Zaner. Martinus Nijhoff: The Hague, 1976.

Cairns, Dorion. 'My Own Life' taken from *Phenomenology: Continuation and Criticism. Essays in Memory of Dorion Cairns*. Edited by F. Kersten and R. Zaner. Martinus Nijhoff: The Hague, 1973.

Deleuze, Gilles. *Negotiations*. Translated by Martin Joughin. Columbia University Press: New York, 1995.

Deleuze, Gilles and Felix Guattari. *What Is Philosophy?* Translated by Hugh Tomlinson and Graham Burchill. Verso: London, 2011.

Fink, Eugen. 'The Problem of the Phenomenology of Edmund Husserl'. *Apriori and World: European Contributions to Husserlian Phenomenology*. Edited and translated by W. McKenna, R. M. Harlan and L. E. Winters. Martinus Nijhoff: The Hague, 1981.

Fink, Eugen. *Sixth Cartesian Meditation: The Idea of a Transcendental Theory of Method*. Translated by Ronald Bruzina. Indiana University Press: Bloomington, 1995.

Gadamer, Hans-Georg. *Truth and Method*. Second, Revised Edition. Translated and revised by Joel Weinsheimer and Donald G. Marshall. Continuum: London, 2012.

Graham, Daniel W. *The Texts of Early Greek Philosophy: The Complete Fragments and Selected Testimonies of the Major Presocratics*. Translated and edited by Daniel W. Graham. Cambridge University Press: Cambridge, 2010.

Günzel, Stephan. 'Deleuze and Phenomenology'. *Metodo: International Studies in Phenomenology and Philosophy*. Volume 2:2 (2014) (pages 31–45).

Heidegger, Martin. *The Basic Problems of Phenomenology*. Translated by Albert Hofstadter. Revised Edition. Indiana University Press: Bloomington, 1988.

Heidegger, Martin. *Basic Questions of Philosophy: Selected 'Problems' of 'Logic'*. Translated by Richard Rojcewicz. Indiana University Press: Bloomington, 1994.

Heidegger, Martin. *Being and Time*. Translated by John Macquarrie and Edward Robinson. First English Edition Blackwell Publishing: Oxford, 1962.

Heidegger, Martin. *Being and Time*. Translated by Joan Stambaugh and Dennis J. Schmidt. New York Press: New York, 2010.

Heidegger, Martin. 'For Edmund Husserl on His Seventieth Birthday. April 8, 1929'. Translated by Thomas Sheehan. Taken from *Psychological and Transcendental Phenomenology and the Confrontation with Heidegger (1927–1931)*. Kluwer Academic Publishers: Dordrecht, 1997.

Heidegger, Martin. *The Fundamental Concepts of Metaphysics. World, Finitude, Solitude*. Translated by William McNeill and Nicholas Walker. Indiana University Press: Bloomington, 1995.

Heidegger, Martin. *The History of the Concept of Time*. Translated by Theodore Kisiel. Indiana University Press: Bloomington, 1992.

Heidegger, Martin. *Introduction to Metaphysics*. Translated by Gregory Fried and Richard Polt. Yale University Press: London, 2000.

Heidegger, Martin. *Introduction to Phenomenological Research*. Translated by Daniel O. Dahlstrom. Indiana University Press: Bloomington, 2005.

Heidegger, Martin. *Kant and the Problem of Metaphysics*. Fifth Edition. Enlarged and Translated by Richard Taft. Indiana University Press: Bloomington, 1997.

Heidegger, Martin. 'My Way to Phenomenology'. *Time and Being*. Translated by Joan Stambaugh. Harper & Row Publishers: New York, 1972.

Heidegger, Martin. *Ontology – The Hermeneutics of Facticity*. Translated by John van Buren. Indiana University Press: Bloomington, 1999.

Heidegger, Martin. 'The Question Concerning Technology' taken from *Basic Writings: Revised and Expanded Edition*. Edited by David Farrell Krell. Routledge: London, 2008 (pages 307–41).

Heidegger, Martin. *Sein und Zeit*. Max Niemeyer Verlag: Tübingen, 2006.

Heidegger, Martin. *Towards the Definition of Philosophy*. Translated by Ted Sadler. Continuum: London, 2008.

Heidegger, Martin. *What Is Called Thinking?* Translated by J. Glenn Gray. Harper Perennial: New York, 2004.

Hopkins, Burt. 'The Essential Possibility of Phenomenology'. *Research in Phenomenology*. Volume 29 (1999) (pages 200–14). A book review of *Edmund Husserl. Psychological and Transcendental Phenomenology and the Confrontation with Heidegger (1927–1931)*. Translated by Thomas Sheehan and Richard Palmer. Dordrecht: Kluwer Academic Publishers, 1997.

Hopkins, Burt. 'The Husserl-Heidegger Confrontation and the Essential Possibility of Phenomenology: Edmund Husserl, *Psychological and Transcendental Phenomenology and the Confrontation with Heidegger*'. *Husserl Studies*. Volume 17 (2001) (pages 125–48).

Hubick, Joel. 'Heretical Hindsight: Patočka's Phenomenology as Questioning Philosophy'. *Journal of the British Society for Phenomenology* (2017). DOI: 10.180/00071773.2017.1387685 (pages 1–19).

Hubick, Joel. 'The Multicultural Philosopher: How the Preservation of Questions Provides Insight into Social and Political Phenomena' taken from *Identity, Belonging and Human Rights: A Multi-Disciplinary Perspective*. Edited by Nasia Hadjigeorgiou. Inter-Disciplinary Press: Oxford, 2016 (pages 3–9).

Hubick, Joel. 'Our Openness to Religious Phenomena: Thinking in Questions as a Way to Understand Possibility'. *ET-Studies*. Volume 7:2 (2016). DOI: 10.2143/ETS.7.2.3170104 (pages 341–9).

Hubick, Joel. 'A Philosophical Response to Plagiarism'. *Teaching Philosophy*. Volume 39:4. DOI: 10.5840/teachphil201612158 (2016) (pages 453–81).

Hume, David. *An Enquiry Concerning Human Understanding and Other Writings*. Edited by Stephen Buckle. Cambridge University Press: Cambridge, 2007.

Husserl, Edmund. *The Crisis of European Sciences and Transcendental Phenomenology: An Introduction to Phenomenological Philosophy*. Translated by David Carr. Northwestern University Press: Evanston, 1970.

Husserl, Edmund. 'Denial of Scientific Philosophy. Necessity of Reflection. The Reflection [Must Be] Historical. How Is History Required?' Appendix IX taken from *The Crisis of European Sciences and Transcendental Phenomenology: An Introduction to Phenomenological Philosophy*. Translated by David Carr. Northwestern University Press: Evanston, 1970.

Husserl, Edmund. 'DIE REINE PHÄNOMENOLOGIE, IHR FORSCHUNGSGEBIET UND IHRE METHODE: FREIBURGER ANTRITTSVORLESUNG'. *Tijdschrift voor Filosofie*. Volume 38:3 (September, 1976) (pages 363–78).

Husserl, Edmund. *Formal and Transcendental Logic*. Translated by Dorion Cairns. Martinus Nijhoff: The Hague, 1978.

Husserl, Edmund. *The Idea of Phenomenology*. Translated by Lee Hardy. Kluwer Academic Publishers: Dordrecht, 1999.

Husserl, Edmund. *Ideas for a Pure Phenomenology and Phenomenological Philosophy: First Book*. Translated by Daniel O. Dahlstom. Hackett: Indianapolis, 2014.

Husserl, Edmund. *Ideas Pertaining to a Pure Phenomenology and to a Phenomenological Philosophy: Second Book. Studies in the Phenomenology of Constitution*. Translated by Richard Rojcewicz and André Schuwer. Kluwer Academic Publishers: Dordecht, 1989.

Husserl, Edmund. *The Logical Investigations Volumes One and Two*. Translated by J.N. Findlay. Routledge: New York, 2008.

Husserl, Edmund. *Phenomenological Psychology: Lectures, Summer Semester 1925*. Translated by John Scanlon. Martinus Nijhoff: The Hague, 1977.

Husserl, Edmund. 'Philosophy as a Rigorous Science' taken from *Phenomenology and the Crisis of Philosophy*. Translated with notes and an introduction by Quentin Lauer. Harper Torchbooks: New York, 1965.

Husserl, Edmund. 'Pure Phenomenology, Its Method, and Its Field of Investigation'. Translated by Robert Welsh Jordan. *The Phenomenology Reader*. Edited by Dermot Moran and Timothy Mooney. Routledge: New York, 2002.

Husserl, Edmund. 'The Vienna Lecture' taken from *The Crisis of European Sciences and Transcendental Phenomenology: An Introduction to Phenomenological Philosophy*. Translated by David Carr. Northwestern University Press: Evanston, 1970.

Ilea, Laura Tusa. 'Heretical Dimensions of Self Responsability by Jan Patočka'. *Investigaciones Fenomenológicas*. Volume 331 (2014). 10.5944/rif.4-I.2013.29752

Ilea, Laura. 'Heretical Dimensions of Self Responsability by Jan Patočka'. *Investigaciones Fenomenológicas*. Volume 331 (2014).

Inskeep, Smith. 'Bob Dylan: A Conversation' www.npr.org. https://www.npr.org/2004/10/12/4080202/bob-dylan-a-conversation (accessed 6th December 2017).

Ionel, Lucian. 'Review of Thomas Sheehan's *Making Sense of Heidegger: A Paradigm Shift*'. Taken from *Choice*. Volume 53:11 (2016) (pages 594–8).

Kant, Immanuel. *The Critique of Pure Reason*. Translated and edited by Paul Guyer and Allen W. Wood. Cambridge University Press: Cambridge, MA, 1998.

Kant, Immanuel. 'Prolegomena to Any Future Metaphysics That Will Be Able to Come Forward as a Science'. Translated by Gary Hatfield. Taken from *Theoretical Philosophy after 1781*. Edited by Paul Guyer and Allen W. Wood. Cambridge University Press: Cambridge, 2002.

Kisiel, Theodore. 'On the Way to *Being and Time*; Introduction to the Translation of Heidegger's *Prolegomena zur Geschichte des Zeitbegriffs*'. *Research in Philosophy*. Volume 15 (1985) (pages 193–226).

Kisiel, Theodore and Thomas Sheehan. *Becoming Heidegger: On the Trail of His Early Occasional Writings, 1910–1927*. Northwestern University Press: Evanston, 2007.

Kuhn, Thomas. *The Structure of Scientific Revolutions*. Fourth Edition. University of Chicago Press: Chicago, 2012.

Macdonald, Iain. '"What Is, Is More than It Is": Adorno and Heidegger on the Priority of Possibility'. *International Journal of Philosophical Studies*. Volume 19:1 (2011) (pages 31–57).

Meacham, Darian. 'The Body at the Front: Corporeity and Community in Jan Patočka's *Heretical Essays in the Philosophy of History*'. *Studia Phænomenologica*. Volume 7 (2007) (pages 353–76).

Melle, Ullrich. 'Husserl's Revision of the Sixth Investigation' taken from *One Hundred Years of Phenomenology: Husserl's Logical Investigations Revisited*. Edited by Dan Zahavi and Frederik Stjernfelt. Springer: Dordrecht, 2002 (pages 111–23).

Merleau-Ponty, Maurice. *Phenomenology of Perception*. Translated by Donald A. Lanes. Routledge: London, 2012.

Moran, Dermot. 'Heidegger's Critique of Husserl's and Brentano's Accounts of Intentionality'. *Inquiry*. Volume 43 (2000). 10.1080/002017400321361.

Moran, Dermot. *Introduction to Phenomenology*. Routledge: London, 2000.

Nietzsche, Friedrich. *Thus Spoke Zarathustra*. Translated by Adrian Del Caro. Cambridge University Press: Cambridge, 2006.

Patočka, Jan. *Body, Community, Language, World*. Translated by Erazim Kohák and Edited by James Dodd. Open Court Publishing Company: Chicago, 1998.

Patočka, Jan. *Heretical Essays in the Philosophy of History*. Translated by Erazim Kohák and Edited by James Dodd. Open Court Publishing Company: Chicago, 1996.

Patočka, Jan. *An Introduction to Husserl's Phenomenology*. Translated by Erazim Kohák and Edited by James Dodd. Open Court Publishing Company: Chicago, 1996.

Patočka, Jan. *Plato and Europe*. Translated by Petr Lom. Stanford University Press: Stanford, 2002.

Petříček, Miroslav. 'Jan Patočka: Phenomenological Philosophy Today' from *Contributions to Phenomenology 61: Jan Patočka and the Heritage of Phenomenology. Centenary Papers*. Edited by Ivan Chvatík and Erika Abrams. Springer: New York, 2011.

Pithart, Petr. 'Questioning as a Prerequisite for a Meaningful Protest' from *Contributions to Phenomenology 61: Jan Patočka and the Heritage of Phenomenology. Centenary Papers*. Edited by Ivan Chvatík and Erika Abrams. Springer: New York, 2011.

Plato. *Laches*. Taken from *Plato: Complete Works*. Edited by John M. Cooper. Hackett Publishing Company: Indianapolis, 1997.

Plato. *Meno and Phaedo*. Translated by David Sedley and Alex Long. Cambridge University Press: Cambridge, MA, 2011.

Plato. *Republic*. Translated by G. M. A. Grube and revised by C. D. C. Reeve. Hackett Publishing Company: Indianapolis, 1992.

Reinach, Adlof. 'Concerning Phenomenology'. Translated by Dallas Willard. *The Phenomenology Reader*. Edited by Dermot Moran and Timothy Mooney. Routledge: London, 2002.

Richardson, William J. *Heidegger: Through Phenomenology to Thought*. Martinus Nijhoff: The Hague, 1963.

Ricoeur, Paul. *A l'école de la phénoménologie*. Vrin: Paris, 1987.

Schuhmann, Karl. 'Husserl's Concept of Philosophy'. *Journal of the British Society for Phenomenology*. Volume 21:3 (1990) (pages 274–83).

Sheehan, Thomas. *Making Sense of Heidegger: A Paradigm Shift*. Roman & Littlefield International: London, 2015.

Sheehan, Thomas. 'A Paradigm Shift in Heidegger Research'. *Continental Philosophy Review*. Volume 34 (2001) (pages 183–202).

Sheehan, Thomas. 'What, After All, Was Heidegger About?' *Continental Philosophy Review*. Volume 47:3 (2014) (pages 249–74).

Sheehan, Thomas. (2013). 'What if Heidegger Were a Phenomenologist?' Taken from *The Cambridge Companion to Heidegger's Being and Time*. Edited by Mark A. Wrathall. Cambridge University Press: Cambridge Massachusetts, 2003.

Shores, Corry. *Difference & Phenomena: A Deleuzean Phenomenal Analysis of Body, Time, and Selfhood*. PhD diss., KU Leuven, 2012a.

Shores, Corry. 'Body and World in Merleau-Ponty and Deleuze'. *Studia Phænomenologica* XII (2012b) (pages 181–209).

Sokolowski, Robert. 'Being, My Way'. *First Things*. Volume 89 (1999) (pages 54–7).

Spiegelberg, Herbert. *Doing Phenomenology: Essays on and in Phenomenology*. Martinus Nijhoff: The Hague, 1975.

Spiegelberg, Herbert. 'From Husserl to Heidegger: Excerpts from a 1928 Freiburg Diary by W. R. Boyce Gibson'. *Journal of the British Society for Phenomenology*. Volume 2 (May 1971): 68 (pages 58–83).

Spiegelberg, Herbert. 'Husserl's Way into Phenomenology for Americans: A Letter and Its Sequel' taken from *Phenomenology: Continuation and Criticism. Essays in Memory of Dorion Cairns*. Edited by F. Kersten and R. Zaner. Martinus Nijhoff: The Hague, 1973.

Spiegelberg, Herbert. *The Phenomenological Movement: A Historical Introduction*. Martinus Nijhoff: The Hague, 1960.

Tolkien, J. R. R. *The Fellowship of the Ring: Being the First Part of the Lord of the Rings*. Second Edition. The Riverside Press: Cambridge, 1965.

Van Breda, Herman. 'Husserl's Inaugural Lecture at Freiburg in Breisgau (1917) Introduction by H. L. Van Breda'. Translated by Robert Welsh Jordan. *Life-World and Consciousness: Essays for Aron Gurwitsch*. Edited by Lester Embree. Northwestern University Press: Evanston, 1972.

Volpi, Franco. 'Phenomenology as Possibility: The "Phenomenological" Appropriation of the History of Philosophy in the Young Heidegger'. *Research in Phenomenology*. Volume 30 (2000) (pages 120–45).

de Warren, Nicolas. 'Homecoming, Jan Patočka's Reflections on the First World War' chapter 10 in *Phenomenologies of Violence*. Edited by Michael Staudigl. Brill: Boston, 2014 (pages 207–43).

Warren, Nicolas, R. Bernet, J. Taminiaux, S. IJsseling, H. Leonardy, D. Lories, Ullrich Melle, R. Bernasconi, D. Carr, E.S. Casey, R. Cobb-Stevens, J.F. Courtine, F. Dastur, K. Düsing, J. Hart, K. Held, K.E. Kaehler, D. Lohmar, W.R. McKenna and B. Waldenfels. (2010). Tamino's Eyes, Pamina's Gaze: Husserl's Phenomenology of Image-Consciousness Refashioned. 10.1007/978-94-007-0071-0_12. 'Tamio's Eyes, Pamina's Gaze: Husserl's Phenomenology of Image-Consciousness Refashioned'. *Philosophy, Phenomenology, Sciences: Essays in Commemoration of Edmund Husserl.* Phaenomenologica 200. Edited by Carlo Ierna et al. Springer: Dordrecht, 2010 (pages 303–32). 10.1007/978-94-007-0071-0_12.

Zahavi, Dan. *Husserl's Phenomenology*. Stanford University Press: Stanford, 2003.

Index

absolute 7, 45, 48, 49, 50, 76–77, 81, 87, 90, 147, 155, 158, 160, 163, 164, 168, 192, 212, 217 n.1, 221 n.17
   absolute meaning 45, 46, 47, 163, 164, 168, 172
   absolute responsibility 87, 147, 155, 158
actuality 41, 42, 51, 72, 74, 81–82, 114, 197, 220 n.15, 221 n.17, 239 n.2
Adorno, Theodore W. 217 n.1, 221 n.17
aletheia 103, 126–135, 129, 130, 131, 235 n.41 *see also truth*
amazement 195
Ancient Greeks 168, 169, 193, 200, 201, 218 n.6 *see also Greeks*
announce, announces 18, 121, 122–126, 134, 135, 153, 205, 233 n.29 *see phenomenon*
answers 1–2, 4–5, 11, 13–14, 17, 21, 24, 26–33, 38, 40, 42, 45–49, 52, 54, 55, 58, 63, 66, 67–69, 74, 83–84, 88, 90, 94, 95–96, 100, 105, 108–109, 115, 116, 138, 158, 166, 179, 181, 196, 206, 231 n.20, 239 n.2
   powerful answers 42, 52, 58, 115, 138, 150, 166, 188–189, 196, 198, 199, 239 n.2
   traditional answers 4, 21, 40, 45–49, 54, 66, 108–109, 115, 116, 158, 179, 181, 206, 231n.20 *see questioning*
appearance 9, 12, 14–19, 22, 23–25, 28, 39, 50, 55, 58–59, 65, 68, 70, 71–72, 76, 78, 80, 84, 89, 95, 104, 113–115, 125–126, 128–129, 145, 146, 151, 156, 158, 161, 170, 173, 175, 196, 203, 205, 206, 207, 216 n.8, 226 n.16, 227 n.25, 229 n.12, 233 n.29, 235 n.38, 237 n.8, 238 n.4 *see semblance, see phenomenon*
   appearance [*Erscheinung*] 18, 117, 120, 121–125, 129, 130, 134, 156, 158, 161, 162, 175, 205, 237 n.8
   mere appearance [*bloße Erscheinung*] 97, 117, 119, 120, 121–125, 129, 130, 132, 134, 156, 175, 205, 237 n.8
Arendt, Hannah 238 n.7
astonishment 49–50
attitude 26, 29, 54, 71, 77–78, 109, 147, 153, 177, 203, 205, 213, 218 n.7
authentic 127–128, 165, 234 n.35, 235 n.37
authority 60, 82, 119, 131, 159, 160, 164, 171, 172

being 4, 7, 18, 21, 31, 98, 108, 110, 115, 127–128, 188, 197, 199
   entities [*Seienden*] 25, 99, 105, 110, 111, 118, 119, 120, 122, 125, 126, 131–132, 134, 136, 148, 228 n.1, 235 n.39
   what is being? 4, 31, 98, 108, 110, 127–128, 188, 197, 199
Bell, David 223 n.2
Bernet, Rudolf 51, 53, 61, 73, 74, 90, 149, 150, 214 n. 3, 215 n.6, 216 n. 7, 224 n.7–10, 232 n.26, 234 n.32, 241 n.7
Borecký, Felix 220 n.14, 237 n.11–12
Buckley, R. Philip 22, 23, 93, 94, 221 n.18, 227 n.23

Cairns, Dorion 82, 83, 102, 217 n.3, 222 n.19, 223 n.3, 224 n.12, 226 n.17, 235 n.42
care, care of the soul 143, 158
certainty 45, 93, 233 n.29
clarification 62, 63, 64, 67, 71, 73, 78, 79, 81, 85, 89, 90, 94, 104, 120, 122, 125, 132, 150, 178, 181, 184, 207, 208, 209, 230 n.15, 232 n.27, 233 n.32
clear 2, 14, 17, 27, 41, 54, 55, 67, 68, 71, 80, 84, 91, 152, 170, 175, 203, 207
concept 2, 8, 9, 13–15, 17, 19, 24–25, 31, 39, 50, 52–53, 60, 64, 69, 70–71, 83–84, 87–89, 91, 96, 107–108, 111, 117–120, 125, 126–135, 140, 148–151, 164, 166, 176, 178–182, 192, 196–197

conceptual responses 14
conceptualize 8, 13, 14, 25, 31, 39, 40, 52, 53, 70, 71, 108, 112, 141, 160, 166, 181, 184, 194, 216 n.7, 231 n.23
phenomenological concepts 28
consciousness 16, 22, 26, 27–30, 40, 43, 59, 60, 68–69, 72–73, 75–81, 83–85, 88, 96, 100, 114, 116, 129, 153–157, 188, 191, 197, 205, 211, 214 n.3, 224 n.9, 227 n.25, 237 n.8
   act of consciousness 28, 68, 79, 80, 103, 153
   appear to consciousness 22, 23, 40, 59, 60, 72, 75, 76, 156, 236 n.8
constitution 22, 27
content 9, 27, 31, 36, 53, 55, 59, 64, 66, 72, 94, 106, 132, 133–134, 140–141, 147, 151, 152–153, 164, 167, 182, 191, 196, 204, 205, 209, 222 n.19, 234 n.33, 237 n.9
   content of phenomenology 9, 27, 55, 59, 134, 147, 153, 204
contrivance 31, 42, 61, 82, 86, 114, 153, 209
correlation 31–32, 68–69, 72, 91, 122, 143, 147, 153, 191, 213, 227 n.25, 232 n.26
covered 14, 29, 31, 99, 107, 114, 124, 131, 132, 136, 206
   concealment 53, 105, 121, 130, 132, 135, 161, 163, 234 n.36, 237 n.8
crisis 149, 167, 168
criticism 35, 37, 38, 43, 62, 89, 104, 118, 136, 142, 143, 144, 154, 158–159, 161–162, 181, 182, 201, 205, 211
Curiosity 176, 184–189, 191, 192–196, 197

Dasein 43, 111, 112, 134–135
De Warren, Nicolas 164, 222 n.20
Deleuze, Gilles 201, 240 n.6
destabilization 7, 164, 189, 190, 193
destruction 53–54, 221 n.18
discourse 12, 127–128, 152, 234 n.33 *see logos*
domain 42, 48, 49, 53, 65, 68, 104, 167, 168, 179, 189, 190, 191, 197
doubt 3, 4, 34, 76, 77, 81, 93, 158
Dylan, Bob 199, 200, 239 n.3
dynamism 9, 14, 15, 19, 23, 25, 42, 48, 57, 68, 132, 150, 151, 156, 184, 188, 194, 204, 210, 212
   see also flux
   dynamism of experience 14, 23, 25, 57, 210
dynamic phenomenon 19, 58

eclipse 5, 9, 10, 14, 17, 39, 42, 58, 64, 65, 71, 99, 100, 104–108, 114, 115, 132, 138, 162, 180, 196, 198, 204, 216 n.8, 221 n.17, 227 n.24
edify, edifying 2, 8–10, 24, 60, 79, 96, 113, 154, 159, 173, 187, 216 n.9, 235 n.41, 239 n.1
eidetics 33, 39, 42
elicit 4, 5, 9, 10, 15, 32, 36, 45, 58, 59, 62, 64, 70, 71, 78, 85, 89, 94, 103–107, 114–116, 128–130, 132, 148, 175, 180, 184, 188, 189, 196, 204, 206, 212, 213, 219 n.10, 226 n.16, 234 n.35
   re-elicit 9, 45, 58, 62, 89, 101, 105, 114, 130, 132, 133, 136, 205
elusive 1, 3, 15, 60, 87, 165, 209
emerge 15, 16, 23, 52, 59, 69, 71, 72, 74, 76, 87, 93, 94, 115, 121, 122, 126, 130, 139, 155, 175, 178, 192, 193, 206, 211, 216 n.7, 231 n.23
   emergence 10, 15, 29, 50, 96, 121, 129, 162, 196, 205, 212
empirical 73, 75, 76, 83, 124–126, 160, 223 n.4
entities *see phenomenon*
epistemology 24, 76, 219 n.12
   epistemological 89–91, 94, 235 n. 43, 237 n.1
epoché 26, 61, 148.
esoteric 161, 162, 223 n.2
essences 22, 30
evidence 8–9, 23, 25–27, 36, 38, 80–83, 94, 96, 114, 119, 134, 144, 181, 203, 206, 222 n.20, 223 n.2, 235 n.42
existence 28, 48, 50, 51, 74, 77, 103, 145, 146, 148, 154, 160, 162, 164, 167–168, 184, 202, 211, 215 n.4, 233 n.31
   existent 29, 45, 49–50, 111
experience 1–19, 22, 25 *see phenomenon*
   dynamism of experience 14, 23, 25, 57, 210
   experience of wonder 7, 36, 176, 186–189, 191, 197

genuine experience 26, 36, 59, 61, 68, 85–86, 90, 91, 107, 116, 128, 130, 149, 153, 181, 185, 194, 195, 196, 209, 211, 214 n.1, 232 n.26
lived experience 73–74, 111, 178, 181
original experience 13–14, 32, 39, 64, 70, 83, 88, 91, 105, 116, 147–149, 178
explore 7, 15, 26, 44, 53, 57, 67, 83, 120, 137, 139, 150, 155–157, 163, 171, 179–180, 188, 191, 204, 207, 227 n.21, 228 n.2
exploration 7, 11, 12, 23, 43, 126–127, 138, 177, 180, 190, 221 n.16

Findlay, J.N. 90, 216 n.10
finesse 177, 214 n.2
finitude 45, 46, 168
Fink, Eugen 27–29, 41, 45, 49–50, 61, 82, 102, 147, 208, 213, 219 n.9, 224 n.6, 225 n.13
flux 3, 9, 15–18, 25–26, 28, 32, 40, 44, 51, 58, 65–70, 72, 78, 114, 121, 130–131, 148, 150, 156, 178, 192–196, 204, 206, 208, 210, 225 n.14, 236 n.8, 239 n.2
fluctuation 3, 25–26, 32, 42, 51, 101, 175, 192, 205, 210, 213
flux of experience 15–16, 32, 57, 68–69, 71–72, 88
flux of phenomena 16, 40–42, 44, 114, 204, 206
freedom 46, 47, 51, 163–164, 212

Gadamer, Hans-Georg 11, 12, 102
genuine, genuinely 9–10, 15, 18, 19, 26, 30–31, 33, 36, 46, 55, 57, 60, 62, 69, 71, 73, 84–85, 86, 89, 92, 105, 108, 117, 128, 130, 147, 149, 162, 168, 177, 179–183, 192, 196, 209
genuine experience 26, 36, 59, 61, 68, 85–86, 90, 91, 107, 116, 128, 130, 149, 153, 181, 185, 194, 195, 196, 209, 211, 214 n.1, 232 n.26
see also genuine questioning *under* questioning
Gibson, W. R. Boyce 30, 217 n.4
grasp 3, 7, 11, 17, 25, 27, 31, 34, 41, 49, 53, 54, 64, 68, 69, 73, 76, 82, 84, 110, 113, 114, 125, 132, 133, 141, 153–154, 179, 180, 188, 203, 205, 207, 222 n.19, 225 n.12, 235 n.40
gravity 10, 14, 33, 54, 115, 180, 198
Gray, J. Glenn 218 n.6
Greeks, 168, 169, 193, 200, 201, 218 n.6 *see also* Ancient Greeks
Guattari, Félix 201

heresy 18, 137, 138, 139–141, 141–143, 143–147, 157, 158–159, 160–163, 171–173, 175, 206, 207, 236 n.4, 237 n.2
heretical 92, 137, 138–139, 141–143, 143–147, 159, 160–163
phenomenological heresy 143–147
Heidegger, Martin *see phenomenology, see phenomenon*
hindsight 137, 139, 140, 171, 173, 189, 236 n.1–2, 237 n.2
history 3, 10, 13, 16, 21, 22, 40, 51, 53, 103–105, 111, 118, 128, 172, 183, 199, 202, 203
history as phenomenon 163–166
what is history? 44–50
Hopkins, Burt 220 n.15
horizon 1, 68, 69, 72, 73, 74, 110, 112, 113, 126, 189, 224 n.7, 234 n.38, 238 n.3
Hume, David 124–126, 129–130, 214 n.4, 233 n.30–31
Husserl, Edmund *see phenomenology, see phenomenon*
motto precedes his method 59–65, 204
list of famous students 102

ideal 22, 28, 42, 68, 73, 81, 91–93, 100, 169, 170, 201, 227 n.22, 230 n.15, 235 n.43, 236 n.8, 237 n.1
Ideality 21, 50, 86, 169
immanent 29, 75–77, 84, 85, 236 n.8
inauthentic 127–128, 234 n.35, 235 n.37
independent 11, 12, 33, 60, 92, 135, 138, 149, 166, 227 n.24
inexhaustible 49, 69, 151, 187, 209, 210
information 4, 36, 109, 128, 135, 184–186, 189
instability 4–5, 7–8, 24–26, 51–52, 54, 94, 99, 106, 121, 156, 176, 178, 186, 189–192, 206
see flux
invariant 162 *see variation*

Kant, Immanuel 11, 92, 117, 124–126, 128–130, 190, 192, 214 n.4, 219 n.12, 226 n.20, 233 n.30–31, 234 n.38, 238 n.4–5
Kern, Iso 61, 149, 150
Kisiel, Theodore 34, 36–38, 120, 217 n.5, 219 n.10
knowledge 3, 4, 6, 10–12, 26, 32, 33, 42, 45, 66, 86–90, 93–94, 103, 105–106, 113, 116, 148, 157, 161–162, 166–167, 172, 173, 182–184, 191, 194–196, 214 n.3–4, 215 n.6, 238 n.7
  theory of knowledge 106
Kuhn, Thomas S. 225 n.14–15

leitmotif 139, 171
lifeworld 137, 143, 147, 147–151, 156, 159–161, 163, 237 n.8
limit 9, 22, 26, 29, 49, 53–54, 65, 70, 83, 89, 94, 104, 144, 154–156, 158–159, 162, 182, 185–186, 189–193, 196, 210, 215 n.6, 227 n.20, 229 n.13, 230 n.15, 232 n.26, 236 n.3, 238 n.7
logic 2, 21, 23, 32, 39–40, 82, 86, 89–91, 94, 104, 107, 116, 136, 178, 197, 202, 212, 230 n.17, 235 n.43, 237 n.1
  what is logic? 39, 107, 197
logos 97, 117, 119, 126–135, 152, 164, 176, 233 n.32, 234 n.36–37
  logos of questioning 175–198

Macdonald, Iain 221 n.17
Macquarrie & Robinson 228 n.1
Mahnke, Dietrich 38
manifest 16, 26, 40, 50, 103, 119, 123, 127–129, 131–132, 145–146, 161, 164, 170, 218 n.7, 222 n.20, 232 n.26, 234 n.33, 234 n.36–38
math, mathematics, mathematical 4, 13, 23, 30, 32–33, 48, 66, 93, 168–169, 227 n.24
Meacham, Darian 220 n.13
Melle, Ullrich 228 n.4, 229 n.6
memory 85
  memorization 92, 179, 181
Merleau-Ponty, Maurice 223 n.2, 240 n.6
metaphysics 31, 42, 86, 111, 114, 126, 147, 152, 153, 190, 192, 209, 219 n.12, 238 n.6
  contrivance 31, 42, 61, 82, 86, 114, 153, 209

mode 12, 25–26, 32, 42, 51–52, 80–81, 98, 105, 119, 125, 133, 140–142, 152, 154, 156–157, 159, 166, 169, 173, 176, 186–187, 196, 205, 209, 215 n.6, 230 n.14
  modality 114, 196, 197
  thinking in a mode of possibility 51, 196–198
Moran, Dermot 62, 89, 224 n. 5–6, 229 n.9, 231 n.25
motto *see Husserl*
multiplicity 3, 78–85, 120
mystery 40, 161–162, 170

Nietzsche, Friedrich 91, 219 n.11
nihilism 45, 47, 165, 200, 211
number 13–14, 21, 23, 32, 39, 53, 68, 75, 81, 127, 185, 197

objectivity 69, 225 n.14
  ideal object 42, 68, 81
  object 3, 5, 8, 10, 12, 22, 24, 26–29, 31, 33, 39, 68–69, 73–75, 79, 80, 81, 83, 115, 118, 132, 151, 153–157, 176, 179, 184, 195, 202, 214 n.3, 217 n.2, 226 n.16, 231 n.22, 232 n.26, 236 n.8
  Object (with a capital 'O') in the pregnant sense 74–78, 79, 81, 226 n.16
  spatiotemporal object 73, 77, 81
observation 77, 131, 155, 161
ontology 53, 98, 111, 114, 115, 117–118, 132, 134, 135
original, original question 5, 6, 10, 21, 27, 31, 39–40, 46, 48–49, 52, 54–55, 62–63, 67–69, 72, 74, 88, 95, 112, 122, 132, 139–140, 142, 144, 156, 158, 179–180, 187–188, 196–198, 205–206, 215 n.4, 220 n.12, 221 n.17
originary 5, 9, 13–14, 70, 89, 107, 129, 130, 133, 175, 240 n.6

participate 40, 55, 81, 83–84, 86, 116, 134, 144, 166, 168, 172, 176, 178–179, 189, 200–201, 208–209, 212
Patočka, Jan *see phenomenology, see phenomenon, see heresy*
perception 16, 22, 25, 31, 52, 53, 72, 75, 78, 80, 85, 114, 127, 131, 154, 197, 216 n.7, 223 n.2, 237 n.9

Petříček, Miroslav 137, 143–147, 152, 158–159
Pfänder, Alexander 37, 102
phenomenological reduction 31, 63, 81, 153, 154, 223 n.4, 232 n.26
phenomenology in general 8–9, 22, 45, 84, 207–210
   Heidegger's definition 40–44, 117–118, 135–136, 175, 181, 197
   Husserl's definition 22–26, 28–33, 58–59, 61–62, 64–65, 150–151, 181, 197, 211
   Husserl's famous students 102
   Patočka's definition 44–45, 137–139, 144–145, 146–147, 151–159, 161–163, 170–173, 197
   phenomenological flux 65–70 *see flux*
   phenomenological seeing 31, 39, 42, 43, 54, 55, 59, 101, 107, 171, 205, 229 n.5–6
   phenomenology as systematic but not a system 32, 39, 42, 58, 60, 61, 64, 67, 86–96, 99, 100, 105–107, 114, 116, 167, 178, 184–185, 194, 208, 219 n.9, 227 n.21, 228 n.2, 236 n.43, 237 n.2
   phenomenology and questioning 50–55, 139–141, 196–198, 204–205, 207–210
   phenomenology as a possibility 18, 41, 113–117, 114, 175
   Reinach's definition 12–14
   shaken but undaunted philosophy 49, 137, 164, 166–170
phenomenon 8–12, 14, 52, 116, 121, 205–206
   Heidegger's definition 105–107, 117, 119–126, 129–135, 156, 205–206
   Heidegger's *phenomenon, semblance, appearance* and *mere appearance* 119–126
   Husserl's definition 26, 57–59, 32, 70–74, 78–85, 150–151, 156, 175, 205–206
   originary / original phenomenon 10, 13–14, 17, 32, 108, 115, 129, 130
   Patočka's definition 138, 145–146, 150, 152, 155, 161–163, 205–206
   phenomenon as a multiplicity 3, 78–85, 120, 121, 205–206
   phenomenon as dynamic 9, 14, 19, 32, 51, 58, 205, 206

potential to further reveal 9, 15, 23, 32, 78, 81, 88, 95–96, 147, 151, 163, 206, 207, 216 n.7
pregnant sense of the word / pregnant objects 74–78
Pithart, Petr 165
polemos 164, 237 n.10
possibility 7, 15, 18, 23, 26, 28, 40, 41–45, 47–53, 68, 74, 77, 151, 155, 161, 164, 169, 175–176, 182, 186, 189–193, 196–198, 204, 207, 212, 214 n.3, 215 n.4, 219 n.12, 220 n.14–17, 223 n.2, 224 n.8, 239 n.2 *see also appearance; phenomenology; phenomenon; questioning*
   possibility of phenomenology 18, 41, 113–117, 114, 175, 220 n.15, *see also chapter 3*
   thinking in a mode of possibility 51–52, 156, 166, 196–198
practise 12, 31, 43, 54–55, 57, 60–61, 70, 83, 106, 179, 181, 206, 209, 214 n.1, 218 n.7, 229 n.13
   primacy of practice 155–157, 192
predicate 13–14, 74–78, 86
   logical predicate 58, 74–78
pregnant, pregnant sense of *see objectivity and Object*
preservation 17, 21, 33–44, 55, 69, 74, 88, 117, 135, 136, 137–138, 141, 144, 146, 166, 172, 180, 200, 205, 206, 216 n.9, 219 n.7, 221 n.17
   preservation of questions 17, 44, 88, 166, 216 n.9, 219 n.7
   preserve 8, 21, 28, 31, 36, 41, 51, 54, 55, 61, 67, 87, 88, 97, 114, 135, 136, 138, 143, 150, 163, 172, 180, 203, 206, 208, 218 n.7
   preserved as a problem 138, 166
problematicity 23, 27, 45, 48, 63, 68, 117, 127–129, 150, 158, 163–164, 166, 167, 172, 180, 193 *see preservation, see questioning*
profile 73, 76–77, 79–81, 205, 232 n.27 *see phenomenon*
progress 28, 42, 45, 49, 66, 91, 93, 138, 143, 167, 172, 173, 188, 190, 196, 225 n.14, 238 n.7 total progress 143, 172

pure 29, 30, 67–68, 79, 81, 84, 86, 90, 91, 100, 147, 149, 155, 169, 178, 190, 223 n.4, 227 n.20, 235 n.43, 237 n.9, 237 n.1
  pure phenomenology 30, 67, 68, 100
puzzle, jigsaw puzzle 185–186, 194, 239 n.1

questioning 1–19, 21–23, 25, 31–35, 43–50, 64, 83, 85, 107–108, 130–136, 152, 170–173, 192, 196–198, 199–213, 216 n.7, 216 n.12, 218 n.7, 220 n.12, 222 n.1, 235 n.42, 236 n.2, 241 n.6
  activity of questioning 2–4, 9–10, 15–19, 21–27, 32, 34–39, 43–50, 64, 83, 85, 107–108, 130–136, 152, 170–173, 192, 196–198, 199–213, 216 n.7, 216 n.12, 218 n.7, 220 n.12, 222 n.1, 235 n.42, 236 n.2, 241 n.6
  colloquial questioning 4, 6–8, 19, 109
  contemplative questioning 4–5, 6–7, 8, 12, 19, 22, 109, 149, 194
  explicitly formulated question 107–113
  Gefragtes, Befragtes, Erfragtes 108–111, 231
  genuine questioning 7–8, 10, 11, 18, 19, 26, 30, 45, 54, 109, 112–113, 115–117, 122, 164, 172, 176–184, 190–191, 201, 204, 206–207, 240 n.6
  philosophical questioning 35–36, 45, 109, 114, 166, 176–177, 179, 181, 186–187, 189–191, 193, 238 n.3
  questioning as phenomenology 50–55, 139–141, 196–198, 204–205, 207–210
  questioning attitude 29, 71, 177, 203
  questioning the things themselves 23, 31, 73
  re-questioning 12, 21, 23, 24–25, 27, 49–50, 65, 73, 81, 86–89, 96, 181
  rhetorical questioning 4, 5–7, 8, 19, 45, 84, 115–116, 165, 180, 188, 208, 211
  stability and instability of questioning 25, 52, 176, 189–192
  transparent question 18, 97, 108–112, 117, 132, 136, 231 n.21

reduction 31, 55, 61, 63, 81, 82, 106, 128, 153, 154, 180, 223 n.2, 4, 26
  phenomenological reduction 31, 55, 61, 63, 81, 153, 154, 223 n.4, 232 n.26

reflection 4, 9, 12, 16, 26, 43, 48, 76, 77, 78, 80, 82, 84–86, 89, 92, 95–96, 135, 146, 153, 159, 167, 184, 193, 208–209, 216 n.7, 219 n.9, 223 n.2, 241 n.6
Reinach, Adolf 12–14, 39, 54, 86–87, 102, 205, 229 n.10
religion 142, 162, 188 *see heresy*
responsibility 87, 142, 147, 155, 158, 164, 217 n.14, 220 n.14, 236 n.4
revitalize 14, 40, 49, 54, 104, 169, 197
Richardson, William J. 34, 107, 218 n.7, 230 n.18
Ricoeur, Paul 46–48, 137, 144, 158, 160–164, 236 n.5
riddle 126–127, 234 n.35
rigour 67, 68, 92–94, 167

science 3, 5–6, 28–33, 43, 51–52, 65–69, 74–77, 84, 86, 90–94, 99–100, 103–105, 114, 128, 134, 145, 148–150, 155, 160, 166–169, 185, 190, 192, 194, 197, 200, 202, 205, 208, 210, 225 n.14, 227 n.22, 25, 229 n.13, 230 n.15, 238 n.3, 5–7, 239 n.2
  rigorous science 67, 91, 92, 155, 167, 227 n.22, 238 n.5
search, searching 3, 26, 32, 47, 50, 67, 90, 108, 127, 149, 162, 165, 172, 187, 190, 216 n.7, 238 n.7
seeing, *see phenomenology*
  phenomenological seeing 31, 39, 42, 43, 54, 55, 59, 101, 107, 171, 205, 229 n.5–6
self-evident 22, 23, 108, 119, 191, 237 n.11 *see phenomenon*
self-reveal 3, 8, 12, 15, 17, 23, 49, 51–54, 57–60, 71, 80, 83, 87, 96, 119, 126, 128, 147, 151, 206, 208, 216 n.8, 226 n.16, 233 n.29 *see phenomenon, see appearance*
shaken 44, 45, 47, 49, 50, 137, 163–166, 220 n.13
  shaken meaning 44, 45, 220 n.13
Sheehan, Thomas 34, 36, 37–38, 218 n.7, 219 n.10, 231 n.22, 24, 232 n.26
sheltered, sheltered life 44–48, 163–164, 168, 172
Shores, Corry 240 n.6
Smith, Elliott 199

Socrates 6, 11, 239 n.1
  Socratic questioning 142
Sokolowski, Robert 107, 224 n.5, 230 n.19
solidarity of the shaken 165
Spiegelberg, Herbert 12, 14, 23, 24, 63, 89, 91, 92, 93, 207, 208, 209, 217 n.4, 222 n.2, 227 n.22–23, 229 n.7, 236 n.6
stable 4, 5, 6, 8, 9, 14, 19, 25, 32, 33, 46, 51, 66, 107, 129, 130, 132, 136, 156, 177, 178, 185, 186, 192, 196, 198, 216 n. 8, 221 n.17
  destabilization 7, 164, 189, 190, 193
  stabilization 9, 18, 25, 33, 43, 55, 71, 74, 104, 105, 116, 121, 129, 130, 131, 132, 156, 164, 178, 184, 192, 205, 213, 229 n.12, 230 n.14
  stabilizing 86, 104, 210
  unstable 3, 19, 42, 51, 104, 130, 131, 154, 156, 186, 192, 196, 205, 237 n.8
Stambaugh, Joan 112, 228 n.1, 231 n.21
subjective 72, 148, 149, 150, 167–168, 223 n.2, 227 n.25
synthesis 48, 89, 96, 136, 137, 139, 166, 222 n.20
system 4, 5, 6, 10, 25, 32, 36, 38, 54, 58, 60–63, 68, 82, 85, 86, 88–94, 101, 103, 106, 111, 140, 142, 152, 177, 178, 185–186, 192–194, 207, 209, 210, 225 n.13, 227 n.21, 24, 228 n.2, 229 n.7, 236 n.43, 237 n.2
  phenomenology as systematic but not a system 32, 39, 42, 58, 60, 61, 64, 67, 86–96, 99, 100, 105–107, 114, 116, 167, 178, 184–185, 194, 208, 219 n.9, 227 n.21, 228 n.2, 236 n.43, 237 n.2
  systematicity 9, 32, 43, 69, 85, 88, 89, 91, 93–94, 186, 227 n.24

thauma 169, 220 n.14, 237 n.11–12 *see wonder*
  thaumasein 176, 186–189, 192–194
  thaumaturge 170
theme 15, 34, 39, 61, 77, 92, 97, 107, 121, 124, 131, 132, 134, 138, 160, 175, 192, 229 n.11
thematic 18, 118, 124, 125, 134, 135

theory 28–30, 57, 74, 85, 106, 168, 208, 222 n.20, 224 n.12, 225 n.14, 230 n.17, 232 n.26
theoretical 29, 72, 77, 86, 97, 108, 157, 165, 202, 203, 211, 232 n.25, 236 n.4
theory of knowledge 106
things, the things themselves 8, 9, 12, 15, 16, 17, 22–23, 27–29, 31, 35, 40, 41, 43–45, 51–53, 55, 57, 59, 60, 63–65, 70–71, 73, 87–88, 93, 95, 98, 101, 114, 116, 118, 133, 135, 138, 150, 158, 159, 170, 171, 175, 197, 204, 207, 209, 213, 214 n.1, 222 n.2
thinking 2–4, 7, 9, 14, 18, 21, 24, 26, 32, 40–41, 45, 47–49, 51–53, 63, 66, 84–85, 94, 98, 101–103, 107–109, 115, 127, 132, 134, 138–139, 141–142, 145, 149–150, 152–153, 156, 159–162, 166, 172–173, 176–178, 180, 182–192, 196–198, 199, 202–203, 205, 207, 209–212, 213, 215 n.6, 216 n.7, 219 n.10–11, 222 n.20, 225 n.14, 228 n.3, 230 n.19, 231 n.25, 234 n.37, 238 n.2, 239 n.1–2
  thinking in a mode 51, 52, 156, 166, 196–198
  thinking in a mode of possibility 51, 196–198
Tolkien, J.R.R. 190
tradition 10, 13, 21, 32, 35, 39–40, 44–50, 52–55, 58, 65–67, 69, 83, 86–88, 92, 104–105, 107–109, 111, 115–116, 118, 131–132, 138–140, 144, 158, 163, 166, 171, 178–183, 188, 192, 195, 197, 202–203, 206, 220 n.12–13, 221 n.16–17, 225 n.14, 231 n.20, 24, 240 n.6
  traditional answers 4, 21, 40, 45–49, 54, 66, 108–109, 115, 116, 158, 179, 181, 206, 231 n.20 *see questioning*
transcendental 11, 29, 39, 40, 58, 61, 92, 116, 117, 124–126, 144, 171, 208, 216 n.11, 222 n.1, 224 n.6, 8, 225 n.13, 226 n.20, 235 n.38, 241 n.7
transcendent 75–77
transparent 9, 18, 26, 53, 97, 108–112, 117, 132, 136, 211, 230 n.20, 231 n.21

truth 1–3, 9–10, 42, 45, 47–50, 52, 54, 66, 68, 69, 82–83, 85, 90, 128–131, 138, 148, 155, 162, 165–167, 172–173, 177, 179, 182, 190, 197, 200–201, 203–204, 225 n.14, 234 n.32, 235 n.39, 41–42, 236 n.43, 240 n.5–6
   truth as *aletheia* 103, 126–135, 129, 130, 131, 235 n.41
Tusa, Laura Ilea 236 n.4

unity 28, 51–52, 78–81, 164, 201, 205, 207, 209, 232 n.27
unsheltered, unsheltered life 44–48, 163–164, 172
unstable 3, 19, 42, 51, 104, 130–131, 154, 156, 186, 192, 196, 205, 237 n.8
   see stability, see instability

valid 28, 49, 83, 85, 127, 235 n.42, 238 n.3
   Validity 61, 75, 83, 85, 111, 148, 227 n.20, 235 n.42

Van Breda, Herman 58
verify 8, 9, 18, 31, 42, 57, 60, 63, 64, 69, 70, 82, 86, 87, 103, 114, 159, 205, 206, 211, 214 n.3, 223 n.4
   verifiable 59, 71, 96
Volpi, Franco 221 n.16

Welch, E. Parl 91
Willard, Dallas 215
wonder 2–3, 7, 15, 29, 36, 42, 46, 49, 88, 92, 136, 138, 146, 147, 161, 164, 169–170, 172, 176, 181, 184, 186–189, 191, 192–196, 197, 213, 238 n.6, 239 n.1
   thauma 169, 220 n.14, 237 n.11–12
   thaumazein 176, 186–189, 192–194
worth 2–6, 11, 36, 165, 169, 197, 199, 203, 214 n.3, 219 n.11

Zahavi, Dan 61, 224 n.11

www.ingramcontent.com/pod-product-compliance
Lightning Source LLC
Chambersburg PA
CBHW071816300426
44116CB00009B/1342